RELIGION IN MODERN INDIA

RELIGION IN MODERN INDIA

Radhika Banerji

MD PUBLICATIONS PVT LTD
NEW DELHI
www.mdppl.com

Published by:

MD Publications Pvt Ltd
"MD House", 11, Darya Ganj,
New Delhi - 110 002
Phone : +91-11-45355555
E-mail : contact@mdppl.com
website : www.mdppl.com

ISBN: 978-81-7533-241-6

Published and Printed by Mr. Pranav Gupta on behalf of **MD Publications Pvt Ltd** at JJ offset Printers, Delhi.

PREFACE

In India, religion is a way of life. It is an integral part of the entire Indian tradition. For the majority of Indians, religion permeates every aspect of life, from common-place daily chores to education and politics. Secular India is home to Hinduism, Islam, Christianity, Buddhism, Jainism, Sikhism and other innumerable religious traditions. Hinduism is the dominant faith, practiced by over 80% of the population. Besides Hindus, Muslims are the most prominent religious group and are an integral part of Indian society. In fact India has the second largest population of Muslims in the world after Indonesia.

Throughout the history of India, religion has been an important part of the country's culture. The vast majority of Indians associate themselves with a religion, and religious tolerance is established in both law and custom. Indian census has established that Hinduism accounts for 80.5% of the population of India. The second largest religion is Islam, at about 13.4% of the population. The third largest religion is Christianity at 2.3%. The fourth largest religion is Sikhism at about 1.9% of India's population.

Other native Indian religions are Buddhism and Jainism. Ancient India had two philosophical streams of thought, the Shramana religions and the Vedic religion, parallel traditions that have existed side by side for thousands of years. Both Buddhism and Jainism are continuations of Shramana traditions, while modern Hinduism is a continuation of the Vedic tradition. These co-existing traditions have been mutually influential. Zoroastrianism and Judaism also have an ancient history in India and each has several thousand Indian adherents.

The preamble to the Constitution of India proclaimed India a "sovereign socialist secular democratic republic". The word secular was inserted into the Preamble by the Forty-second Amendment Act of 1976. It mandates equal treatment and tolerance of all religions. India does not have an official state religion; it enshrines the right to practice, preach, and propagate any religion. No religious instruction is imparted in government-supported schools.

Religion plays a major role in the Indian way of life. Rituals, worship, and other religious activities are very prominent in an individual's daily life; it is also a principal organiser of social life. The degree of religiosity varies among individuals; in recent decades, religious orthodoxy and observances have become less common in Indian society, particularly among young urban-dwellers.

Major religious communities continue to be governed by their own personal laws. Personal laws exist for Hindus, Muslims, Christians, Zoroastrians, and Jews. The only Indian religion exclusively covered under the secular ("civil") law of India is Brahmoism starting from Act III of 1872. For legal purposes, Buddhists, Jains and Sikhs are classified as Hindus and are subject to Hindu personal law.

I am very grateful to Mr. Pranav Gupta, Director of MD Publications Pvt Ltd, New Delhi, for his kind cooperation and support for this book.

Radhika Banerji

Contents

1

Religion
An Introduction

The term "religion" refers to both the personal practices related to communal faith and to group rituals and communication stemming from shared conviction. "Religion" is sometimes used interchangeably with "faith" or "belief system," but it is more socially defined than personal convictions, and it entails specific behaviors, respectively. A religion is an organized approach to human spirituality which usually encompasses a set of narratives, symbols, beliefs and practices, often with a supernatural or transcendent quality, that give meaning to the practitioner's experiences of life through reference to a higher power or truth. It may be expressed through prayer, ritual, meditation, music and art, among other things.

It may focus on specific supernatural, metaphysical, and moral claims about reality (the cosmos, and human nature) which may yield a set of religious laws, ethics, and a particular lifestyle. Religion also encompasses ancestral or cultural traditions, writings, history, and mythology, as well as personal faith and religious experience. The development of religion has taken many forms in various cultures. It considers psychological and social roots, along with origins and historical development. In the frame of western religious thought, religions present a common quality, the "hallmark of patriarchal religious thought": the division of the world in two comprehensive domains, one sacred, the other profane.

Religion is often described as a communal system for the coherence of belief focusing on a system of thought, unseen being, person, or object, that is considered to be supernatural, sacred, divine, or of the highest truth. Moral codes, practices, values, institutions, tradition, rituals, and scriptures are often traditionally associated with the core belief, and these may have some overlap with concepts in secular philosophy. Religion is also often described as a "way of life" or a life stance. Religion has been defined in a wide variety of ways. Most definitions attempt to find a balance somewhere between overly sharp definition and meaningless generalities. Some sources have tried to use formalistic, doctrinal definitions while others have emphasized experiential, emotive, intuitive, valuational and ethical factors.

Definitions mostly include:

- A notion of the transcendent or numinous, often, but not always, in the form of theism
- A cultural or behavioural aspect of ritual, liturgy and organized worship, often involving a priesthood, and societal norms of morality (ethos) and virtue (arete)
- A set of myths or sacred truths held in reverence or believed by adherents

Sociologists and anthropologists tend to see religion as an abstract set of ideas, values, or experiences developed as part of a cultural matrix. For example, in Lindbeck's Nature of Doctrine, religion does not refer to belief in "God" or a transcendent Absolute. Instead, Lindbeck defines religion as, "a kind of cultural and/or linguistic framework or medium that shapes the entirety of life and thought… it is similar to an idiom that makes possible the description of realities, the formulation of beliefs, and the experiencing of inner attitudes, feelings, and sentiments." According to this definition, religion refers to one's primary worldview and how this dictates one's thoughts and actions.

There is a tendency in the sociology of religion to emphasize the problems of any definition of religion. Talal Asad has gone so far as to say "there cannot be a universal definition of religion...because that definition is itself the historical product of discursive processes"

Other religious scholars have put forward a definition of religion that avoids the reductionism of the various sociological and psychological disciplines that reduce religion to its component factors. Religion may be defined as the presence of a belief in the sacred or the holy. For example Rudolf Otto's "The Idea of the Holy," formulated in 1917, defines the essence of religious awareness as awe, a unique blend of fear and fascination before the divine. Friedrich Schleiermacher in the late 18th century defined religion as a "feeling of absolute dependence."

The history of religion refers to the written record of human religious experiences and ideas. This period of religious history typically begins with the invention of writing about 5,000 years ago (3,000 BCE) in the Near East. The prehistory of religion relates to the study of religious beliefs that existed prior to the advent of written records. The timeline of religion is a comparative chronology of religion. The nineteenth century saw a dramatic increase in knowledge about other cultures and religions, and also the establishment of economic and social histories of progress. The "history of religions" school sought to account for this religious diversity by connecting it with the social and economic situation of a particular group.

Typically religions are divided into stages of progression from simple to complex societies, especially from polyt-heistic to monotheistic and from extempore to organised. Thus, the starting point is the tribal band whose religion is animistic and involves shamans and totems. Since the group is tribal, there is no permanent sanctuary. Cultic rites centre on identification with wild animals and appeasing spirits, often of the hunted. As society developed into chiefdoms and small kingdoms, religious rites began to serve different functions. Agriculture became important and so fertility gods were introduced (often female, as it is the woman who has the power to produce life).

The status of the "big man" (or chief) was supported with mythic tales of heroes and demigods, from whom he may be descended. When these small kingdoms merged into larger groups (often through conquest), different cults merged. The conquest of one group by another is therefore recorded in an epic tale of the conquest of the conquered group's god by the victor's (e.g. some Hinduism and the Babylonian Marduk). Another solution was to syncretise different religious traditions, for example, the Romans' identification of their Gods with the Greeks and the Greeks' adoption of Anatolian myths and characters.

Finally, the growth of the city state brought about progression to the most "civilised" level of religion, ethical monotheism. Students of the history of religions often learnt that this began in Egypt with Akhnaten and grew through 7th century BC Judaism, Persian Zoroastrianism and Greek Philosophy to endow Western society with the most progressive form of religion. The historical basis of this—that religion moved from polytheism to ethical monotheism—is now doubted. Nevertheless, it is still widely held that ethical monotheism (e.g. Judaism, Christianity, Islam, some forms of Hinduism and Buddhism) was encouraged by the growth of city states.

This was partly due to the role of a hierarchical society with a god-like absolute ruler. A more powerful social force was the isolation of the individual as he moved from the clan to a more cosmopolitan lifestyle. Questions of justice and value that had been previously answered by the family and small tribe were now to be pursued independently. The relative anonymity of the city afforded the opportunity for not only "sin" but also loneliness.

Ethical monotheism answered society's need for a moral guide and motivation, whilst a unique personal God who was sovereign over all areas of life answered people's feelings of isolation and powerlessness. Good examples of this are the prophetic literature of the Jewish Tanakh (Old

Testament), especially Isaiah, and the wisdom literature of the ancient near east dealing with apparently unjustified suffering. This includes Job, in the Judaeo-Christian Bible, and "The Dialogue of Pessimism", a Babylonian text.

Organized religion

Through the bulk of human evolution, humans lived in small nomadic bands practicing a hunter gatherer lifestyle. The religious practices of hunter gatherers revolve around shamanism, ancestor worship and animism. The emergence of complex and organized religions can be traced to the period when humans abandoned their nomadic hunter gatherer lifestyles in order to begin farming during the Neolithic period. Humans began domesticating crops and animals around 10,000 BCE chiefly in the Near East but independently in a number of locations around the world. The invention of agriculture during the Neolithic revolution was a major event in human history. The increased productivity provided by farming and the relative security of food surpluses allowed these communities to expand.Crop production led to the emergence of the first villages, chiefdoms, states, nations and empires. The societies born out of the neolithic revolution were characterized by high population densities, complex labor diversification, trading economies, centralized administrations and political structures, hiearchical ideologies and depersonalized systems of knowledge.

The transition from foraging bands to states and empires resulted in more specialized and developed forms of religion that were reflections of the new social and political environments. While bands and small tribes possess supernatural beliefs, these beliefs are adapted to smaller populations.

Organized religion emerged as a means of providing social and economic stability to large populations through the following ways:

- Organized religion served to Justify the central

authority, which in turn possessed the right to collect taxes in return for providing social and security services to the state. The empires of Ancient Egypt and Mesopotamia, were theocracies with chiefs, kings and emperors playing dual roles of political and spiritual leaders. Virtually all state societies and chiefdoms around the world have similar political structures where political authority is justified by divine sanction.

- Organized religion emerged as means of maintaining peace between unrelated individuals. Bands and tribes consist of small number of related individuals. However states and nations are composed of thousands or millions of unrelated individuals. Jared Diamond argues that organized religion served to provide a bond between unrelated individuals who would otherwise be more prone to enmity. He argues that the leading cause of death among hunter gatherer societies is murder.

Neolithic Religions

The religions of the Neolithic peoples provide evidence of some of the earliest known forms of organized religions. The Neolithic settlement of Catalhoyuk, in what is now Turkey, was home to about 8,000 people and remains the largest known settlement from the Neolithic period. James Mellaart, who excavated the site, believed that Catalhoyuk was the spiritual center of central Anatolia.

Invention of Writing

Following the neolithic revolution, the pace of technological development intensified. As human society became more complex, more sophisticated accounting systems became necessary. Writing was invented in either Sumeria or Ancient Egypt by 3000 BCE as a means of recording accounting transactions. Subsequently writing would be used to record myth. The first religious texts mark the beginning of religious history. The Pyramid Texts from ancient Egypt are one of the oldest known religious texts in the world dating to between 2400-2300 BCE.Writing played a major role in sustaining organized religion by standardizing religious ideas regardless of time or location.

The "Axial Age"

Karl Jaspers, in his Vom Ursprung und Ziel der Geschichte (The Origin and Goal of History), identified a number of key Axial Age thinkers as having had a profound influence on future philosophy and religion, and identified characteristics common to each area from which those thinkers emerged. Jaspers saw in these developments in religion and philosophy a striking parallel without any obvious direct transmission of ideas from one region to the other, having found very little recorded proof of extensive inter-communication between the ancient Near East, Greece, India and China.

Jaspers held up this age as unique, and one which to compare the rest of the history of human thought to. Jaspers' approach to the culture of the middle of the first millennium BCE has been adopted by other scholars and academics, and has become a point of discussion in the history of religion. In its later part, the "Axial Age" culminated in the development of monism and monotheism, notably of Platonic realism and Neoplatonism in Hellenistic philosophy, the notion of atman in Vedanta Hindu philosophy, and the notion of Tao in Taoism.

Middle Ages

Newer present-day world religions established themselves throughout Eurasia during the Middle Ages by: Christianization of the Western world; Buddhist missions to East Asia; the decline of Buddhism in the Indian subcontinent; and the spread of Islam throughout the Middle East, Central Asia, North Africa and parts of Europe and India. During the Middle Ages, Muslims were in conflict with Zoroastrians during the Islamic conquest of Persia; Christians were in conflict with Muslims during the

Byzantine-Arab Wars, Crusades, Reconquista and Ottoman wars in Europe; Christians were in conflict with Jews during the Crusades, Reconquista and Inquisition; Shamans were in conflict with Buddhists, Taoists, Muslims and Christians during the Mongol invasions; and Muslims were in conflict with Hindus and Sikhs during Muslim conquest in the Indian subcontinent.

Many medieval religious movements emphasized mysticism, such as the Cathars and related movements in the West, the Bhakti movement in India and Sufism in Islam. Monotheism reached definite forms in Christian Christology and in Islamic Tawhid. Hindu monotheist notions of Brahman likewise reached their classical form with the teaching of Adi Shankara.

Modern Period

European colonisation during the 15th to 19th centuries resulted in the spread of Christianity to Sub-Saharan Africa, the Americas, Australia and the Philippines. The 18th century saw the beginning of secularisation in Europe, rising to notability in the wake of the French Revolution. In the 20th century, the regimes of Communist Eastern Europe and Communist China were explicitly anti-religious.

A great variety of new religious movements originated in the 20th century, many proposing syncretism of elements of established religions. Adherence to such new movements is limited, however, remaining below 2% worldwide in the 2000s. Adherents of the classical world religions account for more than 75% of the world's population, while adherence to indigenous tribal religions has fallen to 4%. As of 2005, an estimated 14% of the world's population identifies as nonreligious.

Origin of Religion, Indian Philosophy

The origin of religion in India has a long past. The deification of natural phenomena always has been seen to have a harmful influence on the religious thoughts and practice in India. The world has become alive as the Gods are possessed of the human sense of justice and they are also capable of being influenced by the human qualities like hate and love. In India, the Gods are usually presented in a more humanized manner, as they bear all the human organs like the hands, legs or even the fair skin and long beard. They also have all the human characteristics like happiness, worries, anger and they fight and feast, dance and drink, eat and rejoice, just like the human beings.

The Gods have been the symbols of the nature as well, as they are described as the owners of different natural things like rain, fire, thunderstorm, soil, wind etc. The history of the origin of religion in India therefore unveils the fact that the Indian people also used to fear the Gods, as they can become harmful and cruel, anytime when they are in great anger and they love those Gods, who are helpful in their daily pursuits. Having similarity with this view of Gods, though the Vedic worship of the natural powers is not quite sincere, it is utilitarian.

The history of the origin of religion in India states that the Gods have actually become the sources of material prosperity to the Indian people and as there is a division of functions and attributes, they usually pray to the particular deities for getting some particular things. The ancient Indian philosophers perceived the concept of Gods, as strong rather than good, powerful rather than moral and this type of a religion is quite incapable of satisfying the ethical aspirations of men. The highest religious aspiration of men to get united with the Supreme power has been recognized in the Indian philosophy and the numerous Gods, have been created to help in enabling the people to reach the Supreme.

The origin of religion in India is therefore the saga of taming the masses. In Indian philosophy Gods were created to enable people to reach the supreme. The concept of sacrifices came to the Indian philosophy, as a consequence of the fear to God and also as a mean to satisfy the Gods, so that they do not cause any harm to the devotees. Sacrifices are seen as a symbol of the depth of one's affection towards God, as people usually sacrifice their best property or possessions to the God. However, there have been a lot of debates about the question of human sacrifice, as many of the ancient Indian philosophers raised their voices against this, saying that the concept of human sacrifices is neither allowed nor encouraged in the Vedas.

They quoted the Sama Veda that says, "O, Ye Gods! We use no sacrificial stake. We slay no victim. We worship entirely by the repetition of the sacred verses". The Upanishads and the Buddhist and Jaina schools did adopt this protesting nature at a later period. The sacrifices actually represent the second stage of the Vedic religion, as the first stage talked only about simple prayer. The Parasarasmriti says, "meditation in the Krtayuga, sacrifices in the Treta, worship in the Dvapara, praises and prayers in Kali". The Vishnupurana also says that the rules of sacrifices have actually formulated in the Tretayuga. The growth of religious practice in India has been so far, like from meditation to sacrifice, from sacrifice to worship and then from worship to praise and prayer.

Another aspect of the Indian philosophy in the ancient times is that, the people in ancient India had direct communion with the Gods, without the requirements of any meditation. There were no temples for the Gods in that period and people used to look upon the Gods as friends, rather than worshippers. This is the main reason why the terms like "Father Heaven", "Mother Earth" or "Brother Agni", have emerged from the ancient time in India. The ancient people used to share an intimate personal relationship with the Gods and religion dominated their entire life. They were also completely dependant on the Gods even for the ordinary necessities of their daily life.

The Vedic religion, which tells the origin of religion of India, also described the concept of Sin quite elaborately and according to the Vedic religion, Sin is actually the alienation from God. This definition of Sin in the Vedic religion is quite similar to that in the Hebrew theory and the Vedic religion has described the will of God, as the standard of morality.

The Vedic religion says that the human guilt is shortcoming and people usually commit a sin when they transgress the commands of God, as the Gods are the upholders of the moral order of the world. It is the Gods, who protect the good and punish the wicked. The Vedic religion also says that Sin is not merely the omission of the external duties, as there are both moral and ritual sins. According to the ancient Indian philosophy, the consciousness of sin usually calls for propitiatory sacrifices. As a rule, the Gods of the Rig-Veda are always regarded as the guardians of morality in the Indian philosophy.

Indian Philosophy and Religious Influence

Religion in India was never dogmatic. It was a rational synthesis which went on amassing into itself new conceptions as Indian philosophy progressed. Religious philosophy is experimental and provisional in nature, attempting to keep pace with the progress of thought. Indian thought by its emphasis on intellect, had placed philosophy in the place of religion, thus bringing out the rational character of religion in India. No religious movement has ever come existence without developing as its support, a philosophic content. From such promising information from time immemorial, it stands evident that religious influence on Indian philosophy has been incredible and sublime in its content and making.

Early in the 20th century, several scholars, intellectuals and philosophers looked towards the relationship of religion, Indian religious philosophy and science as an evolutionary one in which the more sophisticated ways of viewing the world simply replaced the older ways. Religion itself was often thought to have arisen from 'magic' and so intelligent schemes illustrated the development of human thought. A book like the Bhagavad Gita is a profoundly crucial religious document for Hinduism, yet it is also one of the funda-mental documents of Indian philosophy. Indeed, the Gita appears to have been produced by Indian philosophy, the Samkhya and Yoga Schools and then been transformed into a religious document. Finally, the text came to be used for both religious and philosophical (by Vedanta) purposes later on.

This kind of aspect makes distinctions between religion and philosophy very difficult in the Indian tradition. India is the home of philosophy, religion and spirituality. In India, spirituality basically adjusts one's mind to consider one's self and others as different from the gross physical body and the subtle mental body and to be beyond the limitations of space, time and causation. Philosophy is the theoretical aspect and religion is the practical aspect of this principle. The 'Indian religious temper', called Hinduism, is more ancient than the oldest known Rig Vedic hymn, which is dated to approximately 5000 B.C. Yet, Indian philosophy is as modern as the school of thought formed in recent past. This dynamic nature of the religion, based on a concrete foundation makes it one of the most knowledgeable and vibrant of religions.

Hence, religious influence on Indian philosophy has been almost historical and intrinsic, making the various emerging schools interlinking themselves in thoughts and principles. The Indian perspective on philosophy is to view all religions as diverse ways to reach the same goal of manifesting the fundamental divinity in man. So a follower of the Indian spiritual tradition accepts all religions to be true and suited for people with various mental structures, if followed in the right spirit. Be it in Hinduism, Jainism, Buddhism or Sikhism, religious influence on Indian philosophy is too profound to be called just mere exaggeration. The ethical doctrines of Jainism are based on the path of liberation, right belief, right conduct and right knowledge.

This very verve of Jainism also contours the vase of the Indian philosophy. The Jains believe in Anekantavada, or the theory that reality is many-sided. This also adds to the base of Indian philosophy and is perhaps the reason why so ideally Indian philosophy negates dogmatism. Buddhism as a religion rejects the "idea of idea of divine providence, but they teach that vices are punished and virtues are recompensed by a fatal necessity"- while this is the kernel of the Buddhist religion, this is also the central idea of Indian Philosophy and explicitly explains the theory of karma. Sikhism is yet another sublime organised religion in India that had originated during the 15th century, precisely in northern India. The principle teachings and scriptures were formulated by Guru Nanak, followed by nine successive gurus.

The basic belief or faith in Sikhism is Vahiguru, symbolised by the sacred symbol of ek oankar (one God). Mirroring the quintessential Punjab in each of their tradition and teaching, adherents of Sikhism initially had begun with a relatively neutral faith system. Sikh gurus had proposed to include the best practices of Hinduism or Islam, which, over time had to be relinquished with, due to crusades with both the mentioned faiths, notably with the Mughals. Sikhism counsels the quest of salvation through disciplined, individual meditation, concentrating on the name and message of God. A key distinguishing feature of Sikhism is a non-anthropomorphic concept of God, to the degree that one can infer God as the Universe itself. Sikh followers believe in equality of all beings and shun favouritism on the basis of caste, creed and gender.

Essentially behaving as a monotheistic religious faction, Sikhism has time and again fixed their impressive religious influence on Indian philosophy. As a matter of fact, religion and philosophy compliment each other in values, spirituality and governance. These theories were explicitly demonstrated by Sri Ramakrishna (1836-1886) during his lifetime. The supremacy of religion and of social tradition in life does not hamper the free pursuit of philosophy.

Religion in India

Hinduism accounts for 80% of the population of India. The second largest religion is Islam, at about thirteen percent of the population. Stating the hospitality of Hinduism towards all other religions, John Hardon writes, "However, the most significant feature of current Hinduism is its creation of a non-Hindu State, in which all religions are equal;..." Other native Indian religions are Buddhism, Jainism, and Sikhism. Ancient India had two philosophical streams of thought, the Shramana religions and the Vedic religion, parallel traditions that have existed side by side for thousands of years. Both Buddhism and Jainism are continuations of Shramana traditions, while modern Hinduism is a continuation of the Vedic tradition. These co-existing traditions have been mutually influential.

About two percent of Indians adhere to Christianity. Zoroastrianism and Judaism have an ancient history in India and each has several thousand Indian adherents. Though inter-religious marriage is not widely practiced, Indians are generally tolerant of other religions and retain a secular outlook. Inter-community clashes have never found widespread support in the social mainstream, and it is generally perceived that the causes of religious conflicts are political rather than ideological in nature. India's religious diversity extends to the highest levels of government. The Constitution of India declares the nation to be a secular republic that must uphold the right of citizens to freely worship and propagate any religion or faith (with activities subject to reasonable restrictions for the sake of morality, law and order, etc).

Indian religions, also called Dharmic religions, are the related religious traditions that originated in the Indian subcontinent, namely Hinduism, Jainism, Buddhism, Sikhism and Ayyavazhi, inclusive of their sub-schools and various related traditions. They form a subgroup of the larger class of "Eastern religions". Indian religions have similarities in core beliefs, modes of worship, and associated practices, mainly due to their common history of origin and mutual influence.

The documented history of Indian religions begins with historical Vedic religion, the religious practices of the early Indo-Aryans, which were collected and later redacted into the Samhitas, four canonical collections of hymns or mantras composed in archaic Sanskrit. These texts are the central shruti (revealed) texts of Hinduism. The period of the composition, redaction and commentary of these texts is known as the Vedic period, which lasted from roughly 1500 to 500 BCE.

The late Vedic period (9th to 6th centuries BCE) marks the beginning of the Upanisadic or Vedantic period. This period heralded the beginning of much of what became classical Hinduism, with the composition of the Upanishads, later the Sanskrit epics, still later followed by the Puranas.

Jainism and Buddhism arose from the sramana culture. Buddhism was historically founded by Siddartha Gautama, a Kshatriya prince-turned-ascetic, and was spread beyond India through missionaries. It later experienced a decline in India, but survived in Nepal and Sri Lanka, and remains more widespread in Southeast and East Asia. Jainism was established by a lineage of 24 enlightened beings culminating with Parsva (9th century BCE) and Mahavira (6th century BCE).

Certain scholarship holds that the practices, emblems and architecture now commonly associated with the Hindu pantheon and Jainism may go back as far as Late Harappan times to the period 2000-1500 BCE. Hinduism is divided into numerous denominations, primarily Shaivism, Shaktism, Vaishnavism, Smarta and much smaller groups like the conservative Shrauta. Hindu reform movements and Ayyavazhi are more recent. About 90% of Hindus reside in the Republic of India, accounting for 83% of its population.

Sikhism was founded in the 15th century on the

teachings of Guru Nanak and the nine successive Sikh Gurus in Northern India. The vast majority of its adherents originate in the Punjab region. India is the only country in the world where a large number of religions have not only evolved but flourished and have grown from strength to strength. Religion is an integral aspect of life in India. Religion has a great impact on the personal lives of people of India on a daily basis. India is a secular state, where the constitution honors all religions equally. India is one of the few countries of the world where the social and religious identity of the nation has remained intact despite numerous invasions, persecution, colonialism and political upsurges.

India has traditionally been a land of faith and spirituality – it is home to the adherents of all the major religions of the world. Out of these, four were born in India while the others came with invaders, travellers and missionaries from abroad. While India is the cradle of Hinduism, Buddhism, Jainism and Sikhism, Islam can be compared to an adopted child as it has been part of our social and cultural fabric for centuries. Judaism, Christianity, Zoroastrianism and Baha'ism also have their followers in India but they are very small in number. Despite the multitude of faiths prevalent in India, the country has by and large, been free of any internecine strife.

Hindus constitute an overwhelming majority in the country and it is a creed which is renowned for its catholicity of outlook. For Hindus, religion is a tool to achieve a one-to-one communication between god and man. However, Hinduism became too ritualistic; and in the 6th century B.C., a great social churning took place in the country – out of which emerged Jainism and Buddhism. Jains place self-conquest above all else – it is one of the most ascetics of faiths, with its votaries living in the most spartan manner imaginable. Buddhism, on the other hand was exported to the Far East, although its philosophy was almost snuffed out in the land of its origin. An iconoclastic faith like Buddhism could not compete with ritualistic Brahminism that cleverly co-opted Buddha into their 'holy pantheon of gods'.

It is not possible to explore India without understanding its religious beliefs and practices. A number of world religions originated in India, and others that started elsewhere strengthened here. To understand India, it is important to understand its religions as religion casts its shadow on every Indian, right from their birth. There are many religions followed here but detail about some of them is given below. Over 80 percent of Indians are Hindu, but there are significant minorities.

Muslims number about 110 million and there are over 20 million Christians, 18 million Sikhs, 6 million Buddhists and a number of other religious groups. The Indian religious and social life is driven by the caste system. While the same has undergone substantial charges since Independence, especially in towns and cities, but most people in India are still clearly identified as a member of a particular caste group. Indian religion is characterized by use of symbols and icons for worship. The chanting of hymns and celebration of the festivals with lot of fanfare is worth a tourist's view for a completely delightful experience.

Hinduism

It has always been easier to define Hinduism by what it is not than by what it is. The name, Hindu name was given by foreigners to the people of the subcontinent who did not profess the other major faiths, such as Muslims or Christians. The beliefs and practices of modern Hinduism began to take shape in the centuries on either side of the birth of Christ. But while some aspects of modern Hinduism can be traced back more than 2,000 years before that, other features are recent.

The four holy abodes for Hindus, where usually "Sanyas" is attained are well visited by all-

- Badrinath - A ice Shiva Linga in the Himalayas
- Puri - the incarnation of Lord Krishna in Orissa

- Ramesvaram - the southern tip of India
- Dwarka - the birth place of Lord Krishna in Gujarat

Buddhism

India was the home of Buddhism, which had its roots in the early Hinduism, or Brahmanism, of its time. Today it is practiced only on the margins of the subcontinent from Ladakh, Nepal and Bhutan in the north to Sri Lanka in the south. Although there are approximately 5 million Buddhists in India, most are very recent converts. The last adherents of the early schools of Buddhism have been killed or converted by the Muslim invaders of the 13th century.

India has sites of great significance for Buddhists around the world. Some say that the Buddha himself spoke of the four places his followers should visit. Lumbini, the Buddha's birthplace, is in the Nepali foothills, near the present border with India. Bodh Gaya is about 80 kilometres south of the modern Indian city of Patna, where he attained what his supreme enlightenment'. The deer park at Sarnath, where he preached his first sermon and set in motion the Wheel of the Law, is just outside Varanasi while Kushinagar, where he died at the age of 80, is 50 kilometres east of Gorakhpur.

Jainism

Like Buddhism, Jainism started as a reform movement of the Brahmanic religious beliefs of the sixth century BC. Its founder was a widely revered saint and ascetic, Vardhamma, who became known as Mahavir - 'great hero'. Mahavir was born in the same border region of India and Nepal as the Buddha, just 50 kilometres north of modern Patna, probably in 599 BC. Thus he was about 35 years older than the Buddha. His family, also royal, was followers of an ascetic saint, Parsvanatha, who according to Jain tradition had lived 200 years previously.

The 18 metres high free-standing statue of Gommateshvara at Sravana Belgola near Mysore (built about 983

AD) is just one outstanding example of the contribution of Jain art to India's heritage.

Sikhism

Guru Nanak, the founder of the religion was born just west of Lahore and grew up in what is now the Pakistani town of Sultanpur. His followers, the Sikhs, (derived from the Sanskrit word for 'disciples') form perhaps one of India's most recognizable groups. Beards and turbans give them a very distinctive presence and although they represent less than two percent of the population they are both politically and economically significant. The Sikhism was propagated through the ten gurus and the code of conduct lay down by them. The famous shrines of Sikhs are Harmandir Sahib in Amritsar, Anandpur Sahib in Punjab, Paonta Sahib in UP, Hazoor Sahib in Maharashtra and Manikaran Sahib in the Valley of flowers.

Islamism

Islam is a highly visible presence in India today. Even after partition in 1947 over 40 million Muslims remained in India and today there are just over 105 million. Islam is the most recent of imported religions. Islamic contact with India was first made around 636 AD and then by the navies of the Arab Mohammad al Qasim in 710-712 AD. These conquerors of Sindh made very few coverts, although they did have to develop a legal recognition for the status of non-Muslims in a Muslim-ruled state. From the creation of the Delhi Sultanate in 1206, by Turkish rather than Arab power, Islam became a permanent living religion in India.

Christianism

There are about 23 million Christians in India. Christianity ranks third in terms of religious affiliation after Hinduism and Islam and there are Christian congregations in all the major towns of India. The great majority of the

Protestant Christians in India are now members of the Church of South India, formed from the major Protestant denominations in 1947, or the Church of North India, which followed suit in 1970. Together they account for approximately half the total number of Christians. Roman Catholics make up the majority of the rest. Many of the church congregations, both in towns and villages, are active centres of Christian worship.

A Country of Diverse Religion

Four main religions were born in India while the others came with invaders, travellers and missionaries from abroad. Despite the multitude of faiths prevalent in India, the country has by and large, been free of any internecine strife. Hindus constitute an overwhelming majority in the country and it is a creed which is renowned for its catholicity of outlook. For Hindus, religion is a tool to achieve a one-to-one communication between god and man.

However, Hinduism became too ritualistic; and in the 6th century B.C., a great social churning took place in the country – out of which emerged Jainism and Buddhism. Jains place self-conquest above all else – it is one of the most ascetics of faiths, with its votaries living in the most spartan manner imaginable. Buddhism, on the other hand was exported to the Far East, although its philosophy was almost snuffed out in the land of its origin. An iconoclastic faith like Buddhism could not compete with ritualistic Brahminism that cleverly co-opted Buddha into their 'holy pantheon of gods'.

Dominance of Islamic Religion

By the 12th century, India began to get coloured with a distinctly Islamic flavour as wave after wave of Islamic hordes descended on the country. Drawing sustenance from the Koran and the Sunnah (sayings of Prophet Mohammad), their missionary zeal was unmatched. Although Islam (which has two main sects – the Shias and the Sunnis) is as distinct from Hinduism as chalk from cheese, the two faiths learnt to coexist with each other, cheek by jowl and the confluence of the two religions produced a cultural syncretism, which is exemplified by the Urdu language – an amalgam of Persian and Hindi and out of the fusion of the two cultures arose new religious denominations – uniquely Indian, which characterised the Hindu-Islamic interface.

The best example of that synthesis are the Ahmediyas – a sect that abides by the Holy Koran and the Prophet, yet practises idolatry which is a decidedly Hindu custom. Christianity and if you think that Christianity came to India with the Europeans – you would be off the mark by 1500 years. For St. Thomas came to India in 50 A.D. and brought the teachings of Jesus along with him – even before the Messiah was adopted by Europe. But the Europeans did bring with them a scientific temper and the Indian Renaissance of the 19th century, was largely due to their influence. As Albert Einstein said "religion without science is mere superstition" and men like Raja Ram Mohan Roy and Swami Vivekananda strove to inculcate a rational outlook among their countrymen. Vivekananda put it eloquently when he said that "I do not believe that a god, who cannot provide me food to eat on earth, will ever give me paradise in heaven".

Religion in Positive Manner

Suffice to say in the end that we could actually work miracles if we used religion in a positive manner. India is a land which has always been tolerant of people belonging to different races and religions. After all the Jews who have been persecuted the world over, have never been discriminated against in India and the Zoroastrians fled Iran in the eighth century and sought sanctuary in India, when they suffered maltreatment in the former country. Small wonder then that most major religions have made their presence felt in India.

The Theosophical Society

The Theosophical Society was inspired by the philosophy and mysticism inherent in Hinduism and came into being through the efforts of the celebrated Russian born occultist, H.P. Blavatsky and her American colleagues, B.S. Olcott, W.Q. Judge and thirteen others who established the society in New York on 17 November 1875. Their motivation was the "wisdom of the East" and their desire for the "spiritual regeneration of man". They declared themselves to be the disciples of an Indian mahatma, a `jivanmukta` (liberated soul) dwelling in the Himalayas. He was himself a member of `samsara` (the ocean of births and deaths) but who remained "in incarnation to help the world on its upward path" and they turned to India for inspiration and strength.

In 1882 they chose a site on the banks of the Adyar, Madras for its permanent headquarters which is visited by numerous people every year and is a holy shrine for all religions. The main hall has bass reliefs representing the founders of the world religions. It comprises of Christ knocking at a closed door; Buddha in meditation; Krishna, flute in hand, leaning on a cow; Zarathushtra; a verse from the Koran inscribed on the wall; symbolic representations of Jainism, Buddhism, Judaism, Sikhism, Confucianism and other faiths, such as, the beliefs of ancient Egypt and Mexico and Mithraism. The origins of the Theosophical movement were therefore deep rooted in one pattern of socio-religious dispute within western civilization of India.

The term 'Theo-sophy' or divine wisdom evolved and also became popular in the seventeenth century. As Theosophy developed into a movement in India, it exploited ideas and symbols from Egyptian, Hindu, and Buddhist religions as justification for its criticism of contemporary life in Europe and America. Helena Petrovna Blavatsky and Henry Steel Olcott brought about this movement in 1875 after becoming acquainted through a shared interest in spiritualism. Alice Bailey, Annie Besant, Geoffrey Hodson,

C.W. Leadbeater, Alfred Percy Sinnett, Rudolf Steiner and Abner Doubleday are the prominent personalities who worked with the Theosophical society.

The Theosophical Society was the organization formed to advance the spiritual principles and search for Truth known as Theosophy. The main objective of the Theosophical Society was the investigation, study and explanation of mediumistic phenomena. After a few years Olcott and Blavatsky traveled to India and established the International Headquarters at Adyar, Madras (Chennai). There, they also became interested in studying Eastern religions, and these were included in the Society's agenda.

By 1889 when Blavatsky wrote Key to Theosophy, it mentioned the aims of the Theosophical Society, which are as follows:

- To form the nucleus of a Universal Brotherhood of Humanity without discrimination of race, color, or creed.
- The society promoted the study of Aryan and other Scriptures, of the World's religion and sciences, and to vindicate the importance of old Asiatic literature, namely, of the Buddhist, Brahmanical, and Zoroastrian philosophies.
- To inspect the hidden mysteries of Nature under every aspect possible, and the supernatural and spiritual powers dormant in man especially.

As early as 1889 Blavatsky also claimed a group of Theosophical students that the real purpose of establishing the Society was to prepare humanity for the reception of the international teachings when he appeared again, in addition to the stated objectives. This declaration was again repeated again more publicly by Annie Besant in 1896, five years after Blavatsky's death. After Helena Blavatsky's death in 1891, the Society's leaders apparently worked together peacefully, however this did not last long. Olcott and Annie Besant accused the judge of forging letters from the Mahatmas. Finally, the batch ended his association with

Olcott and Besant in 1895 and took most of the Society's American Section with him. The original organization supervised by Olcott and Besant is still in India and is known as the Theosophical Society - Adyar.

The section led by Judge is today known as the Theosophical Society, but often with the advisory statement, "international headquarters, Pasadena, California". A third society, the United Lodge of Theosophists or ULT, in 1909 got separated from the latter organization, and various small fragment groups began to evolve including the Palmers Green Theosophical Lodge under the leadership of Thomas Neumark-Jones that was influential among British New Liberal intellectuals. In 1902, Rudolph Steiner became General Secretary of the German/Austrian division of the Theosophical Society, he maintained a Western-oriented course, comparatively self-governing from the Adyar headquarter led by Besant and Olcott.

After grave philosophical disagreements, primarily on the spiritual allegation of Christ and on the status of the young boy Krishnamurti, most of the German and Austrian members divided into other groups in 1913 and formed the Anthroposophical Society that remains very active and influential today and has branches in almost all western communities, including the US and Canada. Theosophists have worked for the promotion of harmony, understanding and mutual respect among the religions. Much of theosophical lecturing and literature has concerned itself with the comparative study of religions, tracing their essential unity and reverentially analyzing, their teachings.

The society's Adyar library and research centre has books on ideology and the promotion of oriental learning. Started in 1886 by Olcott, it has some 17,500 palm leaf and paper manuscripts from many countries and more than a hundred and fifty thousand books on the religions, philosophies and cultures of the world, and on occultism and the spiritual life, in most of the major languages.

Theosophists all over the world regard India as the home of true religion and as the spiritual teacher of the world. The Indian section is numerically the largest national section of the society and has influenced large numbers who are not professed theosophists. There are several organisations somewhat parallel to the Theosophical Society at Adyar which draw their inspiration and their teaching from Blavatsky. However, these have a separate and independent existence.

There are many branches of the Theosophical Society in the world they are as follows:

- Theosophical Society at Pasadena, California
- Theosophical Society, Unterlengenhardt, Germany
- United Lodge of Theosophists, Los Angeles

Anthroposophical Society, Germany, was also a part of this society. But it broke away from the parent body Adyar and today it is still active in some countries. There is a great deal of co-operation between these offshoots of the theosophical movement, which is given voice through the monthly journal, Theosophists Reunite. It is published in California.

Racial Beliefs in Theosophical Society

Blavatsky declared that humanity had come down from a series of "Root Races", and named the fifth root race (out of seven) the Aryan race. The Root Races were evolutionary stages, each new Root Race being more evolved than the previous one. She thought that the Aryans originally came from Atlantis, who was part of the fourth Root Race. The Aryan Root Race was only one more step in the evolutionary progress and a more spiritual Root Race; the sixth would eventually supersede it. Blavatsky believed that Semitic peoples were later Aryans who have disintegrated in spirituality and thus perfected in materiality. Blavatsky did not encourage any feeling of superiority by any person or race and thus effectively spread the idea of the common origin and destiny of all humanity, and establishing the principle of universal brotherhood as the primary aim of the Theosophical Society.

This society looked for one single goal to form the nucleus of a Universal Brotherhood of Humanity without any discrimination amongst race, colour, or creed. Thus, she declares that Theosophists actually respect the Bible as much as they do the sacred books of other races and religions. The theosophists find the declarations of all the holy book it the same eternal truths as in the Vedas, the Tripitakas, and the Zend-Avesta and so on. Guido von List and his followers Lanz von Liebenfels, later started to follow some of Blavatsky's ideas, mixing her philosophy with patriotic and fascist ideas. These ideas and the system of thought became widely known as Ariosophy. Alike Theosophy, Ariosophy had based on rational expositions of ethnic development.

The Bhagavadgita and its Philosophy

The Mortal and the Immortal

The First Chapter of the Bhagavadgita pinpoints the basic difficulties which a spiritual seeker may face in the long run, in spite of the preparations that he might have made with all his logical conclusions and sincerity of purpose. In the earlier stages of our aspirations we do not fully realise the problems that are hidden deep, invisibly beneath the outer layers of our personality, not directly connected with our daily life. We have an unconscious personality apart from the conscious one limited to this bodily existence, and this unconscious level of ours is larger in its content than the little expression of it we visualise outside as the body and its sensory relations. There are fears of various types which keep us secretly unhappy, and many of the activities of life in the conscious level are attempts to brush aside these fears; and then we imagine that they do not exist at all. We occupy ourselves so busily with works of various types as a kind of outlet or counteracting power against these fears, usually known in the language of psychology as 'defence mechanisms.'

We protect ourselves by certain psychic mechanisms which we have formed within ourselves as a kind of self-deception, we may say, finally. This is the attitude of the ostrich which is said to bury its head in the sand when it is threatened with any kind of fear outside. It hides its head in the sand so that it cannot see things outside, and when nothing is seen outside, it thinks that nothing exists outside. This is not merely the ostrich's way, but, perhaps, the attitude of every human being when he is faced with insoluble difficulties. The problems are mostly in the unconscious level; they are not always on the conscious surface.

It may not appear to us that they exist at all. We are comfortably placed in a sensory world wherein the senses are fed to surfeit and they keep us completely ignorant of the dangerous abyss through which we may have to pass in the future stages of our life. We are brain-washed by the impetuous activities of the senses to such an extent that we cannot be aware of what is ahead of us, what may happen tomorrow. Because, if we can be awakened to the fact of all things that are to be faced in the future, we may perish just now with a fear of it, and Nature does not want anybody to die like that, and defeat its purpose. Nature keeps everything as a secret and lets the cat out of the bag only when necessary.

Now, when the tremendous confrontation of the Mahabharata battle was there staring at the face of the otherwise heroic Arjuna, what was unconsciously present in the human being that he was came off and spoke in its own voice. Fears which were otherwise unknown and undreamt of manifested themselves as the only realities and gripped Arjuna with such power that his personality changed completely, and he was not the man that he was before. We can suddenly become different persons in a moment if serious conditions overtake us. Just a second is enough to transform one into a different personality altogether, and one can be a personality of any type, because we are everything inside us. Everything that is anywhere exists also within us. And anything can come out under a given condition. It all depends upon the particular button that is pushed, and there you have the genius coming up, as if we have rubbed the lamp of Alladin, which you hear in the stories of the Arabian Knights.

Great fears overpowered Arjuna's mind like serious diseases. Doubts of various kinds harass our minds when we begin to tread the path of the spirit because of a basic misconstruing of the very meaning of the path chosen, which mistake we commit due to a lack of proper training in the art of living the spiritual life. An emotional stirring up of oneself into the enthusiasm of love of God, due to the study of scriptures or mystical texts, or listening to the sermon of a master, cannot be regarded as a reliable support for all time to come. There must be a conviction which must go deep into the heart, and as long as the head and heart stand apart like the two poles of the earth, there is the likelihood of the psychic apparatus getting out of order and throwing us in different directions as scattered pieces of our personality, so that we may lose even the little that we had earlier.

This is what they call the 'fall' in the language of mysticism, religion and spirituality. This happens because we are not studying ourselves properly and we had a wrong notion of ourselves based upon what we know through sense-perceptions, social relationships, etc. The doubts that arise in the mind later on, when we advance sufficiently on the path, can be many, but those that are recorded in the first chapter of the Gita, as those that occurred to the mind of Arjuna, are a few. He had a few serious difficulties which he posed before Krishna. All this is the preparation for the war, the battle in which the seeking spirit is confronting Nature as a whole, and the society outside. "Can this adventure be a mistake on our part?" "Have I committed a blunder with no proper thought?"

When we grow older in age, these doubts can come to the mind. "Is there not something different from what I am seeking just now?" I have made an evaluation of human society, my relationship with human society, and the world as a whole; and have come to a conclusion that they are to be faced in a storm if it becomes necessary. They are to be subdued and thrown out, abandoned, put down for the purpose of the achievement of spiritual victory. But is this a proper attitude? Shall we face in a war those things, those persons, who have been our support and in regard to whom we are certainly required to per form certain obligations?

There is what is called ethics and morality; there is etiquette and goodness, a charitable feeling, all of which is quite different from the spirit of battle or war with the atmosphere outside. Are we to consider it friendly and accommodate it with our relationships in the world of sense? Or, are we to fight with everything? What should be our spirit, our attitude in relation to the world and human society? A spirit of accommodation is one thing and a spirit of war is another thing. Are things to be completely put down with the power of our arms? Or, can this attitude be an error on our side?"

Arjuna puts this question: "Is this not a mistake? Are we expected to face our brethren, our nephews, our relations, our grandsire, our teachers as if they are our opponents? Is the world our enemy? Are we to confront society as an unfriendly environment? This is one difficulty. Secondly, if we set this example before other people, naturally, we expect others also to follow the same thing as a permissible attitude. The world will follow suit along this line, which will end in a chaos of the entire society, a destruction of all human values, and a defeat of the very purpose of creation. Is this not a sin that we commit? Are we to create disorder in human society in the name of a so-called victory, in the name of an idea that we have placed before ourselves calling it Dharma or justice?

But, there is another difficulty, yet. Is it certain that we are going to win victory in this battle? The world is mighty enough, and human society is very complicated in its make. Are we sure that we are to be the winners, or can it be the other way round? We may be overpowered by the powers of Nature or we may be destroyed by the ethics of society. Considering all these aspects of the situation it appears to me that all these engagements of ours are a futile attempt. We have to think thrice before we take a step. To me, at least, it appears that there is a basic error in the entire outlook with which we have embarked upon this war. "I shall do nothing," says Arjuna, and throws down the weapon of all effort, enthusiasm and aspiration, and reverts to the level of the ordinary human being of sentiments and sense-ridden satisfaction.

The difficulties mentioned, in a few words, in the first chapter of the Bhagavadgita are not ordinary jokes or mere stories told to us for our cajolement. These things are the difficulties of human nature as such. It is not just my difficulty or your difficulty. Anyone who is human shall have to pass through these stages. Who can ever gainsay that one does not think in terms of gains and losses, in the light of one's relationship with the world outside and human society externally. We love and hate and have our ways in this complex of relationship in the world and in all human affairs. Where does God come in here into this picture? The notion of God has also been a frightening factor many a time in the history of human thought. And there have been as many ideas of God as there are people in this world.

There are those who denied the very existence of such a thing as God, because of the fact that there are no proofs adequate enough to convince us of God's existence: All our arguments are sensory in the end, the logic of philosophy is a phenomenal argument and it can not touch what we imagine to be the noumenon, or a transcendent Being, because the substantiation of the existence of anything transcendent cannot be achieved through the instrument of phenomenal reason. There are people who have been totally agnostic. God may be, or may not be. Even if He is there, it is all something impossible for us to understand with the faculties with which we are endowed at present. But more serious difficulties are those which faced Arjuna's mind, and which gradually creep into our own minds, and keep us inwardly insecure and anxious.

The anxiety of a spiritual seeker is due to doubts as to the possibility of success in the spiritual path, doubts concerning the correctness of the approach which one has launched, doubts as regards the duties one owes to the world and to human society, and, finally, doubts even concerning what will happen to oneself, taking for granted that this realisation takes place. These doubts are not ordinary ones. They are present, perhaps, in every one of us, in some measure, in some proportion. And nothing can be more frightening to the ego of the human being than to be told that God is All-Power and the experience of God means an abolition of individuality. No one expects this, and one keeps that situation as far away from oneself as possible, postpones it to an indefinite future and closes one's eyes to such a possibility at all. What can be a greater fear than that of losing oneself, even if it be in the ocean of God Himself? We would not want to be drowned even if it be in a sea of nectar.

Now, the sum and substance of the first chapter of the Bhagavadgita is this much;—a relinquishment of all effort, which originally was the spring of action of the seeking state. After years of spiritual practice one may content oneself with being the very same person that one was many years back and lead the little life of the man of the street either due to incapacity or due to a total disillusionment here. There are several types of spiritual seekers who may have to face the same problems, no doubt, but who will be taken along different paths on account of the varying extent of the clarity of their spirits and the sincerity of purpose with which they have started the adventure of spiritual life.

When our search is sincere and hundred percent genuine, notwithstanding the fact that we have not understood things entirely, we will be taken care of by the powers of the world and we will see light rising in the horizon, and a Guru, or a teacher, or a master like Krishna, will be there in front of us, and we will be placed in the context or juxtaposition of such a master by the nature of the universe, by the very law of creation, by the justice of God. In the earlier stages one may be reluctant even to receive the advice of the master fully. Even when one is face to face with a competent teacher, one may not be prepared to act upon the teaching entirely. This happened to Arjuna also by a circumstance described in the very beginning of the second chapter.

The great teacher told him, "This is an unworthy and unbecoming attitude on your part at this crucial moment of time." The retort of Arjuna was, "I am sorry; however, I have decided that I am not going to take up arms. What is the good of all this bloody warfare whereby everything is going to be destroyed! Everything is to be swallowed up by the gaping mouths of doom." Then a necessity arises for the teacher to take the disciple along the proper course and lead him up, stage by stage. A competent teacher understands the level of the mind of the student and takes his stand on that level, which is sometimes called the Socratic method of teaching.

The teacher does not impose himself upon the student, because a flowering of the bud of the mind of the student is essential. We cannot forcefully open it, for, if it is done, there would not be a blossomed flower. "All right," says Krishna, "I understand what you say. You have a fear that you may not win victory. You may have other difficulties apart from this, namely, the social catastrophe that may follow the destruction." Any argument or logical approach should take into consideration what is called the 'universe of discourse.' One must know the field in which the reason is operating at any given moment of time. One cannot jump into another field altogether different from the one in which the reason operates. We argue as a citizen of the world, a unit in human society, or we argue on the basis of our being a metaphysical unit.

A metaphysical argument should not be employed to solve problems which are purely social and personal, too intimate perhaps, material or physical. Similarly, purely social and economic arguments should not be used in the description or understanding of metaphysical realities. Everything has to be taken at the level in which it is. And Arjuna made a mistake of mixing up his arguments. He was on the one hand fear-struck with the possibility of death and destruction in the war, he might die and he might lose everything; and the question of success or victory in war does not arise if that predicament takes place. On the other hand, he had a fear from society, the fear of committing sin by way of destruction of values conducive to social solidarity.

And he did not understand what would happen to him as a result of these errors that he might commit in the name of war. The metaphysical side of human nature is in a peculiar manner connected with the empirical features. In the very beginning of the second chapter, Krishna resorts to the principle of the immortality of the soul. Do we die, really? The phenomenon of death is analysed threadbare. Who dies? And what is the meaning of death? Death is generally regarded as destruction. Does it stand to reason to say that anything can be totally destroyed? Is there a real destruction of anything? Now, destruction is the total negation of what is, and what is, is called the real. When some thing really exists, it cannot be called a phenomenon or a passing phase. A real thing cannot pass away, and that which passes away cannot be called the real. The real has to 'be', and, therefore, it is called the real.

The unreal cannot be, and there is no necessity to entertain any kind of fear or doubt in regard to it either that which dies is real or unreal. We cannot have a third alternative to imagine. Something dies, or someone dies. Is that thing or that person real, or unreal? We have to be clear in our minds when we consider this process of arguing. If we say that the thing that has died was real, then we are contradicting ourselves, because, if it had been real, it could not be destroyed; there is no death for it. It is already declared that it is real, and the real cannot not be and the unreal cannot be. Thus, that which is, that which is real, cannot be regarded as destructible. If we say that the thing that has died is not real, that it is unreal, then there is no question of its death; it has already been dubbed as unreal. The destruction of a non-existent thing is unthinkable.

And a destruction of an existent thing, also, is equally unthinkable; because, that which is existent cannot be destroyed, and that which can be destroyed cannot be regarded as existent. Then, what is it that dies? The phenomenon of death is visible before our eyes because of a mixing up of standpoints. This mixing up is called, in philosophic language, Adhyasa, a superimposition of one thing on another thing. We read one meaning in another and that meaning in this, and so on. That which exists is not that which dies. And that which does not exist is not that which dies. Therefore, one cannot say what dies. The process of death is one of transition, and is not a 'destruction' of anything. A change of condition is what we call death, which is a change that is required by the law of the evolution of the universe. In fact, we die every moment.

Every cell of our body changes constantly and it is opined by biologists that after every seven years we become entirely changed personalities, physically. All the cells of the body renew themselves in such a manner that we are new beings after many years. Not merely that; every day there is transformation as we grow. We have grown from baby-hood to this adulthood of today. But we have never seen how we have grown. This process of growing was imperceptible. And, if growth is nothing but change, how is it that it could not be perceived? We never knew that we are becoming something else every moment. All change is perceptible, visible, recognisable. But in our own case of growth, for instance, we never knew, we never recognised, we never felt that we are changing; all this because there is something in us which does not change. That character of this mysterious entity in us which does not change is the real reason behind the fear of death and the love of life. Change is only a condition and not a substance; it is not a thing. It is, therefore, not a reality. But it appears as if some tremendous event takes place at the time of death, for all our practical purposes.

We are horrified at the very name of death. The horrific nature of death is due to the identification of characters belonging to two levels of our being, the spiritual or the metaphysical getting transferred to the temporal or the transitional, and vice versa. We see two things at the same time imagining that it is one thing and that the experience is not constituted of two different things. There is a procession of events, a continuous change of process charged with a unitary invisibility of being which our basic essentiality is. We call it the Atman, the soul, the self, consciousness, etc. There is an indestructible element in us, and that has got mixed with the condition of change which infects every thing that is finite. We are imbued with the world of finites, of the bodily individuality of ours, and even the psychic isolation of ours is a character of our finitude.

The finite struggles to align itself with the Infinite, to which it really belongs, and this struggle of the finite to move towards the Infinite is the whole story of evolution. Any change, any transformation, any movement whatsoever, anywhere in this world, at any time, is a consequence of this impulse from the finite in the direction of the Infinite; and no one can remain for ever as a finite, inasmuch as the finitude of being is an unnatural state of being. The unnatural cannot always be, it tries to overcome and transcend itself and expand itself into the higher stage which moves gradually towards an infinitude of realisation. This tendency of the finitude in us towards the Infinite that is really there is the reason behind transmigration, birth and death. What we call birth-and-death, or rebirth, transmigration, metempsychosis, etc., is a necessary obligation on the part of everything that is finite in the light of the all-comprehensiveness of the Infinite.

We cannot maintain our individual personalities continuously intact. As a matter of fact, we cannot be the same individuals even for two seconds together. Every moment we change and move and urge in the direction of a larger achievement. But, because of the fact that our consciousness is tethered, somehow, to the finitude of body and mind, it appears as if the whole of our 'being' has changed. And when the change becomes so intense as to make it impossible for the mind to contain it within itself, when the change that is to take place for this purpose becomes marked in the sense of a total change in the form of this finitude, it appears as if our essential being itself has undergone a process of destruction. There are two kinds of change; that particular series of changes which we pass through everyday as in the case of our growth, for instance, from baby-hood to adulthood, etc., and the other one which we usually call death.

While the constituents of our finitude change in the manner of a growth in a new form, we do not feel this transformation or change in a marked manner, because this complex we call the body in this space-time world somehow maintains its particular form of complexity, and as we are living in a world of senses, and the senses regard this body as the self, we do not feel that anything serious has taken place to us in this frame of space-time. As long as this form is maintained we feel ourselves intact, but when the conditions of the process of evolution require a change in the very form of this finitude, and we are to be shifted from one spacetime order to another space-time realm, it appears that there is a total annihilation of personality. Death is a transformation of us from one space-time order to another space-time structure. We move from one continuum of space-time to another continuum. It does not mean that the universe is made up of one type of space-time only.

The present system is one particular arrangement of space-time and this particular body of ours is in consonance with the requirements of the order of space-time in which we are at present. When the time-series and the spatial order changes in the higher ascent of us, the whole physical form has to be shed completely and a new form has to be assumed for this purpose. But inasmuch as our consciousness, the soul, is connected with this particular bodily complex, we imagine that this transformation of ourselves from one space-time order to another is a destruction of ourselves, and as destruction is fearsome, we hate death. Now, therefore, the fear of death is due to a misconception in our minds on account of a lack of understanding of what the universe requires from us. We are not punished by death. We are only educated by it. And the Bhagavadgita gives a simple analogy to explain what actually happens in the process of death. We cast off one garment when it is worn out and put on another which is new.

When we throw off old clothes and put on new ones, we do not imagine that we have lost something valuable. Likewise is the change of body, and we should not imagine that there is a real loss in death, this process being a necessity, and also because of the fact that we are entering into a new life altogether in the direction of a personal transvaluation of values for the growth of our personalities, because the justice of God shall reign supreme finally, and the truth of the universe shall assert itself eternally. The assertions of the universe in experience are the various series of phenomena to be seen in the world. All change, whatever be its nature, throughout human history, is a requirement of the assertion of the cosmic justice, and birth and death are part of this requirement.

So, "Arjuna, you are unnecessarily weeping over something in regard to which wise ones will not grieve. Birth and death do not become the causes of sorrow to people who are endowed with wisdom, who can see through things and not confine their vision merely to the outer form of the events of the universe. Your sorrow is because of the fact that your vision is limited to your senses merely, and you are unable to think in the light of the higher requirement of the law of the cosmos. Thus, your argument that death is an undesirable consequence that follows the battle of life is fallacious." And the knowledge that is positive in the light of the ultimate reality of things will follow.

2

Modern India
Religion, Law, and Judiciary

Among the seven nations of South Asia forming the South Asian Association for Regional Cooperation (SAARC), India stands out as the only country that has declared itself a secular State. In each of the remaining six nations, one or another spiritual faith has the status of the officially adopted or legally promoted religion-Buddhism in Bhutan and Sri Lanka; Hinduism in Nepal; and Islam in Bangladesh, Maldives, and Pakistan. Constitutionally, India is a secular country and therefore has no State religion. However, it has developed over the years its own unique concept of secularism that is fundamentally different from the parallel American concept of secularism requiring complete separation of church and state, as also from the French ideal of la cit.

Despite the clear incorporation of all the basic principles of secularism into various provisions of the Constitution when originally enacted, its preamble did not then include the word secular in the short description of the country, which it called a "Sovereign Democratic Republic." This was, of course, not an inadvertent omission but a well-calculated decision meant to avoid any misgiving that India was to adopt any of the western notions of a secular state. Twenty-five years later-by which time India's peculiar concept of secularism had been fully established through its own judicial decisions and state practice, the preamble to the Constitution was amended to include the word "secular" (along with "socialist") to declare India to be a "Sovereign Socialist Secular Democratic Republic."

This briefly states and explains the constitutional, statutory, and judicial framework of India's religion-state relations, and the unique balance that is found in that framework between secularism and freedom of religion-namely that, in India, the law of the land determines the scope of religion in society; it is not religion that determines the scope of the law.

Constitutional Foundations

Constitutionally, India is a secular nation, but any "wall of separation" between religion and state exists neither in law nor in practice-the two can, and often do, interact and intervene in each other's affairs within the legally prescribed and judicially settled parameters. Indian secularism does not require a total banishment of religion from the societal or even state affairs. The only demand of secularism, as mandated by the Indian Constitution, is that the state must treat all religious creeds and their respective adherents absolutely equally and without any discrimination in all matters under its direct or indirect control.

In this Part, Section A below describes the constitutional mandates that apply to all religions, and Section B discusses the provisions that relate to certain religious communities and their faiths. The Constitution of India contains in its chapter on Fundamental Rights several provisions that emphasize complete legal equality of its citizens and prohibit any kind of religion-based discrimination between them. Among these provisions are the following:

"The State shall not deny to any person equality before the law or the equal protection of the laws within the territory of India."

"The State shall not discriminate against any citizen on grounds only of religion, race, caste, sex, place of birth, or any of them."

"No citizen shall, on grounds only of religion . .be subjected to any disability, liability, restriction or condition with regard to access to or use of various public places."

"No citizen shall, on grounds only of religion. . .be ineligible for, or discriminated against, in respect of any employment or office under the State."

Regarding the people's right to religious liberty, the Fundamental Rights chapter in the Constitution provides in general terms that:

All persons are equally entitled to "freedom of conscience and the right freely to profess, practice and propagate religion."

Every "religious denomination or any section thereof" shall have the right (a) to establish and maintain institutions for religious and charitable purposes; (b) to manage its own affairs in matters of religion; (c) to own and acquire movable and immovable property; and (d) to administer such property in accordance with law. The State may, however, pass laws providing for "social welfare and reform," and may also freely regulate or restrict "secular activity"economic, financial, political, etc.-even though it may be traditionally associated with religion.

There shall be "freedom as to payment of taxes for promotion of any particular religion"-by virtue of which no person shall be compelled to pay any taxes where the proceeds are specifically appropriated in payment of expenses for the promotion or maintenance of any particular religious denomination. No religious instruction is to be provided in the schools wholly maintained by State funding.Those attending any State recognized or State-aided school cannot be required to take part in any religious instruction or services without consent.

"Any section of the citizens residing in the territory of India or any part thereof having a distinct language, script or culture of its own shall have the right to conserve the same." Religious minorities are free to establish and administer educational institutions of their choice, which shall not be discriminated against by the State in the matter of giving aid. But no institution maintained by the State or receiving aid from it is to deny admission to any citizen only on the ground of religion.

The chapter on Fundamental Duties under the Constitution includes the following among the basic national obligations of all the citizens:

"to promote harmony and the spirit of common brotherhood amongst all the people of India transcending religious, linguistic and regional or sectional diversities," and "to value and preserve the rich heritage of our composite culture."

Community-Specific Provisions

Side by side with the aforestated general provisions relating to religious neutrality of the state and religious liberties of the people, we find within the Constitution of India a number of religion-based and religion-related provisions for particular communities. Among these are the following:

- A provision in the chapter on Directive Principles of State Policy requiring legal prohibition of the slaughter of cows and calves (in an obvious recognition of the Hindu reverence for the bovine creatures).
- A provision in the chapter on Fundamental Rights saying that carrying the sacred kirpan (a small sword) in public places would be regarded as a "fundamental right" for the Sikhs.
- An explanatory provision in the chapter on Fundamental Rights enabling the State to legislate for

removing all sorts of caste-based restrictions on entry to Hindu, Buddhist, Jain, and Sikh temples.

- A special provision in the chapter on Finance for specified annual maintenance-allowances to be given from the State exchequer for the upkeep of Hindu temples of a certain denomination in two South Indian states-Kerala and Tamil Nadu.

Two separate provisions in the chapter on Special Provisions providing for the protection of religious customs prevalent among the tribal communities of two Christian-dominated states of North East India-Nagaland and Mizoram. There is, thus, a rather curious blend of secular and religious elements within the text of the Constitution; and it is this judicious blend that defines and determines the contours of secularism to be acted upon by the state and the religious freedom to be exercised by individuals and communities in modern India.

Legislation & State Practice

There is a large body of legislative enactments in India dealing with, or having a bearing on, religious matters pertaining to various faith groups. All this legislation, as well as the established state practice, fully conforms to the Constitutional dictates relating to secularism and parameters of religious freedom. The various sections in this Part illustrate how secularism is balanced with freedom of religion under India's legislative enactments and how religious matters are controlled by state practice, both in accordance with the basic Constitutional provisions in this context.

Religious Conversion and Renouncement

During the British rule in India, with a view to protecting the interests of converts to the rulers' religion (viz., Christianity) a law called the Caste Disabilities Removal Act was passed in 1850. The Act, of course, provided in general terms that:

So much of any law or usage now in force in India as inflicts on any person forfeiture of rights or property, or may be held in any way to impair or affect any right of inheritance by reason of his or her renouncing, or having been excluded from the communion of, any religion, or being deprived of caste, shall cease to be enforced as law in any court.

This Act remains in force to date in the whole of India except the state of Jammu and Kashmir. On the other hand, also during the British rule, some princely states outside the boundaries of what was called "British India" had enacted certain laws meant to protect the local people against the evangelic activities of the foreign Christian missionaries.

After independence from the British rule, although Parliament has never enacted any law on this subject, several states have introduced local laws imposing restrictions on religious activities (mainly on Christian missionary activities, although no law would expressly say it) that are believed to be aimed at converting people from one religion to another. The first among these local laws was the Orissa Freedom of Religion Act of 1967, providing that no person shall "convert or attempt to convert, either directly or otherwise, any person from one religious faith to another by the use of force or by inducement or by any fraudulent means."

Next came the Madhya Pradesh Freedom of Religion Act of 1968, also prohibiting conversion by "force or allurement or by fraudulent means" and requiring registration of every case of conversion with the local state authorities. Ten years later, the Arunachal Pradesh Freedom of Indigenous Faith Act of 1978 similarly prohibited conversions by force or threats, including "threat of . . . divine displeasure or social excommunication." This Act also requires that every religious conversion must be duly registered with the local govern-mental authorities.

In the current millennium, similar anti-conversion laws were enacted in the states of Tamil Nadu and Gujarat, but the former state repealed its law following a public outcry. The last state so far to enact an anti-conversion law is Rajasthan, where a Religious Freedom Bill was passed by the state legislature in March 2006.

Religious Endowments in General

During the British rule in India, three general laws were enacted one after the other to regulate the working of the endowments and trusts of a religious or charitable nature. These were the Religious Endowments Act of 1863, the Charitable Endowments Act of 1890, and the Charitable and Religious Trusts Act of 1920. The Religious Societies Act of 1880 was enacted during the British rule "to simplify the manner in which certain bodies of persons, associated for the purpose of maintaining religious worship, may hold property acquired for such purpose."

Providing guidelines for the management of property held in trust by religious societies, this law was enacted mainly for the benefit of the Christians and was not applied to the Hindus, Buddhists, and Sikhs. Also during the British rule, the provincial legislature in the Sikhdominated state of Punjab had enacted a law to regulate the management of the Sikh shrines (called gurdwaras). Known as the Sikh Gurdwaras Act of 1925, this law has remained in force after independence subject to certain amendments.

Since the advent of independence, a large body of local legislation has grown to regulate the management and working of Hindu religious endowments and trusts. Among these local laws are the Bihar Hindu Religious Trusts Act of 1950, Orissa Hindu Religious Endowments Act of 1969, and Tamil Nadu Hindu Religious and Charitable Endowments Act of 1959. No central law has yet been enacted to regulate the Hindu religious places in general. For regulating the management of the Muslim religious endowments (called wakfs) a brief central law known as the Wakf Act of 1923 was enacted during the British rule. After independence, several states including Delhi, Bihar, West Bengal, Uttar Pradesh, and Jammu and Kashmir, enacted local laws for regulating the wakfs located in their respective territories. Then, in 1954, Parliament enacted the first central law on the subject, called the Wakf Act, which was replaced four decades later with the new comprehensive Wakf Act of 1995 now in force.

Particular Shrines

Several legislative enactments-both central and local-impose state surveillance on the management of particular shrines belonging to various religious communities. The Bodh Gaya Temple Act of 1949, relating to the largest Buddhist shrine in India, provides for the "upkeep and repair" of "the great temple built by the site of the Mahabodhi Tree near the village of Bodh Gaya" in Bihar State. There are similar special laws for several Hindu shrines situated in different parts of the country, including the famous Nathwara Temple of Rajasthan, the Jagannath Temple of Orissa, and the Mahabaleshwar Temple of Madhya Pradesh. The only special law for a Muslim shrine is the Dargah Khwaja Saheb Act of 1955, relating to the Dargah of Khwaja Moinuddin Chishti at Ajmer in Rajasthan.

Protection of Religious Places in General

Two central Acts enacted in the recent past relate to the protection of religious places in general. The first of these, the Religious Institutions (Prevention of Misuse) Act of 1988, makes it an offence to use religious sites to harbor an accused or convicted criminal, or for any political purpose. The second statute, the Places of Worship (Special Provisions) Act of 1991, prohibits forcible conversion of any place of worship of any religious denomination into a place of worship of a different religious denomination, and requires preservation of the religious character of all places of worship-except the disputed mosque site in Ayodhya-as they existed on August 15, 1947, the date of India's independence.

The first of these laws was enacted with a view of curbing the Sikh insurgency in Punjab, which was at its height in the 1980s, while the second law was meant to prevent the occurrence of communal incidents like the one in which an old mosque in the holy city of Ayodhya was forcibly demolished and converted into a makeshift Hindu temple in an act of mob frenzy.

Foreign Pilgrimages

Parliamentary legislation regulates arrangements for the Muslims of India to participate in the great Haj pilgrimage annually taking place in the holy city of Makkah in Saudi Arabia to which Muslims throng from all parts of the world. During the British rule, local "Haj committees" were set up in the three major port cities of India to organize the Haj pilgrimage in accordance with the Port Haj Committees Act of 1936. After independence this law was replaced with a new Haj Committee Act enacted in 1959.

The Indian government similarly organizes the annual Hindu pilgrimage to the holy Mansarovar site, situated outside India in and around Tibet. Delegated legislation exists for it in the form of executive regulations. Both the Haj and the Mansarovar pilgrimages are subsidized by the state and are managed by separate special departments in the Union Ministry for External Affairs.

Religious Laws of Family Relations

Side by side with the secular laws of marital relations and property, India has retained the system of religion-based and community-specific "personal laws," offering individuals a choice between their respective personal laws and the parallel secular laws. The personal laws applicable to various communities have been codified and reformed to varying extents. Given below is an account of the religious elements found in the codified personal laws currently in force.

Personal laws of the Christians and Parsis

In 1866, during the British rule in India, the Native Converts' Marriage Dissolution Act was enacted and enabled married Indians converting to Christianity to seek divorce from their non-converting spouses who might have deserted them on account of the change of religion. In 1869, the British rulers enacted for the Christians an Indian Divorce Act, and three years later a Christian Marriage Act, both based on ecclesiastical law.Both these Acts have remained in force in independent India but have been subjected to certain amendments.The Indian Succession Act of 1865, enacted mainly for the Christians, was later incorporated as one of the chapters into the Indian Succession Act of 1925, which remains applicable to the Christians in independent India.

The British rulers had enacted an inheritance law for the tiny Parsi Zoroastrian community of India. Known as the Parsi Succession Act of 1865, this law was also later incorporated as a special chapter into the Indian Succession Act of 1925, which is still in force. The old Parsi Marriage and Divorce Act, also enacted in 1865, was replaced in 1936 by a new Act.58 Both the special chapter on inheritance for the Parsis under the Indian Succession Act of 1925 and the Parsi Marriage and Divorce Act of 1936 were retained in force after independence but have now been subjected to some amendments.

Personal laws of the Hindus, Buddhists, Jains, and Sikhs

In 1955-56 Parliaments enacted four religion-based personal laws applicable to the Hindus, Buddhists, Jains, and Sikhs-viz., the Hindu Marriage Act of 1955, and the Hindu Succession Act, the Hindu Adoption and

Maintenance Act, and the Hindu Minority and Guardianship Act, all three enacted in 1956. It was only for the sake of brevity that the word "Hindu"-denoting the largest of the four communities to be governed by these laws-was used in the titles of these Acts; this certainly had no reflection on the independent religious status of the other three communities. Side by side with their provisions commonly applicable to the four communities, these Acts in fact protected quite a few of their different customs and usages.

Under the Hindu Marriage Act 1955, both parties to a marriage must be Hindu, Buddhist, Jain, or Sikh, and conversion by either spouse from any of these to any other religion after marriage would be a ground for divorce available to the spouse who retains his or her faith. Conversion to any religion other than Hinduism, Buddhism, Jainism, or Sikkhism is seen as a civil offense also under each of the other three Hindu-law enactments of 1956, resulting in loss of succession, guardianship, maintenance, and adoption rights.

Thus, parents ceasing to be Hindu, Buddhist, Jain, or Sikh lose guardianship of their minor children, while convert wives and children are deprived of their right to be provided maintenance by their husbands and parents, respectively. While only a Hindu, Buddhist, Jain, or Sikh child can be adopted; abandoned children and those of unknown parentage are presumed to belong to any one of these religions so as to facilitate their adoption. If a Hindu converts to Christianity or Islam, children born to him or her after his or her conversion cannot inherit from any of their Hindu relatives unless they reconvert to Hinduism before the opening of succession.

Personal Law of the Muslims

The Muslim Personal Law (Sbariat] Application Act of 1937 directs the civil courts to apply Muslim religious law to Muslims in all matters relating to family relations, property, and succession. The Dissolution of Muslim Marriages Act of 1939 specifies the grounds on which a woman married under Muslim law can seek a judicial divorce, including obstruction by a husband of his wife's religious practices.

Contrary to the provision of Hindu marriage law of 1955, which recognizes post-marriage conversion by a spouse to an alien religion as a ground for divorce, this Act declares that the renunciation of Islam by a woman married under Muslim law would not ipso facto dissolve her marriage. The Muslim Women (Protection of Rights on Divorce) Act of 1986 has codified the traditional Islamic law on divorced women's rights to dower, maintenance, and marital properties to be speedily implemented by the lower criminal courts.

Misuse of Religion for Electoral Gains

In the domain of public law, the Representation of the People Act of 1951 prohibits the use of religion and religious symbols with a view to promoting one's candidacy for a public election or for adversely affecting the election of another such candidate. Making an appeal to vote or refrain from voting for any person on the ground of his religion, race, caste, community, or language, as well as the use of or appeal to religious symbols for the furtherance of the prospects of one's election or for prejudicially affecting the election of any candidate, is a "corrupt practice" under this law resulting in the vitiation of the election and possible criminal punishment.

Offenses against Religion

Chapter 15 of the Indian Penal Code is dedicated entirely to punishments for offenses relating to religion. In many cases, the punishments for these offenses are quite severe. Section 295 states:

Whoever destroys damages or defiles any place of worship, or any object held sacred by any class of persons with the intention of thereby insulting the religion of any class of persons . . . shall be punished with imprisonment of either description for a term which may extend to two years, or with fine, or with both.

When such acts are done deliberately or maliciously, the prison sentence may be increased to three years. It is also a crime under the Indian Penal Code to disturb a religious assembly. Though such a crime does not merit the same punishment as defiling a place of worship, it carries a sentence of up to one year in prison, fines, or both. One year in prison may also be sentenced upon any person who trespasses into a place of worship or burial site with the intention of "wounding the feelings of any person" or of "insulting the religion of any person."

Finally, under the Indian Penal Code, it is a crime punishable by up to one year in prison if anyone "utters any word or makes any sound in the hearing of that person or makes any gesture in the sight of that person or places any object in the sight of that person" with the deliberate intent of wounding the religious feelings of that person. The law reports of India abound with judicial decisions interpreting the various provisions of the Indian Penal Code relating to offenses against religion.

Commissions for Religious Minorities

The religious minorities in India have the protection of a number of national and state-level commissions, both statutory and nonstatutory, that were established to oversee the enforcement of their constitutional and legal rights. The first such national-level commission, now known as the National Commission for Minorities (NCM), was set up by a Union Cabinet Resolution in January 1978. Fourteen years later it was given a statutory status and judicial powers by the National Commission for Minorities Act 1992. Two more commissions of a quasi-judicial nature have been set up for the minorities in recent years. One of these-the threemember National Commission for Minority

Educational Institutions (NCMEI)-has come into existence under an Act of 2005, and looks after the implementation of Article 30 of the Constitution of India relating to the educational rights of the minorities.

Very recently the one-year old statute of the Commission has been amended to extend the sphere of its activities. The second quasi-judicial Commission, set up in 2005 by a Cabinet Resolution, is the five-member National Commission for Religious and Linguistic Minorities (NCRLM). This Commission was charged with the responsibility of suggesting the criteria for identifying educationally and economically backward sections among the minorities, and recommending measures for their uplift, along with the constitutional, legislative, and administrative steps that may be necessary for implementing its recommendations.

Later, when the statutory provision relating to "Scheduled Castes"-select castebased groups picked up under a constitutional provision for preferential treatment in educational and employment opportunities, and under which only a Hindu, Buddhist, or Sikh can be a member-was challenged for its legal validity before the Supreme Court of India, the government referred this contentious issue to the NCRLM.

Judicial Rulings and Attitudes

All the constitutional provisions and legislative enactments relating to religion and religious rights and freedoms have been applied and interpreted in various ways by the higher courts in the country. Read together, these judicial decisions define the role of religion in state affairs and the role of the state in religious affairs, in addition to laying down the contours of religious rights and freedoms of the individuals and communities.

The judiciary in India has been actively involved in adjudicating religious affairs. In the process of reviewing these affairs, it has resolved many religious disputes between the people and the state on one hand, and between various communities, sects, and groups on the other. Among the major judicial rulings on religion and religious matters, those listed below in the nine sections of this Part deserve a special notice.

The Concept of Hindutva

Certain political parties who give the Hindu religion a central place in their ideology and programs have been using the vernacular term "Hindutva" claiming that it has "national" and "patriotic" connotations and is not just an equivalent of "Hinduism." From the late 1980s through the early 1990s, some politicians sought a judicial pronouncement on the legal permissibility of using Hindutva in political speeches.

In December, 1995, the Supreme Court of India pronounced seven judgments together making some pronoun-cements on the concept of Hindutva and the legal validity of its use in elections. The main thrust of these judgments was that the Hindu religion was indeed not merely one of the religions of India but was identifiable with the "culture and heritage of India, the Indian social ethos and the way of life of the people in the subcontinent."

As India's top legal minds criticized these judgments for their apparent effect of giving a free hand to votaries of communal politics, disposing of a review petition, the court quickly issued a clarification of its earlier judgments, stating it did not mean for its ruling to have such an effect and that it had no intention of diluting the constitutional principle of secularism.

Status of Some Religious Groups

In a very recent case the Supreme Court has decided that the Jains-although mentioned in the Constitution and also enumerated in the Census Reports of India as an independent religious community-are not a religious minority, as their religion, in the opinion of the court, is merely "a reformist movement amongst Hindus."

In an earlier case the Kerala High Court ruled that the Ahmadi Qadianis-although they recognize another prophet living long after the age of Prophet Muhammad, generally regarded by the Muslims as the Last Prophet-was part and parcel of the Muslim community.

Right to Convert Others

In Stainislaus v. Madhya Pradesh & Ors, considering the constitutional validity of the anti-conversion laws of Orissa and Madhya Pradesh, the Supreme Court held that the right to propagate religion, guaranteed by Article 25 of the Constitution, should be interpreted as "not the right to convert another person to one's own religion, but to transmit or spread one's religion by an exposition of its tenets."

Singing the National Anthem

India's National Anthem-a Bengali-language song composed by the late Rabindra Nath Tagore-is believed by some people to be in conflict with monotheistic religious beliefs. A group of school students in the state of Kerala belonging to the Jehovah's Witnesses used to stand up in respect when the National Anthem was sung in their morning assembly, but did not participate in singing the anthem. The school took disciplinary action against them, which the students challenged in court. The Supreme Court decided that the National Anthem of India is to be duly respected by all but need not necessarily be sung by those objecting to it on religious grounds.

Ascertaining Essential Religious Practices

In several cases, the courts have assumed and exercised the power to ascertain if a religious practice followed by any community is indeed an "essential practice" of its religion, holding that only such "essential" practices are entitled to protection under Article 25 of the Constitution that guarantees freedom of both belief and practice of religion. In a recent case, the Supreme Court held that offering prayers in a mosque is not necessarily an "essential practice" in Islam.

The ruling was given in a case in which the Muslims had challenged, on religious grounds, the validity of a law enacted for state acquisition of the land on which had stood the mosque in Ayodhya that had been demolished in a communal frenzy. In another case, the Supreme Court held that the so-called "tandav" dance (worshippers dancing with human skulls in their hands) is not an essential practice of the Anandmargi Hindu faith, notwithstanding the contrary claim of religious leaders of the community.

Teaching Vedic Astrology

In a 2004 ruling, the Supreme Court decided that Vedic astrology-although associated with the Hindu religion-could be lawfully taught in the State institutions of higher learning. The University Grants Commission (UGC), which is charged with introducing courses and curriculums into public universities and providing funding for new courses, decided to introduce "jyotir vigyan" (the science of astrology) as a course of study in several Indian universities.

The UGC decision was challenged by various university professors and other interested parties seeking to prevent the state from funding courses in astrology. The Supreme Court sided with the UGC and held that there was no infringement of state secularism by allowing astrology to be taught in the universities.

Residential Colonies for Particular Communities

In a recent case involving the Parsi Zoroastrian community, the Supreme Court held that a particular religious community can lawfully build and maintain a residential colony restricted to its own members.

Protecting the Sacred Cow

Notwithstanding the citizen's constitutionally assured fundamental right to adopt and carry on any profession or trade of their choice, in order to respect the religious sensitivities of the Hindus, the slaughtering of the cows and other bovines can be prohibited even for religious purposes and on non-Hindu religious occasions. The Supreme Court of India has upheld this legal position in several cases, including one decided in 2005.

Sanctity of Scriptures

Several judicial decisions have established the rule that religious scriptures and holy books shall not be subjected to judicial construction to test the conformity of their tenets with the principles and provisions of the Indian Constitution and legislation. In a 1979 case, it was disputed whether certain individuals belonging to the Hindu "lower castes" had been legitimately ordained. The lower court opined that some of the rules for eligibility to be so ordained were no longer valid as they contradicted fundamental rights guaranteed in the Indian Constitution.

The Supreme Court criticized this approach, stating that those constitutional rights did not touch upon the "personal laws" of the parties. The Court assertively said that in interpreting Hindu religious law, courts were not to introduce their "own concepts of modern times," but are to enforce the law "as derived from recognized and authoritative sources of Hindu law."

A 1986 petition asked the Calcutta High Court to determine the validity of the Holy Qur'an on the touchstone of the Indian Penal Code.Rejecting the petition, the court observed that like the Holy Vedas and the Bible, the Qur'an too was above judicial scrutiny and could not be "examined" to check its conformity with the modern laws of the country.

3

The Brahmo Samaj for India's First Religious Reform

In 1828 Ram Mohun founded the Brahmo Sabha, which became famous as Brahmo Samaj in 1830. The Samaj laid emphasis on the worship of one omnipresent God. In the weekly meetings of the Samaj, the Vedic hymns were first recited in Sanskrit and later the Bengali version of the hymns was also read on every Saturday evenings. In these meetings about 50-60 persons participated. His main aim in founding the Samaj was to solve the problem of ordinary English educated families of Bengal, which were greatly disturbed by the propaganda of Christian missionaries. The Christian missionaries vehemently criticized doctrines and practices of Hinduism. Ram Mohun accepted only those doctrines, which were common to all the three religions namely Hinduism, Islam and Christianity.

The Christian missionaries did not support the Brahmo Samaj, as their aim in cooperating with Ram Mohun was to spread Christianity. Brahmo Samaj laid emphasis on the worship of one formless omnipresent God. In the worship only excerpts from the Vedas and the Upanishads were recited. Ram Mohun never claimed that he had founded a new religion different from Hinduism. Probably he started the practice of weekly prayer meetings as a result of his contact with the Christian missionaries.

In founding Brahmo Samaj the aim of Ram Mohun was to purify Hinduism and to preach the worship of one God. The Samaj was based on those teachings of the Vedas and the Upanishads and also those of other religions, which had some rational basis. The Brahmo Samaj has played a significant role in the renaissance of India, and the roots of much of the modern thinking in India can be traced back to the Brahmo movement. Rabindranath Tagore, the Nobel Laureate, was one of the luminaries of the Brahmo Samaj. The movement was started on 20th August 1828 by Raja Rammohun Roy and his friends (Brajosundar Mitra and others) when they opened a place for public worship, Brahma Sabha on Chitpore Road Kolkata, India. It was publicly inaugurated on 11th Magh or 23rd January 1830.

The former date is celebrated as Bhadrotsab and the latter as Maghotsab. Raja Ram Mohan Roy found responsive echo in his heart towards Missionary attacks on idolatry. He found studies of the Upanishads as very rewarding. He was as much impressed by the monotheistic doctrine of the Upanishads. He began to consider reform of Hinduism by abolishing idolatry and establishing in its place the principle of 'one true god'. The orthodox section of Brahmins developed a hostile attitude towards his preaching. In 1820 he published a book 'The Percepts of Jesus, the Guide to Peace and Happiness'. Deserted by the Orthodoxy he found his own sect of Unitarianism, along with the Baptist missionary William Adam.

Hindus considered it to be a Christian sect. Meetings of the Samaj were held every Saturday evenings. These meetings started with recital of the Vedas in a side room, screened from the view of the people attending worship, where non-Brahmins were not admitted. Though the procedure has been oriented on lines of Christian Church practices, the Primary belief of this Brahmo Samaj were not different from the Upanishads. English educated Hindus found an easy outlet in Brahmo Samaj from their divided loyalties between Church and Temple. As there was no idol to be worshipped, the place of worship was called church and not temple.

But Saturday prayers and preaching were modeled on the Rig Veda and Upanishads. This was sort of a worship of Nirguna Brahman-the one True Attribute less God. The Orthodox Hindus were, however, incensed at this open revolt against the Hindu practices and rituals. They felt their religion was in danger with the founding of this new Church. The fundamental principles of the Brahmo Samaj, founded by Raja Ram Mohan Roy in 1828 are:

1. There is only one God, who is the creator, and the saviour of this world. He is spirit, infinite in power, wisdom, love, justice and holiness, omnipresent, eternal and blissful.
2. The human soul is immortal and capable of infinite progress, and is responsible to God for its doings.
3. Man's happiness in this and the next world consists in worshipping God in spirit and in truth.
4. Loving God, holding communion with Him, and carrying out His will in all the concerns of life, constitute true worship.
5. No created object is to be worshipped as God, and God alone is to be considered as infallible.

But the worship of one omnipresent formless god soon excited the hostility of the orthodox citizens of Calcutta, who started a rival organization named the Dharma Sabha with its organ the Samachar Chandrika. This Samachar Chandrika opposed Ram Mohun Roy's Bengali Weekly named 'Samvada Kaumudi'. After Ram Mohun's death in 1833, the Brahmo Samaj had practically no organization, no constitution, no membership, no covenant, and no pledge up to 1841. Maharshi Devendranath Tagore was prominent in the time frame of 1817-1905. He entered the Samaj in 1843 and he gave the Samaj a new life within five years. He introduced a regular form of church service, including thanksgiving, praise and prayer. Previously it was the old practice of mere expositions of passages from the Upanishads attended with sermon and hymn.

Mr. Keshav Chandra Sen was another important member of Brahmo Samaj. His emphasis on Christian and Vaisnava teachings and forms and the rapidity with which social reform was proceeding under his leadership led to a breach with the more conservative members of the Samaj. Keshav Chandra took a leading part in the passing of the Marriage Act of 1872. This act among other things wanted to discourage child marriage, and for the minimum age of men and women marrying under that Act was at eighteen and fourteen years respectively. When Keshav Chandra married his daughter under fourteen to the Maharaja of Cooch-Behar who was below sixteen years of age there was a split in the Samaj. The Samaj actively supported the movement for widow remarriage, abolition of polygamy, women's education. Thus Brahmo Samaj played a consistent role in the social and religious reforms of the nineteenth century.

Reform movement in Hinduism

From the earliest times the history of Hinduism has been marked by repeated endeavours at reform. Almost at every epoch there has been some effort to purge and purify the current religion and to establish in its place the spiritual worship of the One True God. From the times of the Rishis of the Upanishads there has scarcely been a generation but, in some part of India or other, some nobly inspired soul has raised his protest against the idolatry, unspirituality and ceremonialism of the popular religion.

Gautama Buddha, Nanak, Kabir, Tukaram, Sri Chaitanya are only a few of the more prominent and successful spirits amongst a host of religious reformers in the long, mostly unwritten annals of Hinduism. The Brahmo Samaj is the latest attempt at religious reform in Modern India, and Raja Ram Mohun Roy a direct lineal descendant of the Rishis and saints of Hindusthan.

Brahmoism

Modern India represents an epoch of great interest and importance. In the history of India it has a unique signi-ficance, never before did the country pass through such a momentous change in all spheres of national life. The political, social, industrial structure of the nation is undergoing a radical transformation. Nay, we may say that in Modern India is being enacted a momentous drama of world-wide interest.

Brahmoism, the religion of Future Humanity: Now and here, for the first time in the history of the world, the Eastern and Western civilisations, like two mighty rivers after a long parallel march, have at last met together at the feet of the Himalayas to give birth to a truer, fuller and completer civilisation for future humanity; and Brahmoism is the religion of that future humanity born of the union of the East and the West.

Ram Mohun the prophet of the World Religion

To its founder, Raja Ram Mohun Roy, was vouchsafed the sublime ideal of a universal religion which knew no barriers of caste, colour, race or nationality but united men and women of all classes and countries in the spiritual worship of the One Eternal God, the Creator and Father of all.

Ram Mohun Roy was eminently fitted, as though by a special ordination of God, to be the prophet of this world-religion, in that he combined and harmonised in himself the spiritual culture of all the great existing religions. Born and brought up in an orthodox Hindu family and possessed of a thorough and intimate knowledge of the profound spiritual culture and vast religious literature of Hinduism, the Rajah early in his life came into close contact with Islam and made an earnest study of its literature. Later in his career, he made a strenuous and searching study of Christianity, having learnt Greek and Hebrew in order to be able to study the Bible in the original. He had also opportunities of being acquainted with Buddhism in close quarters, having spent some time in Tibet in search of religious truth in early manhood when turned out of home by his father on account of his bold religious speculations.

Ram Mohun's Message and Method

After a varied and eventful career, in the course of which he traveled far and wide even beyond the borders of India to the then unknown Tibet, learnt sixteen languages and studied the Hindu, Mahommadan, Jewish and Christian Scriptures in original, he at length settled down to Calcutta in 1814, at the age of forty, with the object of propagating his religion among his countrymen and the world at large. To this task he consecrated all his resources time, power and energy.

Foundation of the Brahmo Samaj

For fourteen years he laboured on his mission, delivering his message in earnest conversation to the circle of friends who clustered round him and through written discourses to the wider public. The generality of Hindus and Christians failed to understand him and attacked him vehemently. Rajah Ram Mohun Roy tried to silence both by the authority of their own respective scriptures. To the Hindu opponent he showed that the most ancient and authoritative scriptures of Hinduism enjoined the worship of One Eternal God who is without form or shape; to the Christian he proved that the religion of Jesus was the pure universal theism of the Fatherhood of God and the Brotherhood of Man.

Single-handed and under very trying circumstances, he fought against the assaults of bigoted Hindus and orthodox Christians to establish the universal religion of 'One God, one humanity', till at length on the 2nd August, 1828, he succeeded in organising a weekly meeting for the worship of God irrespective of caste and creed in a hired house in the northern part of Calcutta.The First Congregation: Two years later, with the help of some friends, he erected a modest building for the Theistic Church or the Brahmo Samaj, as it came to be called, in a central part of Calcutta; and this exists and is known as the Adi Brahmo Samaj.

Here, week after week, a motley gathering used to meet for the worship of the One God without regard to caste, creed or colour. The worship consisted in reciting verses from the Upanishads and singing hymns and reading religious discourses written by Ram Mohun Roy. Prior to this public service, portions of the Vedas used to be read by Brahmins in a back-room to which only Brahmins were admitted.

Ram Mohun's visit to England and Death

In August 1830, Rajah Ram Mohun Roy embarked for England, leaving the infant church in the care of Ram Chandra Vidyabagish. And there he died on the Brahmo Samaj in Calcutta gradually 27th September, 1833. In the meanwhile, languished; most of its members, who had been drawn to it mainly through the influence of Rajah Ram Mohun Roy, ceased to take any interest in it after his departure for England. Only the faithful Ram Chandra Vidyabagish remained steadfast; and for seven years he regularly and punctually conducted the weekly service, as directed by Rajah, often alone like the solitary watcher by the dim burning pyre at the burning ghat. At length, help came from an unexpected quarter.

Conversion of Devendra Nath Tagore

In the year 1838, Devendra Nath Tagore, eldest son of Dwarka Nath Tagore, a friend and fellow-worker of Rajah Ram Mohun Roy, began to take interest in the Brahmo

Samaj. As a boy, Devendra Nath had often seen Raja Ram Mohun Roy and had been, in fact, a pet of his. It is said the Rajah foresaw the young boy would grow to carry on his own life-work. But, for many years, there was no sign of any religious tendency or interest in Devendra Nath. His early youth was like that of any other scion of wealthy families.

In the year 1838, while attending on his grand-mother in her last moments at the burning-ghat, a strange feeling came over him: he experienced an indescribable joy in the felt presence of God. The pleasures and riches of the world appeared trivial to him. From that time a great change came over his life. He spent many days in meditation and felt that the idols they worshipped were nor God, that God was one and could not be perceived by the senses. Then the memory of Rajah Ram Mohun Roy came back to him; he inquired about his Brabmo Samaj and sent for its Minister, Ram Chandra Vidyabagish.

Tattwabodhini Sabha

Devendra Nath began to read the Upanishads under Ram Chandra Vidyabagish and established a society. The Tattwabodhini Sabha for the study and diffusion of the ancient Theistic literature of India. This institution, which was at first composed of the brothers and cousins of Dvendra Nath, began to expand rapidly. Ram Chandra Vidyabagish was appointed its minister; its anniversary was celebrated with great eclat in 1840. The Brahmo Samaj at this time was at the lowest ebb of its life. Fortunately, the Tattwabodhini Sabha came to its rescue at this juncture. The members resolved to take charge of it; the separate monthly service of the Tattwa Bodhini Sabha was discontinued and they began to attend the services of the Brahmo Samaj.

Through their youthful energy and enthusiasm the Brahmo Samaj soon revived; and a period of great and growing activity followed. The faithful old Minister of the

Brahmo Samaj, Pandit Ram Chandra Vidyabagish, had at last the satisfaction of seeing his devotion rewarded. Bit for his loyal perseverance, the sapling planted by Raja Ram Mohun Roy might have perished in the dark days following the death of the founder.

Rapid progress of the Brahmo Samaj

The Brahmo Sama; now passed into the safe keeping of Devendra Nath. Drawn by his influence, many young men joined the Samaj. His active mind devised many new measures for the development of the Samaj. In 1842 the Tattwabodhini Patrika was founded as the organ of the Brahmo Samaj which exercised a very powerful influence over the rising generation of Bengal. The Brahmo Samaj, up to the time when Maharshi Devendra Nath Tagore joined it, was nothing but a motley congregation which occasionally met together in a half-serious, half-comical mood for listening to hymns, recitations from the Sanskrit Scriptures and religious discourses. There was neither any definite aim nor any settled conviction.

The noble provision of the Trust Deed about the equal rights of all without regard to caste, creed or nationality was openly violated by disallowing the presence of nonbrahmins at the reading of the Vedas; doctrines about idolatry and incarnation were often preached from the pulpit. No sooner had Maharshi Devendra Nath joined the Brahmo Samaj than he turned his attention to rectifying these irregularities. Institution of a Brahmo Covenant and Initiation: Under his influence and inspiration, it soon developed into a purely theistic congregation, He found that those who came to the service of the Brahmo Samaj were not inspired and animated by one common Conviction. In their individual lives and at their homes they were idolaters as the ordinary Hindus.

Nucleus of a Brahmo Community

In order to make the Brahmo Samaj a body of men

believing in the One True God and worshipping Him in truth and spirit only, Devendra Nath drew up a Brahmo convenant containing a number of vows enjoining the renunciation of idolatry, the worship of the One Only in the Vedanta and the practice of virtue. God as described Devendra Nath himself took the lead in being initiated into Brahmoism by Ram Chandra Vidyabagish by signing this Covenant in Dec. 1843 ; twenty of his friends followed him in this new and momentous departure, Thus was formed the nucleus of a Brahmo community; and by 1874 the number of covenanted Brahmos rose to 767.

Infallibility of Vedas Discarded

Up to this time, Brahmoism was tacitly under stood to be based on the Upanishads. In his religious controversies, Rajah Ram Mohun Roy used to refute the arguments of his Hindu opponents by citing passages from the Upanishada in support of his views, as, in his Controversies with Christian opponents; he would refute theirs by the authority of the Bible. In order to show to his countrymen that all Hindu scriptures were not idolatrous, he published some of thc Upanishads in original Sanskrit and also translated them into English and Bengali.

His followers took it to mean that he based Brahmoism on the Upanishads. The religion of the Brahmo Samaj at the beginning was, known to be Vedantism. The doctrine of the infallibility of the Vedas was tacitly accepted by the Brahmo Samaj. It found a stimulus in the ill-feeling against the Christian missionaries which was at that time raging strong on account of the conversion of a Hindu lad of a respectable family into Christianity.

Compilation of Brahmo Dharma

Though the genesis of Devendra Nath's own faith in Brahmoism was independent of the Upanishads he had a great reverence and predilection for them and was rather disposed to accept them as the basis of Brahmoism, rejecting all other Hindu scriptures including the Samhitas. But by this time a younger generation had grown up who were not ready to accept even the Upanishads as infallible. The controversy went on in the Brahmo Samaj for several years. Maharshi Devendra Nath had the question carefully considered. He sent four students to Benares to study the four Vedas. He himself went to Benares to discuss the question with reputed Vedic teachers.

At last, to his great regret, he found that the doctrine of the infallibility of the Vedas or of the Upanishads was untenable and, much against his natural inclination, he gave it up in 1848; thus the early Vedantic Unitarianism came to be superseded by natural Universal Theism. Soon after, he compiled a book called the Brahmo Dharma, a collection of theistic passages from the Upanishads dictated by him from memory and taken down by Babu Akshaya Kumar Dutt, the whole work being finished in two hours.

Missionary Activities of Devendra Nath

All these changes were formally announced during the anniversary festival of 1850, which was now being celebrated on the 11th of Magh, the day on which the Prayer Hall at the Chitpore Road had been consecrated. The reconstructed Samaj entered upon a carer of great propagandistic activity. Maharshi Devendra Nath visited different parts of the country and established many new Samajas in mofussil towns. He also trained up a small band of preachers who carried the message of Brahmoism throughout Bengal. For several years the work went on with unabated enthusiasm.

In 1857 Maharshi Devendra Nath retired to the Himalayan regions near Simla to spend his days in study, meditation and communion. He had no desire to return to the bustle and tumult of society. But, at the end of a year and a half, one day he felt a distant call to go down and work among his countrymen, however unpleasant the task might be. Sorely against his will he came back to Calcutta.

The result was a period of unusual sctivity and enthusiasm in the Brahmo Samaj. The sermons he used to deliver at this time from the pulpit of the Samaj kindled a new fire among the younger generation.

Association of Keshub Chandra Sen with Maharshi Debendra Nath

Already during the absence of Maharshi Devendra Nath, Babu Keshub Chandra Sen joined the Brahmo Samaj. The kindred souls soon recognised each other. Keshub looked upon Maharshi with unbounded regard and love, and Maharshi rejoiced at the accession of this gifted young man from a respectable family and treated him with fatherly affection and solicitude. For a time they worked together in perfect harmony and their combined influence created a new life among the younger generation of Calcutta and Bengal. Hundreds of young men joined the Samaj.

The younger party threw themselves heart and soul into the work of propagation. They went about to all parts of the country preaching the new faith, establishing new Samajes and gaining many sympathisers for the cause. In 1864, Babu Keshub Chandra Sen visited Madras and Bombay; and his visit was instrumental in rousing public interest in the cause in those parts and as a consequence the Veda Samaj of Madras was established in that year and the Prarthana Samaj of Bombay came into existence in 1867. The Veda Samaj after undergoing many reverses of fortune was finally transformed into the Southern India Brahmo Samaj.

Idolatry and Caste Strictly Interdicted

There was also a great development in the faith and practice of the Brahmo Samaj during this period. The Brahmos, though they had ceased to worship idols, were not able to get rid of caste distinctions as yet. On occasions of domestic ceremonies, such as, marriages, sraddhas (funeral rites) idolatrous practices, Young Keshub and his friends declared that such association with idolatry was inconsistent and unworthy and they resolved strictly to abjure idolatry and caste. Maharshi Devendra Nath had already shown the way by refusing, against the universal wish of his relatives and to the consternation of the entire Calcutta society, to perform the sraddha of his father according to orthodox Hindu rites in 1846. But so far none had dared to follow him. Now at last in Keshub and his young friends he found the men after his mind. He heartly sympathised with the new aspirations of the younger generation he himself threw away his 'sacrificial thread'.

In 1861, Maharshi Devendra Nath married one of his daughters according to Brahmo rites; other Brahmo marriages followed. For a time the progress of the Brahmo Samaj, both within and without, was rapid and extensive. But unfortunately within a few years differences sprang up between Devendra Nath and Keshub. The immediate cause of the misunderstanding was in the old ministers of the Brahmo Samaj who still retained the sacrificial thread. Keshub insisted that those who retained these symbols of idolatry and caste should not be allowed to officiate as ministers.

Maharshi Devendra Nath felt unwilling to deal harshly with old members and workers. Keshub was supported by the younger generation, while the older members naturally stood by Devendra Nath. Thus there grew up two parties, the conservative and the progressive, in the Brahmo Samaj. Devendra Nath at first yielded; those of the old ministers who retained the sacred thread were not allowed to conduct the service and in their place two younger men of the progressive party who had formally given up caste were appointed as assistant ministers.

First Inter-caste Marriage

About this time the progressive party solemnised an intercaste marriage in the Brahmo Samaj. This further alarmed Maharshi Devendra Nath. Soon after, he reinstalled the old ministers without consulting the progressive party and protested against it. As the sole surviving trustee of the Samaj, Devendra Nath withdrew all the powers he had conceded to the younger men, dismissed them from their offices and removed the Tattwabodhini Patrika from under their management. Babu Keshub Chandra Sen and the progressive party tried for some time to preserve the union and retain their hold on the affairs of the church by organising a Pratinidhi Sabha or representative association.

But, failing in this, they formed themselves into a separate organisation called the Brahmo Samaj of India in November, 1866. The bulk of the younger and progressive Brahmos joined the Brahmo Samaj of India, the work of which was carried on with great vigour and enthusiasm. Freed from the restraining influence of the conservative party, the Brahmo Samaj of India now entered on a career of reform and expansion all round. The work of propagation was taken up with laudable zeal. Missionaries of the Brahmo Samaj of India began to visit every part of the country. Books and pamphlets on Brahmoism were issued in rapid succession. In 1870, Babu Keshub Chandra Sen, accompanied by a few friends, paid a visit to England, where he was well received by the British public and succeeded in creating a lively interest in the Brahmo Samaj.

Developments under the Brahmo Samaj of India

Internally also the foundation of the Brahmo Samaj of India was followed by many radical changes and developments. One important departure under the Brahmo Samaj of India was in the direction of greater catholicity. Under Devendra Nath the Brahmo Samaj had confined itself practically to Hindu influence and inspiration. Keshub Chandra Sen gave it a more universal character. He began to draw upon the scriptures and living inspirations of all the principal historical religions of the world. Devendra Nath, as we have already seen, had compiled a Manual of Brahmoism from the Upanishads. Now as a mark of the catholicicy of its principles, a book was published under the auspices of the Brahmo Samaj of India containing passages from all religious scriptures.

Another remarkable feature of the Brahmo Sarnaj of India was the substitution of the vernacular. Bengali, in place of Sanskrit in Brahmo liturgy. Greater simplicity and spontaneity were allowed in the divine services. Individual lives as well as prayer meetings were marked by greater devotional fervour. Sentiments about prayer, repentance and conscience gained wider currency in the Samaj. Of all these developments Keshub Chandra Sen was the soul. Under his leadership, the progressive Brahmos moved the Government of India to clear up the uncertainty as to the legality of the Brahmo marriage and got a law passed in the year 1872, thenceforth known as Act III of 1872, which laid down fourteen as the minimum marriageable age for women and eighteen for men.

Dissatisfaction for want of a Constitution

Things went on well for some time. But ultimately Keshub Chandra Sen also failed to retain the confidence of the entire, growing body of his followers. With the Brahmo Samaj of India, again, there appeared a progressive section which did not like the latter-day autocratic methods of Sen. They clamoured for representative organisations for conducting the work of the Samaj and for more radical reform in social life, specially as regards the position of women. Under an apparently smooth and prosperous surface, there was a strong pent-up dissatisfaction with the methods of Keshub and his immediate encourage.

The Cooch Behar Marriage

At this juncture, there happened a fateful event in the history of the Brahmo Samaj. In the beginning of 1878, the Brahmo Community was taken by surprise at the intelligence of the proposed marriage of the eldest daughter of Babu Keshub Chandra Sen with the young Maharaja of

Cooch Behar. Both the bride and the bridegroom were below the minimum marriageable age, fourteen and eighteen respectively, fixed by Babu Keshub Chandra Sen himself and adopted by the Brahmo community.

The bridegroom was not a Brahmo; and it was rumoured that the marriage was to be celebrated according to the idolatrous Hindu ritual of the Cooch Behar Raj family. Earnest protests poured in from many Samajes and individual Brahmos, expressing the widespread concern of the whole Brahmo community. It was feared that such a compromise with the principles of the Brahmo Samaj by its leader and minister would discredit and ruin the cause irretrievably. Babu Keshub Chandra Sen gave no heed to the protests and proceeded in person to Cooch Bchar to celebrate the marriage. When it actually came off, the requirements of a Brahmo marriage were dispensed with and there were other features highly objectionable in the eyes of the Brahmos.

The second schism

As Babu Keshub Chandra Sen returned from Cooch Behar, the protesters wanted to move a vote of censure against him at a meeting of the Brahmo Samaj of India but Babu Keshub Chandra Sen, who was the Secretary of the Samaj, foiled their attempts by putting obstacles in the way of holding the meeting. They, however, passed a resolution at a meeting of the congregation deposing him from the office of Minister. But Babu Keshub Chandra Sen did not give any heed to constitutional laws of the Samaj and forcibly retained the post of Minister with the help of the Police. The protesters in despair and indignation formed themselves into a separate organisation, called the Sadharan Brahmo Samaj, the work of which would be carried on according to strictly constitutional methods.

Inauguration of Sadharan Brahmo Samaj

The Sadharan Brahmo Samaj was formally inaugurated at a public meeting held in the Town Hall of Calcutta in

May, 1878. The majority of the mofussil Samajes associated themselves with it. The first care of the new organisation was to provide against the possibility of the assumption of all power by one person enabling him to set at naught the views and opinions of the entire body, as had been the case On the occasion of both the schisms. A thoroughly representative constitution was given to the new body. The governing body was to be elected annually by the votes of the entire body of members, The mofussil Samajes were entitled to send their representatives to the governing body. The new organisation soon became the main channel of Theistic life and work in India. By 1880, a spacious Prayer-Hall in the central part of Calcutta was constructed for it.

Renewed effort of Keshub Chandra Sen

Babu Keshub Chandra Sen and those Brahmos who remained with him also redoubled their energy. They were in possession of the Prayer-Hall and all the properties and resources of the old united Samaj, and had thus a great advantage over the new organisation. Moreover, almost all the missionaries, personally very much attached to Babu Keshub Chandra Sen, stood by him. With their loyal co-operation he sent out mission parties to different parts of the country. He also introduced many novel mystic forms of religious practice and in 1880 he changed the name of his Church into the 'New Dispensation' and selected twelve of his missionaries to be called the Apostles of the New Dispensation.

Keshub's Death

His unique career, however, was soon cut short by the hand of death. The strenuous labours of the past years and the pain caused by the secession of the majority of Brahmos and Brahmo Samajes and by the internal dissensions among his own missionaries told heavily on his health; and in January 1884, he passed away from this world. After his death, the Church of the New Dispensation became still more disorganised. The apostles and missionaries could not agree among themselves. But, though the common organisation has broken down, many of the missionaries have been individually carrying on the work with exemplary devotion and self sacrifice.

Progress under the Sadharan Brahmo Samaj

The foundation of the Sadharan Brahmo Samaj was marked by another outburst of propagandist activity. There was a general enthusiasm among the Brahmo public. Many new congregations were organised and old congregations drawn closer, forming an influential Church. Several new and powerful institutions were started in Calcutta, which have ever since been doing valuable work in the field of religious and social reform. The organisation of the Brahmo Samaj seems now to have at last found a stable form. More than thirty years have elapsed since the formation of the Sadharan Brahmo Samaj. But, whereas the previous thirty years witnessed two violent and disastrous schisms, the subsequent history has been one of smooth, steady growth.

In the free atmosphere of a progressive church like the Brahmo Samaj, differences of opinion are inevitable and natural. Such differences there undoubtedly are among the members of the Sadharan Brahmo Samaj; but with its broad, liberal, representative constitution founded on the principle of unity in essentials, difference in non essentials and charity in all, men and women of all shades of theistic belief have found it possible to co-operate for the glory of God and the good of man. The genesis of Indian renaissance has often been traced to 1815 when Rammohun Roy (1772 - 1833) moved to Calcutta and founded the Atmiya Sabha and began his campaign for religious and social reform.

The effects of the British on India had then just begun to be felt. In the cultural front exposure to western ideas and education generated lively debates and discussions among the Indian intelligentsia on the merits and demerits of India's age-old religious beliefs and practices. Rammohun represented a new group in Bengal society who had lost faith in some of the beliefs and practices of orthodox Hinduism, which they regarded as irrational and inhumane. They were looking for a rational religion commensurate with their western education and professional outlook. Rammohun protested against idolatry and sought to establish a universal religion based on the idea of the unity of Godhead.

To give shape to his religious ideas in 1828 Rammohun founded the Brahmo Sabha, a universalistic, theistic society that later on was renamed as the Brahmo Samaj. In this Unit you will be introduced to the origin and the basic objective of the Brahmo Samaj, its further developments and significance in the religio-cultural movements of India. You will also be familiarized with the ideas and activities of the Prarthana Samaj, which was based in Bombay. Like the Brahmo Samaj followers the activists of the Prarthana Samaj disapproved of idolatry and believed in worshipping one God. Both these movements can be considered as attempts to reform Hinduism from within and to restore Hinduism to its primitive purity.

Religious Ideas of Rammohun Roy

Beginning of nineteenth century marked the emergence of an English educated class of Indians who were exposed to the rational and scientific ideas of the West. This was also the time when enlightened Europeans like Sir William Jones, H.H. Wilson, H.T. Colebrooke and others revealed by comment and by translation the treasures of ancient Indian wisdom. Rammohun Roy was a product of this transitional phase in our history. What made him stand out from his peers was his questioning mind. Apart from knowing several languages he was a Sanskrit and an Arabic Scholar and studied several religions. In 1804 he wrote a book in Persian, with a preface in Arabic, entitled Tuhfat-ul-Muwahhidin (A gift to monotheists).

The book revealed his knowledge of Sufism. It also showed that he was acquainted with Mutzalites, a rationalist school of Muslim thought of the eighth century which spoke of freedom of thought and will. Tuhfat-ul-Muwahhidin has been variously admired for its radicalism, uncompromising rationalism, and devastating Aristotelian logic and for its frontal attack on religious orthodoxy and obscurantism. Rammohun used the twin criteria of reason and social comfort with great effect to establish the startling proposition that "Falsehood is common to all religions". He argued that only three basic tenets are common to all religions - a belief in a single creator, existence of a soul and a faith in an afterworld where rewards and punishments will be duly awarded. Tuhfat-ul-Muwahhidin is a compelling statement of a simple and impassioned monotheism with a humanistic essence.

Here one sees the beginning of Rammohun's belief in One Supreme Being who is the source and fountainhead of all creation. According to Rammohun, this belief in one eternal being often gets lost in irrational beliefs and dogmas, superstitions and absurd and socially detrimental forms of worship. Hundreds of useless privations and hardships regarding eating, drinking, purity, pollution, auspicious, inauspicious creep in, as a result of which true religion is lost sight of. Tuhfat-ul-Muwahhidin shows the influence of Islamic monotheism on his thinking. Rammohun was acquainted with the Serampore missionaries William Carey, Marshman and Ward. He learnt Hebrew and Greek to read the Bible in the original.

Rammohun was deeply impressed by the moral teaching of Christianity. He denied the divine Christ but accepted the ethical Jesus. He found the doctrines of Christianity more conducive to moral principles and better adopted to the use of rational beings than those of other religions. In 1820, he wrote the Precepts of Jesus, the guide to peace and happiness, under the pseudonym of Prasanna Kumar Tagore. The book was a series of extracts from the Gospels according to

St. Matthew, St. Luke, St. Mark and St. John. According to Rammohun, Christ was a theist but his disciples misunderstood him. The publication of the extract got him involved in a controversy with Christian Missionaries.

Between 1820-23, Rammohun wrote Three Appeals to the Christian Public in defense of his position, which was very close to that of Unitarians. In 1823, he, together with Dwarkanath Tagore and William Adam had established the Calcutta Unitarian Society. This society had been described as assembly of near-atheists. Rammohun put forward his religious views in his first journal, the bilingual Brahmanical Magazine (1821-23) in which he displayed his deep love for the best traditions of India and defended the intellectual consistency of Hindu theism. He published a series of polemical tracts in which he pronounced a scathing attack on priests who taught superstition and idol worship to the masses and discouraged vernacular translation of Sanskrit scriptures. These attacks on the orthodoxy were reminiscent of Luther's attack on the Papacy and Catholic priests during the Reformation. Rammohun advocated a rational approach to religion and exposed the logical absurdities of idol worship.

For him, religion could not be judged solely on its own internal scriptural evidence, but had to be measured by reason and shown to be free of contradictions to uphold a beneficial social order. Once proper belief was established, erroneous customs such as sati, debarring women from education and property rights would disappear. In 1818, he published A Conference between an Advocate and an Opponent of the Practice of Burning a Widow Alive. He cited scriptural evidence to justify his contention that sati was not required by Hindu law and was instead an erroneous accretion, an example of degenerate Hinduism. Rammohun was the first Indian to take up the cause of Indian women. Roy's primary concern was to maintain the unity of God against all false ideas and techniques devised by man to adulterate the purity of monotheistic faith. Thus, he repudiated all myths, miracles and images which made a mockery of the unity of godhead. But Rammohun's monotheism was not based on Bhakti, but on rational, philosophical analysis.

Rammohun and the Brahmo Samaj

In order to carry forward his religious ideas in an organised manner Rammohun Roy founded the Brahmo Samaj at Calcutta in 1828, which was initially known as 'the Brahmo Sabha'. The deed of the first Samaj building declared its purpose to be '... a place of public meeting of all sorts and descriptions of people, without distinction, as shall behave and conduct themselves in an orderly, sober, religious and devout manner: for the worship and adoration of the Eternal, Unsearchable and Immutable Being, who is the Author and the Preserver of the Universe...'. The Brahmo Samaj preached and devised a pure form of worship and ceremonials. The ideas of the Brahmo Samaj were based on the Vedanta and the Upanishads. It believed that God cannot be seen but his existence can be read in his works of nature.

The Brahmo Samaj declared a war on popular religious practices and rituals. It denied that ceremonies and rites were necessary to true religion. Any representation of God was impossible and hence idol worship was a useless, foolish, puerile practice in which only the weak, ignorant and those of feeble intellect indulged in. Idol worship was not for the wise; it was not only an intellectual error, but it also carried with it evil consequences. It was responsible for the decay of Hinduism and had led to slackening of true religion. Hindus had got involved in ceremonies and the social evils reflected the loss of their grip on true religion. Brahmo Samaj preachings also contained a severe indictment of priesthood whom it blamed for the sorry state of the Hindu society. The priests deliberately deceived ordinary people. Selfish motives and greed activated them. They depended on temples and idol worship for their livelihood.

The Brahmo Samaj defended the vernacular versions of the sacred scriptures. Brahmo Samaj prayers were held on a Sunday, where a sermon was preached which was followed by communal singing of hymns and monotheistic devotional songs. Congregational prayers and hymn singing were Christian influences. The weekly sermon was initially in English but later in Bengali. The essence of the new worship was an attempt to reach God directly without priests as intermediaries. The pivot of Rammohun's worship was the ancient formula Om-tat-sat- object contemplated by Om could be described only as 'that' which exists. The religious ideas of the Brahmo Samaj were based on the Upanishads. Rammohun believed in immortality of the soul, which was eternal and not liable to birth or death.

The individual soul- Atman was merged with the universal spirit Brahman. Evil thoughts and actions were sinful. Sin was not connected to observance of fasts, rituals or dietary restrictions. Rammohun did not discuss his belief in Karma and reincarnation and thus it is not clear whether the Brahmo Samaj believed in them. Rammohun can be regarded as Bengal's first non-conformist of importance and therefore her first intellectual, who symbolized in himself the inauguration of modern India. He could not suffer his environment passively and fought valiantly to compel it to respond to human needs and aspirations more satisfactorily. He insisted on the sovereignty of reason and on the right of the individual conscience to judge what was good. In his day the Brahmo Samaj was a source of social dynamism in Bengal. After his departure for England in 1833 and his death there in the same year, the Brahmo Samaj fell into a moribund condition.

Debendranath Tagore and the Brahmo Samaj

After Rammohun, the leadership of the Samaj fell into the hands of Pandit Ramchandra Vidyavagish, one of his devoted followers. However, he lacked Rammohun's charismatic leadership and the Brahmo Samaj became weak. It managed to survive because of the patronage of Dwarkanath Tagore. In a decade the fortunes of the Brahmo Samaj began to rise because of the spiritual leadership of Dwarkanath's son, Maharshi Debendranath Tagore (1817-1905). Debendranath had established in 1839, a society of young intellectuals who dissatisfied with orthodox Hinduism, were in search of new spiritual ideas- the Tattvabodhini Sabha (truth teaching association) which had informal associations with the Brahmo Samaj. The society had weekly religious discussions and monthly meetings.

It merged with the Brahmo Samaj in 1859. Under Debendranath's leadership, the Brahmo Samaj became predominantly a religious body. His intense religious devotion and ability to organize religious services of worship had little social reform impact on Brahmos, much less on Hindu society in general. Debendranath tried to counter Christian missionary propaganda and began publishing Tattvabodhini Patrika in 1843 which became a forum for religious discussion and an outspoken critic of missionaries. Debendranath wrote the Brahma Covenant, a statement of the basic creed of the Brahmo Samaj in 1843.

In 1850, he released a volume of scriptures, the Brahmo Dharma, for use in private and public worship. In 1861, he revised the Hindu Life cycle rituals giving them a new Brahmo form, though these were not significantly different from the Hindu Sacraments which already existed. The new statement of faith developed by Debendranath was: "God is a personal being with sublime attributes. God has never become incarnate. God hears and answers prayers. God is to be worshipped only in spiritual ways. Hindu asceticism, temples, and fixed forms of worship are unnecessary ..... all castes and races may worship God acceptably. Repentance and cessation from sin are the only ways to forgiveness and salvation. Nature and intuition are sources for the knowledge of God."

Keshub Chandra Sen and the Brahmo Samaj

Debendranath Tagore's successor was Keshub Chandra Sen (1838-1884) who gave a new direction to the Brahmo Samaj movement. According to Keshub Chandra Sen's biographer 'from the moment he had entered the Brahmo Samaj, he had taken the vow of finding in it a religion of life as opposed to a religion of theories. Every principle that he developed, every reform that he undertook, was the result of that vow. In his lecture Sen stressed that once people came under one Church and one God caste distinctions would naturally perish. In 1860 Sen founded the Sangat Sabhas (Believer's Associations) whose followers wanted to abandon caste and the sacred thread and work for women's equality. Sen and his disciples urged a more radical approach to religious ideas and greater efforts for social reform. They argued in favour of inter caste marriages and widow remarriage.

They emphasized the critical non-conformist intellectual tradition of the Brahmo Samaj and were influenced by Comte, Bentham and rationalist ideas. In 1864, the Samaj building was damaged in a cyclone and the Samaj meetings were shifted to Tagore's residence. Debendranath allowed those who were not against wearing the sacred thread. Sen objected and in 1865 withdrew his section of the Samaj. This decision along ideological and generational lines was formalised in 1866 when Sen organized the Brahmo Samaj of India. Those loyal to Tagore, formed the Adi Brahmo Samaj. The younger liberals rallied behind Keshub Chandra Sen. They wanted Brahmos to live up to their liberal, rational religious and ethical ideals.

They insisted that ministers remove both their sacred threads and caste marks, that the ministry be earned by merit rather than be awarded for caste; that inter-caste marriage be encouraged and child marriage discouraged; that Bengali and no Sanskrit be used in worship. They wanted the Samaj to join other progressive groups in promoting social reforms. The younger Brahmos were particularly concerned with women's emancipation. Keshub threw himself into the struggle for change as spokesman of the young liberals. The Adi Brahmo Samaj had little interest in social reform. With Debendranath's death in 1905, the Adi Samaj's effective role came to an end. Keshubites declared that men and women of every nation and caste who believed in the fundamental doctrines of Brahmo dharma could be eligible to be members of the Brahmo Samaj of India. They made a compilation of theistic texts from all the scriptures of the world, which led to the sloka sangraha which was used in Brahmo services.

When a new edition was published in 1870, on the title page was inscribed the motto "The wide universe is the temple of God." The architecture of the Keshubite mandir opened in 1869 proclaimed the universalism of the Brahmo Samaj of India. It was the blend of a Hindu temple, a Muslim mosque and a Christian church. No idols were to be worshipped and no scripture was to be considered to be infallible. No prayer, no hymn, sermon or discourse was to be delivered in the temple, nor was it to encourage any manner of idolatry, sectarianism or sin. Men and women of all castes, colour and conditions could participate in the services. For a brief while, Keshub's popularity in Bengal and India increased rapidly. In the 1860s and 1870s, the Samaj established new branches and won new recruits.

By 1872 there were nearly a hundred branches, mostly in Bengal but also in Bihar, Orissa, Assam, U.P., Madhya Pradesh and even in Madras and Kerala in the South and in Western India. Sen went to England, met Queen Victoria and on his return established the Indian Reform Association and a journal Sulabh Samachar to spread his ideas. In 1872, the Samaj was rocked by the controversy over the Special Marriage Act, which legalized Brahmo marriages but did so by declaring that Brahmos were not Hindus. There was also dissatisfaction with Sen's attitude towards women's rights. Ananda Mohan Bose, a "wrangler" from Cambridge and Durga Mohan Das, a lawyer, protested that women should be allowed to sit with their male relatives during Brahmo services. In 1875, Keshub, who ten years earlier had championed constitutionalism and liberal reform against Debendranath, now found himself opposing liberalism in his own Samaj. The samadarshi faction challenged Keshub's leadership and accused him of authoritarianism as well as of misuse of Samaj funds and property.

By 1876, Keshub was no longer interested in active social reform and turned more and more to meditation and comparative study of religions. He was also accused of hypocrisy as he arranged the marriage of his daughter to the maharaja of Cooch Behar. The marriage violated the Brahmo Marriage Act because of the bride's age and the proposed use of idolatrous rituals. The progressive faction led by Ananda Mohan Bose, Shivnath Sastri and others called themselves the Sadharan Samaj and thus the second split in Brahmo Samaj took place in 1878. Sen became more and more interested in bhakti and universalistic religious ideology. In 1881, he founded the Nava Vidhan (New Dispensation) symbolised by a red banner bearing the name of his church, plus the Hindu trident, the Christian cross and the Islamic crescent. He started a news paper the New Dispensation and a new code, the Nava Samhita which replaced the Brahma Dharma. Keshub died in 1884 and the movement broke under the impact of factionalism.

Shivnath Sastri and the Brahmo Samaj

The breakaway group from Kushub Ch. Sen founded the Sadharan Samaj led by Shivnath Sastri and Ananda Mohan Bose. The Sadharan Samaj gave a rational, monistic interpretation of the Upanishads and admitted the essential unity of the universal self and the individual self. It continued to have a weekly Sunday service and the members expressed their faith in one God in congregational prayers. They held Keshub guilty of indulging in mysticism and sentimentalism. However, the new group also emphasized Brotherhood, opposed caste distinctions and argued for freedom of conscience.

The Samaj was, unlike Keshub in his later years, interested in social reform. It opened a Brahmo School for girls in Calcutta, a welfare institution for untouchables, small hospitals, orphanages, leper asylums, legal aid cells for women and worked among Khasi hill tribals. The Sadharan Samaj allied with Veeresalingam, a Telugu reformer in Andhra Pradesh and continued to expand in Bengal. Pratap Chandra Mazumdar, a leader of the Sadharan Brahmo Samaj, carried the ideas of the Samaj to England and America. In 1893, he addressed the Chicago World Parliament of Religions. The Sadharan Samaj, like the Adi Brahmo Samaj and the Brahmo Samaj of India, remained a small elitist organization.

Importance of the Brahmo Movement

The Brahmo Samaj, an acculturative movement among the Bengali Hindus was led by high caste members of the English educated elite and was supported by them. It never gained mass popularity. It originated in the colonial environment of Calcutta and spread to other cities, mainly in Bengal, but elsewhere also through the travel of its leaders. Brahmo ideology was a reinterpretation of Hinduism. It adopted Western organizational pattern of a voluntary religious association, with society officers, bank account, printed literature, congregational meetings and a creed. The Brahmo Samaj provided a new reformed Hinduism and a model of religious organization to other reform movements.

The original Samaj split into three, the Adi Samaj which looked back to Hinduism, the New Dispensation towards a cult centered on Keshub Chandra Sen and focusing on bhakti and the Sadharan Samaj that followed the original teachings of Rammohun Roy. The Brahmo Samaj played an important role in the Bengal renaissance and in shaping the modern Bengali Bhadralok culture. Rammohun's response to the West became the model for subsequent generation of Hindu modernizers. He neither defended everything in traditional Hinduism, nor accepted everything Western, but chose the difficult middle path of modernizing India by accepting which was rational and humane in India's past and tried to borrow the new knowledge from the West. Thus Rammohun began the process of modernization of Hinduism.

He has been called "the father of modern India", though more recently his links with the past have been stressed. It has been argued that there were similarities between his thinking and those of the bhakti movements of Kabir, Nanak and Chaitanya. While there may be some truth in this, Roy's ideas do constitute a break with the past. The Brahmo Samaj bequeathed a reformed Hinduism and worldly social Hindu ethic similar to the Protestant or Puritan ethic of the West. The crusade to abolish Sati, remarry widows, abolish child marriage, encourage inter-caste marriage, discourage kulin polygamy, eliminate prostitution, extend equality of education to women, give property rights to women, support professional opportunities to women– these were all begun by Brahmo efforts. Thus the Brahmo Samaj movement in spite of the differences within is considered as a major effort to reinterpret Hinduism in the light of rationalist and humanist spirit.

Origin of the Prarthana Samaj

The spirit of religious reform found its manifestation in Bombay with the establishment of the Prarthana Samaj. The Paramahansa Sabha preceded by Prarthana Samaj. In Bombay, the Paramahansa Sabha had been founded in 1849 consisting of radical students of Elphinstone Institution. Their main object was the breaking of caste rules and at secret meetings they ate forbidden food cooked by persons of low caste and other religious faiths and consumed alcoholic drinks. These secret meetings were discovered and the boys were threatened by their parents which led to the breaking up of the society in 1860. Four years later, Keshub Chandra Sen visited Bombay and returned again in 1867. The trips generated considerable interest and excitement among the western educated elite of Maharashtra. In 1867, Atmaram Pandurang (1823-1898) and some of his friends established the Prarthana Samaj (Prayer Society).

The Prarthana Samaj disapproved of idolatry and caste and supported widow re-marriage, late marriage and women's education. This was the beginning of the Prarthana Samaj in Bombay. Several of its members had been associated with the Paramahans Mandali. The leaders of the Samaj were all respectable Chitpavan or Saraswat brahmins. Not only were they members of the highest caste, but were also western educated professionals. They were extremely successful as 'wranglers', judges, medical doctors, professors and civil servants.

Dr. Atmaram Pandurang was a well-known physician, Bal Walgle was a barrister, Janardan Sakharam was a journalist. The famous elitist Prarthana Samaj trio- Sir G.R. Bhandarkar, Narayan Ganesh Chandavarkar and Madhav Govind Ranade all responded enthusiastically to Keshub's call for social reform. Bengal continued to provide assistance to this new organization through visits by distinguished Brahmos. In 1871, a Bengali civil servant from Lahore, Navin Chandra Ray, came and lectured on the virtues of progressive Brahmoism. The next year Pratap Chandra Mazumadar spent six months in Bombay where he helped organize a high school for the education of working classes and helped in starting the journal Subodh Patrika. Despite the help and inspiration provided by the Bengali Brahmos, the Prarthana Samaj leaders refused to call themselves 'Brahmos' or to formally link their society with the Brahmo Samaj. The Prarthana Samaj continued as an independent reform movement.

Ideas And Activities Of The Prarthana Samaj

The Prarthana Samaj movement was a religious movement within Hinduism. Based on theistic philosophy in their religious reform they stressed on social reform such as— the abandonment of caste, widow remarriage, female education, etc. Their theism was based on ancient Hindu texts and their doctrine was as follows:

1. God is the creator of this universe. He is the only true God; there is no other God beside him. He is eternal, spiritual, infinite, the store of all good, all joy, without parts, without form, one without a second, the ruler of all, all-pervading, omniscient, almighty, merciful, all-holy and the saviour of sinners.
2. His worship alone leads to happiness in this world and the next.
3. Love and reverences for him, an exclusive faith in him, praying and singing to him spiritually with these feelings and doing the things pleasing to him constitute His true worship.
4. To worship and pray to images and other created objects is not a true mode of divine adoration.
5. God does not incarnate himself and there is no one book which has been directly revealed by God or is wholly infallible.
6. All men are His children; therefore, they should behave towards each other as brethren without distinction."

The Vaishnava bhakti devotional movement that developed in the thirteenth century in Maharashtra around cult 'Vitthala' had strong influence on the Prarthana Samaj. The devotional poems of Vitthalas, particularly those of Tukaram, formed the basis of the Prarthana Samaj worship. The Prarthana Samaj was an association with a managing committee and its own rules and byelaws. Weekly meetings were held each Sunday where bhakti hymns, lectures and readings from various scriptures were recited. The Prarthana Samaj showed a syncretic acceptance of all religions. They drew upon Christian and Buddhist texts as well as Hindu Scriptures while composing their weekly services. The Samaj was pledged to worship one God and seek truth in all religions. They condemned idolatry and the existing corruption of Hindu religions. Ranade tried to create an ideological base for the Prarthana Samaj in his A Theist's Confession of Faith. In it, he stressed the compassionate, omnipotent God similar to the divine figure found in the writings of the Maratha bhakti saints.

'To Ranade religion was as inseparable from social reform as love to man is inseparable from love to God'. The Prarthana Samaj was involved in various social reform activities. It wanted to provide education to women and all sections of society, to end the ban on widow re-marriage and to abandon all caste restrictions. But it did not want a complete break with Hindu society. Branches of the Prarthana Samaj were started in Poona, Satara and Ahmednagar and different cities of Maharashtra.

After the split occurred between Keshub Chandra Sen and the Sadharan Brahmos in 1878, the Prarthana Samaj in Western India moved closer to the latter. In conjunction with the Indian National Congress, the Prarthana Samajists and Sadharan Brahmos started the Social Reform Association in 1888 which used to meet every year in the same venue after the Congress session was over. In Gujarat, there were various religious sects like the Vallabhacharyas, the Kabir Panthis, Dadupanthis and the Swami Narayans.

The Swami Narayan sect who originated in the 18th Century was a reformist sect who wanted to remove the corruption then prevailing in the Vaishnava sects. Among the modern religious reform associations in the nineteenth Century were the Param Hansa Sabha and the Manav Dharma Sabha. In 1858, to draw the attention of the youth to true religion and encourage proper moral conduct, the Dharma Sabha was started in Ahmedabad. Not much work was done by this association beyond the publication of some devotional songs.

Bholanath Sarbhai who was one of the active persons behind this organization, together with Rancchodlal

Chhotalal, the founder of the first textile mill in Ahmedabad, Mahipatram Nilkanth and a few others founded the Gujrat Prarthana Samaj. All of them belonged to the Nagar Brahmin caste, the highest caste in Gujarat. Pratap Chandra Mazumdar visited Ahmedabad. Satyendranath Tagore was posted for some time as District Judge in Ahmedabad. Many young Gujaratis, educated at Elphinstone College in Bombay, had imbibed the ideas of the Prarthana Samaj. All this led to the foundation of the Gujarat Prarthana Samaj whose aims and objectives were the same as those of the Prarthana Samaj in Bombay.

4

Major Movements of Reform in Modern India

Arya Samaj

A powerful movement on similar lines as Brahmo Samaj under the leadership of Dayanand Saraswati was started in 1875. He was a sannyasi (renouncer) who believed in the infallible authority of the Vedas. Dayanand advocated the doctrine of karma and reincarnation, and emphasized the ideals of brahmacharya (chastity) and sanyasa. One Shivratri day when Dayanand Saraswati was just 14 yrs old, near the diety of Lord Shiva, his father asked him to recite 'Om Namah Shivaya' constantly all night. While he followed his father's instructions, he was aghast on the sight of a mouse playfully mounting the phallus symbol of Lord Shiva and taking away offerings place before the diety. He then thought to himself "What is this God who could not protect himself from the impertinence of such a little creature?" He woke his father and the priest and pointed out the helplessness of the diety. They argued with him, but to no effect.The boy left for home breaking his fast.

The air was thickening with the missionary propaganda that idol worship was mere stone-worship and that only the half-civilised barbarians indulged in it. He began to analyse the problem and stealthily left his house and began practicing yoga. He met one Sanayasi named Brijanand who initiated him to preach the Vedic truths avoiding Puranic practices of idol worship. Dayanand did not know English, so he established rapport with the elite who had no English education. Brahmo Samaj was confined to English-educated classes. Therefore dayanand could not win over the Brahmo Samaj leaders to his point of view. He also appro-ached Prarthana Samaj leaders in Ahmedabad, but could not win them over also. Reason being both of these movements could not accept the infallibility of the Vedas or the transmigration of the souls. Dayanand then founded his Arya Samaj on 10th April 1875 at Mumbai.

He translated Vedas, wrote his 'Magnus Opus Satratha Prakash'. He gathered a large number of followers in Punjab.Under the influence of Christian missionary propaganda; it had become a fashion with these new reformers to denounce castes to derecognise the superiority of the Brahamanas and to look upon idol worship. Inter-caste marriage was recognised. Minimum age of marriage was fixed at 16 for girls and 25 for boys. Arya Samaj upholds the sanctity of the cow, Samakars, oblations to fire, and social reform, including the education of women. The main thrust of Arya Samaj was however at Shuddhi.He advocated the return of converted Christians and Muslims to their original faith, namely the Hindu.This attracted wide attention amongst all sections of Hindus, but it was strongly resented by Muslims.

Arya Samajists also advocated the spread of English education. Dayanand Anglo-Vedic College at Lahore under the principalship of Lala Hansaraj became a foremost agency to preach this gospel of Independence. The two other Brahmo and Prarthana Samaj, were founded in Vedas, yet they lacked that militancy of Arya Samaj and were movements politically leaning on the British rule. Arya Samajists insisted on fighting Christianity and Islam with their own weapons. Dayanand and other Arya Samajists insisted on emphasing that the Vedas and other ancient literature of ours had been much more inspiring than the borrowed thoughts from Europe for more liberal thought or for more pure religion. Dayananda Saraswati's strong advocacy of the vedic infallibillity turned the tide against the then current submissive approach of the English educated elite.

The 10 Principles of the Arya Samaj

1. God is the original source of all true knowledge and all that is known by the physical and spiritual sciences.
2. God is Existent, Intelligent and Blissful. He is Formless, Almighty, Just, Merciful, Unborn, Infinite, Unchallengeable, Beginningless, Incomparable, the Support and Lord of All, Omniscient, Imperishable, Immortal, Fearless, Eternal, Holy and the Maker of the Universe. To God alone is worship due.
3. The Vedas are the scriptures of true knowledge. It is the duty of all noble individuals to read them, to hear them being read and to recite them to others.
4. One should always be ready to accept truth and give up untruth.
5. One's actions should always be performed in conformity with Dharma (righteousness), i.e., after due consideration of right and wrong.
6. The primary aim of the Arya Samaj is to advance the good of all, i.e., to promote physical, spiritual and social well-being.
7. One's dealings should always be regulated by love and due justice in accordance with the dictates of Dharma.
8. One should aim at dispelling ignorance and promoting knowledge.
9. One should see one's own greatest welfare as residing in the welfare of others.

10. One should regard oneself as being under the restriction of the altruistic rulings of society, while one should be free in matters of individual welfare.

Out of these ten, the first three principles are seen as comprising the doctrinal core of the Arya Samaj, as they summarize the member's beliefs in regards to God, the nature of Divinity and the authority of the Vedas. The remaining seven principles reflect the reformative ambitions of the Samaj in regards to both the individual and society at large. However, nothing beyond these 10 Principles has any binding force on any member of the Arya Samaj.

For this reason, the early Samaj proved to be attractive to individuals belonging to various religious communities, and enjoyed a notable degree of support from segments of the Hindu, Sikh and Muslim populations of Indian society. Drawing what are seen to be the logical conclusions from these principles, the Arya Samaj also unequivocally condemns practices such as polytheism, idolatry, iconolatry, animal sacrifice, ancestor worship, pilgrimage, priestcraft, the belief in avatars or incarnations of God, the hereditary caste system, untouchability and child marriage on the grounds that all these lack Vedic sanction.

The Theosophical Society

In 1877, a meeting occurred in America between some leading members of the Theosophical Society, founded in 1875, and Mulji Thakarshi, an individual who had played an instrumental role in the establishment of the Bombay Arya Samaj that same year. During the course of the exchange, it became clear that the two societies held many views in common, and efforts were undertaken to bring their respective leaders into closer contact.

As a result, correspondence began between Henry Steel Olcott, one of the co-founders of the New York Theosophical Society, and Harish Chandra Chintamani, the then acting president of the Bombay Arya Samaj. At the suggestion of Chintamani, Olcott composed a letter addressed to Swami Dayanand dated the 18th of February, 1878. Unwilling to wait for what they were led to believe would be a positive response, the heads of the Theosophical Society decided to go ahead with their plans to recast their organization as a branch of the Arya Samaj. On the 22nd of May, 1878, the Theosophical Society was renamed 'The Theosophical Society of the Arya Samaj of Aryavarta' and Swami Dayanand was announced as its director in chief.

Reconsideration and Reorganization

This unilateral move on the part of the Theosophists, however, eventually proved to be grossly miscalculated. While Olcott's open profession of faith in the Vedas was positively received and publicly praised by Swami Dayanand on more than one occasion, when he came to learn of the details of the tenets held by the Theosophists, including their belief in ghosts, mediumistic abilities, miracles and other occult matters, the Swami, taking up the role of teacher, was quick to admonish Olcott for what he termed 'humbuggery' and 'superstition' unbefitting of a seeker of truth.

The Theosophists, however, were unwilling to give up their faith in these matters, and the gulf which had always existed between the two societies suddenly became apparent to all involved. Therefore, in September of 1878, the Theosophical Society was reverted to its former status as an independent organization. However, a second organization was simultaneously formed and given the now familiar name 'The Theosophical Society of the Arya Samaj of Aryavarta'. It was agreed that membership of the new society, which itself was to remain a common branch of both the Theosophical Society and the Arya Samaj, would be open to any persons who wished to remain associated with both societies.

Irreconcilable Differences

This tentative solution, however, proved incapable of

bridging the growing divide. Between 1879 and 1881, the founders of the Theosophical Society, Henry Olcott and Helena Blavatsky, paid Swami Dayanand several visits while touring India. Through the course of their discussions and correspondence, it became clear that the differences between the two societies were not, as previously assumed, limited to relatively minor issues, but in fact extended to what the Swami viewed as central tenets of the Vedic Religion. The main point of contention was in regards to the nature of God.

While the Theosophists asserted that the highest Divinity is an impersonal Principle, Swami Dayanand maintained that the Vedas and their allied literature clearly teach that God is a personal Being - in his words, "the Personification of Being, Knowledge and Bliss". Thus, the line dividing the two organizations was clearly identified and neither party saw themselves in need of reconsidering their views. Therefore, on the 28th of March, 1882, Swami Dayanand announced that the Arya Samaj had officially cut off all ties with the Theosophical Society.

It has been stated that many of the difficulties and subsequent hostilities which arose between the Theosophical Society and the Arya Samaj were due to an unfortunate combination of personal intrigue and poor translations. Both parties have claimed to have been misrepresented on several occasions and members of each have accused the other of being responsible for the failure of the undertaking. Regardless, the theological and ideological differences between the Theosophical Society and the Arya Samaj persist to this day.

On April 10th, 1875, the organisation called "Arya Samaj" was formally registered in Bombay (Mumbai), India. Arya Samaj, as the name signifies, is a Samaj (Organisation) of Aryas (people who are noble). Further clarified, the Arya Samaj is a Society of Noble People, who follow the Veda (the Word of God handed down to mankind in the begining) and try to behave in accordance with the teachings of the Vedas.

The Arya Samaj was founded by Maharishi Swami Dayananda Saraswati, a scholar who believed in the authority of the Vedas. The motto of the Arya Samaj, taken from the Vedas, is "Krinvanto Vishwam Aryam" (Rig Veda 9.63.5) - Make ALL men arya (noble and cultured)." Hence, by being a part of a Noble Society (Arya Samaj), you enjoin with a commitment of becoming an arya (noble person), who gathers in religious assemblies to propagate the teachings of the Vedas, so that you can ennoble (make noble) those who aren't noble - Making the Universe Noble.

The purpose of creating the Arya Samaj

The society of the Arya Samaj was created in an effort to preserve the original values and beliefs of Hinduism as stated in the original scriptures of Hindus: The Vedas.

Women

According to the Vedas, women of all races should be given an equal opportunity to education as men. At the time of the creation of the Arya Samaj, Hindu women were not allowed to study religious scriptures; they were not allowed to be priests or preach the word of God; they were denied access to education; they were treated as second class citizens below men; widows were treated as outcasts; they had to burn themselves on their husbands funeral pyre, their families were forced to produce a dowry before a man's family accepted them into their family; and they were forced into child marriages with older men. The Arya Samaj fought against all of these injustices then and continues to champion the rights of women all over the world. In many societies, you will find that only Arya Samaj women are given the opportunity to become Hindu priests.

Society

The Arya Samaj believes that every individual shall be

judged by his character and actions and not by his birthright. Due to the unscrupulous manipulation of the caste system, those of high caste families were given honour and respect and those of low caste and their children were deemed "untouchables" and were ill-treated and suppressed. The Arya Samaj fought against these injustices against the untouchables and embraced them, educated them and welcomed them in their satsangs and religious gatherings.

Education

The Arya Samaj pioneers education for all. In India, many institutions of learning (schools, colleges, gurukuls) were created for men, women and children. The Arya Samaj is very vociferous in encouraging the common man to learn and read the scriptures. This society is against the practice of having only one selected group of individuals indulging in the reading and preaching from the scriptures.

Social Welfare

The Arya Samaj plays an active role in the welfare of the needy. Many orphanages, homes for abused women and widows and homes for the elderly have been established in India and other parts of the world. The society is also involved in providing relief during times of famine, drought, earthquakes and other natural disasters.

Politics

The Arya Samaj propagates patriotism and dedication to serving the interest of one's nation and motherland. In the times of the British Rule in India, the Arya Samaj was one of the foremost organisations to champion the cause for political freedom and independence.

Religion

The Arya Samaj propagates the motto "Back to the Vedas" and promotes these scriptures as the one true source of all knowledge. The Arya Samaj holds the Vedic principle of monotheism - that there is ONE GOD who is formless, ever-existent and all powerful. Due to the fact that God is all-powerful with many attributes he is referred to by many names such as Creator (Brahma), Preserver (Vishnu) and Dissolver (Rudra). For hundreds of centuries Hindu sects and scholars had accepted the Vedas as the original Hindu scriptures but due to passage of time and destruction of Hindu scriptures and the introduction of other texts and interpretations, many deviations to the original teachings crept into Hinduism.

The Arya Samaj promotes the Veda as the original scripture of all mankind and teaches that the acceptance of this will bring about a unity in the religious thinking of Hindus. The Vedas promote universal peace and its teachings are universal in character and apply to ALL people at ALL times.

The Arya Samaj rejects the belief of blind faith, animal sacrifices, idolatry, priestcraft and superstitions brought about by ignorance and fear. It promotes the philosophy of Karma (receiving the fruits of one's deeds). Suffering is the logical consequence of one's action (the law of cause and effect) and hence, superstitious belief does not eradicate suffering.

The Arya Samaj is NOT a religion. It is a society that was formed, not as a new religion, but as a coming together of men and women of noble thoughts and actions who (irrespective of their social, ethnic or racial origins) believe in the underlying principles of Vaidik Satya Sanatana Dharma (commonly called "Hinduism"). In simpler terms, the Arya Samaj is a society of Hindus that propagates selfless action for the development of humanity and congregates for the common purpose of preserving the pristine values of Hinduism. As was said by Maharishi Swami Dayanand: "I have not come to preach a new dogma or religion, or to establish a new religious order, or to be proclaimed a new messiah or pontiff. I have only brought before the people, the light of Vedic Wisdom which has been hidden during the centuries of India's thraldom."

Prarthana Samaj

On the lines of Brahmo Samaj and under the inspiration of its very dynamic leader K.C.Sen, Dr. Atmaram Pandurang founded Samaj known as Prarthana Samaj which means Community wedded to prayerful worship of One True God. Like Sen's Samaj, it believed in the Unity of God and denounced idolatry as a special sin. But it did not abandon Hindu practices nor did it advocate definite exclusion of idolatry or abolition of castes. It was confined to a small group of intellectuals who were advocates of reforms of the social system of the Hindus.

Prarthana Samaj is milder and less radical in its principles. Theistic worship comes first, followed closely by social reform - the abandonment of caste, widow-remarriage, female education, and the abolition of child-marriage. Many members hold the view that definite beliefs and theological thought are not necessary for a free theistic movement. Others have produced theological and devotional books. Though their theism is based on ancient Hindu texts, they have practically given up the inspiration of the Vedas and belief in transmigration.

Two secret societies preceded the Prarthana Samaj. The Paramahamsa Sabha established by Ram Balkrishna Jaykar and others followed this in 1849. Members had to eat bread baked by Christian and drink water brought by a Moslem. Orthodox opposition resulted in the documents being stolen in 1860 and the names of the members being made public. This caused panic. Some members became Christian, while others held to their convictions. Those who held to their convictions became the founders of the Prarthana Samaj in Bombay in 1867. These were educated Indians from Bombay and their leader was Dr. Atmaram Pandurang (1823-1898), a personal friend of Dr. Wilson, founder of Wilson College in 1835.

The Brahmo Samaj made an important impression on these men. In 1872 one of the great Brahmo, Pratap Chandra, stayed for six months at the invitation of the Prarthana Samaj. During his visit there was a plan to make Prarthana Samaj a branch of Brahmo Samaj. This was prevented by Mahadeo Ranade pointing out the splits among the Brahmos of Bengal that might be echoed in Bombay, while Dr. Bhandarkar did not approve of the extremism and Christian bias of Keshub. Similarly, when Dayanand came to Bombay in 1874, there was great interest in his lectures and the next year he founded the Arya Samaj in Bombay. However, his ideas on the Vedas stopped the Prarthana Samaj from joining him.

So the Prarthana Samaj continued as an independent reform movement. In Bombay this was the most important and well-organized movement of the time, being sponsored by leaders of society. P.C.Mazoomdar came from Calcutta in 1872 for six months and increased the worshippers, started night schools for workers, and also a journal, the Subodh Patrika. Their own building was erected in 1874 at Girgaum, Bombay. The mildness of the Prarthana Samaj has meant that there have never been groups of missionaries as in the Brahmo Samaj. With only one or two missionaries the movement has not spread widely. However, the mildness of the Samaj has been attractive in the South, in Andhra Pradesh and Tamil Nadu, where the Prarthana Samaj is the most popular of the Samajas.

The Samaj runs the Young Theists Union, the Postal Mission to send religious literature, the Subodh Patrika, night schools, and a Ladies Association. It is also associated with The Students Brotherhood, an Orphanage and Foundling Asylum in Pandharpur, and the organization of the Social Reform Movement and the Depressed Classes Mission. Every year both the Brahmo and Prarthana Samajas attend an All-India Theistic Conference.

The Samaj defines its faith as:

1. God is the creator of this universe. He is the only true God; there is no other God beside him. He is eternal, spiritual, infinite, the store of all good, all joy, without parts, without form, one without a second, the ruler of all, all-pervading, omniscient, almighty, merciful, all-holy and the saviour of sinners.
2. His worship alone leads to happiness in this world and the next.
3. Love and reverence for him, an exclusive faith in him, praying and singing to him spiritually with these feelings and doing the things pleasing to him constitute His true worship.
4. To worship and pray to images and other created objects is not a true mode of divine adoration.
5. God does not incarnate himself and there is no one book which has been directly revealed by God or is wholly infallible.
6. All men are His children; therefore they should behave towards each other as brethren without distinction.
7. This is pleasing to God and constitutes man's duty.

This doctrine was very similar to the Brahmo Samaj but with one significant difference. The Prarthana Samaj bases its worship on the devotional poems of the Vitthalas, especially those of Tukaram. The Vitthalas or Varkari Panth, 'pilgrim's path is the cult of Vitthala, the Vaishnava bhakti devotional movement that rose in the thirteenth century and is centered on Pandharpur in the far south of Maharashtra. Though the Prarthana Samaj is opposed to image-worship, in practice members follow the ceremonies of Hinduism though regarding them as of no religious importance. Thus Samaj members can still practice image-worship in their homes and be part of the caste system. It is said that the Prarthana Samaj pays allegiance to Hinduism with a protest. Their own services use hymns of the old Maratha poet-saints, especially Tukaram.

Yogoda Satsanga Society of India, British India

Paramahansa Yogananda formed Yogoda Satsanga Society of India in 1917. The headquarters or the Yogoda Satsanga Math is situated on the banks of the Ganges at Dakshineswar, near Kolkata. Another branch of this math is at Ranchi, Jharkhand and also many more branch centers. Other than meditation centers throughout India, there are twenty-three educational institutions, from primary through college level all controlled by Yogoda Satsanga Society of India. "Yogoda," is a term coined by Paramahansa Yogananda. The term is derived from Yoga, union, accord, balance; and the term da, means, "that which imparts". "Satsanga" is the term made of Sat, truth and Sanga, fellowship. For the west, Paramahansaji translated the Indian name of Yogoda Satsanga Society of India as "Self-Realization Fellowship (SRF)."

The Society publishes Paramahansa Yogananda's priceless writings, lectures, and informal talks - including his all-inclusive series of Yogoda Satsanga Lessons for home study, publishes, audio and video recordings based on his teachings; oversees its ashrams, kendras, and meditation centers, and its monastic community; conducts lecture and class series in almost each and every city all across the Indian subcontinent; and coordinates the Worldwide Prayer Circle. A wide network of groups and individuals dedicated to praying for those in need of physical, mental, or spiritual aid and for global peace and harmony are welcomed at the Yogoda Satsanga Society of India. Yogoda Satsanga Society of India answers all the inquiries about the teachings of Sri Sri Paramahansa Yogananda from the countries like Bangladesh, Bhutan, India including Andaman and Nicobar Islands, Nepal, Maldives Islands and Sri Lanka. The programmes executed at the Yogoda Satsanga Society of India include Kriya Yoga Diksha Ceremonies, Conducted Spiritual Retreats, Janmotsav at Ahmedabad and Bangalore (to be held in 2009) and Sadhana Sangam Delhi in October.

Shuddhi Movement

It was started by Arya Samaj in early 20th century to bring back those Hindu people back to their religion, who had converted themselves to Islam and Christianity. Dayananda Saraswati claimed to be rejecting all non-Vedic beliefs altogether. Hence the Arya Samaj unequivocally condemned idolatry, animal sacrifices, ancestor worship, pilgrimages, priestcraft, offerings made in temples, the caste system, untouchability and child marriages, on the grounds that all these lacked Vedic sanction. It aimed to be a universal church based on the authority of the Vedas.

The nature of scriptural authority in Hinduism is different from Islam and Christianity in the sense these two world religions claimed more or less exclusive divine authority for their books, the Veda never put up any such claim. Hinduism thus suffered from the universal character of their scriptures. Dayananda was aware of this disadvantage and was moved by the evalengical spirit of Christianity & Islam to create a similar militancy in Hinduism itself. He therefore, moved to give the Vedas the same degree of supernatural authority, which was claimed by the Koran and Bible.

By doing so Dayananda made a departure from the line of ancient Hindu fathers, but by doing so he rendered an immense service to the new nationalist movement in India. He saw these world religions making deep inroads into India and realized that unless action was taken, India would in course of time ceased to be the land of the Hindus. Dayananda was impressed by the credal universalism of Christianity and Islam that he wanted to seek it for his own religion. Thus the logic behind statement on the Infallibility of the Vedas was that he wanted to build Hindu society and Hindu nation.

The process of reconverting Hindus, who had embraced Islam known as Shuddhi, was accompanied by a Sanghathan movement, which was launched to unify the Hindus and organize them in self-defence. Literally speaking Shuddhi means purification but when used by the Arya Samajists, it means reconversion. The Samaj being a Vedic church received a considerable success in reconverting Hindus.

But this provoked the Muslims. "How could the Arya Samaj break their 1200-year-old monopoly", this though led to the murder of Lala Ram Chandra in Kashmir in 1923. This was followed by the foul murder of Swami Shraddhananada. The Swami was the founder of the Gurukul at Kangri, a unique educational institution, respected by the Hindus and Muslims during the Non-Cooperation Movement. He was also arrested during the Khilafat movement.

After his release he found that Muslims were harassing Hindus, converting them. He launched the Shuddhi movement. Because of his saintly character, courage and moving oration more than 18,000 Muslims returned to Hindu fold in some parts of U.P. alone. They also succeeded in reconverting a number of Hindus who had been forcibly converted to Islam during the Moplah rebellion in Kerala in 1920. The Muslims were upset, oddly though some Hindu Congress leaders joined the Muslim chorus in denouncing the Swami.

The Swami narrated one more incident in his journal Liberator "As regards the removal of untouchability, it has been authoritatively ruled several times that is the duty of Hindus to expiate for their past sins and non-Hindus must have nothing to do with it. But the Muslims and Christian Congressmen have openly revolted against this dictum. Even such a unbiased leader such as Shri Yakub Hassan, openly called upon Muslims the duty of converting all the untouchables in India to Islam".

India's first President Dr Rajendra Prasad exposed the double standards adopted by the critics of the Swami. "It is difficult to understand how Christians and Muslims can object to the Shuddhi movement on its merits. The Hindus must have the same rights as propagating as others have". On 23 December 1926, when the Swami, after a serious attack of pneumonia, was lying in his bed, a Muslim by the name Abdul Rashid came to see him, asked for a glass of water and when the attendant went in, took out his revolver and shot at the Swami four times.

When Rashid was caught and charge sheeted the Muslims collected a large fund for his defence. Quoting Pattabhi Sitaramayya at the Gauhati Congress session of 1926 "Gandhi expounded what true religion was and explained the causes that led to the murder. Now you will perhaps understand why I have called Abdul Rashid a brother and I repeat it. I do not regard him as guilty of Swami`s murder. Guilty indeed are those who excited feelings of hatred against one another".

Brahma Kumaris

To develop the inner strength, to cultivate the inner values and above all to teach a practical method of meditation The Brahma Kumaris World Spiritual University recognizes the very inherent goodness of all people.

It's just not the history but a tale of growth, an account of development and the moving document of moving from nothingness towards a mammoth growth. Brahma Kumaris rich history is an amalgamation of all these and much more.

World Headquarters of Brahma Kumaris

The year 1950 was indeed an important year in the history of Brahma Kumaris. It is in this year the community moved to Mount Abu. Mount Abu has been credited for its serenity and pristine splendor and certainly for its age-old heritage. Perched high in the Aravalli Mountains, Mount Abu with its divine grandeur had all those ex factors, to be the right place for reflection and contemplation. Perhaps this was the reason why the community moved the headquarters to the Mount Abu. Named as Madhuban (Forest Of Honey) in a rented building there at Mount Abu the community established the University's World Headquarters.

Expansion of Brahma Kumaris in India

The expansion of Brahma Kumaris in India is again a tale of a ceaseless journey. Dada Lekhraj better known as Brahma Baba felt the sheer necessity to share the knowledge he did receive, with the rest of India. The year was 1952 and with the greater intention of implementing his plans sent a few young women members to Delhi and the then Bombay to establish study centers to teach Raja Yoga meditation. The expansion of Brahma Kumaris in India thus began humbly however today; a single town in India could not be found without a Brahma Kumaris study center.

The organization did expand rapidly. It was in the year 1971, the permanent centers were established in London and Hong Kong. This further strengthened the roots of the organization whilst leading towards a colossal worldwide expansion in terms of both geographical growths as well as in the growth of overall membership.

World Spiritual University

Today there are thousands of students attending thousands of meditation centres in nearly one hundred countries. Madhuban serves as the nucleus of all the BK centers, This Madhuban complex now includes two campuses, located elsewhere on the mountain, and Shantivan. There is also the Academy for a Better World, also known, as Gyan Sarovar. All these 3 campuses attract 2.5 millions individual every year. From its modest beginning the organization has come indeed a long way.

Brahma Baba, Founder of Brahma Kumaris

Born in the year 1876 into a humble home as Lekhraj Kripilani, Brahma Baba was the son of a schoolteacher. Strict Hindu tradition was induced in him from his early days. In the year 1836, Baba begun his journey, the journey in understanding the truths of life and founded the Btahma Kumaris.

Spiritual Leaders of Brahma Kumaris

A number of spiritual leaders further carried away the unfinished task of Brahma Baba. Dadi Janaki, Dadi Gulzar is some of the names.

Brahma Kumaris Administration

The World headquarter is ideally seated at the Mount Abu, Rajasthan. It comprises the Administrative Head, Additional Administrative Head, Joint Administrative Head, a Governing Board and a Management Committee.

Students of Brahma Kumaris

Brahma Kumaris offers education in moral and spiritual value. Individuals aged above 18, whoever support the guiding, teachings and philosophy of the BKWSU can attend the daily classes twice a week on a regular basis. There is an option of free enrollment also. The students from all strata of the society here at the BK centre thus mirror a variety of backgrounds, echelon of education, profession and age. Current data show that the University has 825,000 students and over 8,500 centres in 100 countries and territories.

Indian Caste System

When the British first gained a foothold on the Indian subcontinent in the 18th century their concern was profit. The men who administered the territory for the East India Company were more inclined to profiteering than to attempting to establish an effective government. By the beginning of the 19th century this type of attitude had begun to change. A series of conquests expanded the territory held by the British and the idea of responsible trusteeship began to creep into the thinking of the individuals charged with governing British India. The freebooters of the 18th century were giving way to the bureaucrats of the 19th century. Ironically, it is highly debateable which of the two, freebooters or bureaucrats were the most dangerous to the people of

India. Treasure can be replaced. Cultures, once tampered with, are nearly impossible to reclaim.

The men charged with the governing of British India in the 19th century were creations of the society that they had left behind in Britain. That society had become increasingly intrigued with methods of social management and improvement. Moreover, as the 19th century progressed, it progressively appeared that the British were destined to lead the world. Victorious in the Napoleonic wars and with an empire growing at an unprecedented rate, the British became ever more confident that their destiny was to lead the way to civilization and rise up the lesser races. The British Empire was believed to be the natural heir to the classical Roman Empire. From this mix of belief in their superiority and fascination with methods of social management and improvement, came a variety of so called sciences. These included such things as phrenology and eugenics but at the heart of any of the movements to study either man or society was statistics.

The term statistics can be traced to the 1797 edition of the Encyclopedia Britannica and was defined as a "word lately introduced to express a view or survey of any kingdom, county, or parish." This definition gives no indication of any kind of methodological approach being used as would be evident at the end of the 19th and the beginning of the 20th centuries. Rather, the word statistics seems to have been used to indicate a simple compilation of raw numbers used to describe the demographics of a given geographic area. However, while a strict methodological model would not develop for many years, it did not take as long for individuals and groups to begin to collect data on a wide variety of interest areas. By the 1830s statistics were being gathered on everything from crime and occupations to sewage systems.

None of this work, however, was done by individuals who were professional statisticians. Indeed, statistics was not recognized as a science and was not taught in any of the universities in Britain. Rather, these figures were collected by politicians, economists, government officials, physicians, and a few mathematicians. The object of all of this data collecting was to obtain information about the society that would be politically useful and would indicate new means of social improvement and control. Within this framework developed the London Statistical Society. This society had as its goal, the furtherance of statistics as a science and among its many endeavours it gave advice to the government on the types of information that the society felt should be collected as part of the various censuses that were done periodically in the British Isles.

One of the main points that the Statistical Society repeatedly recommended be included in the census was a question regarding religious persuasion as may be seen when the Society stated that: "An accurate knowledge of the religious persuasions of its people is requisite for every state. The ascertainment of it we see to be neglected by few claiming a high rank in civilization; and England ought assuredly not to be of that number." While this question was included in the Irish census, it was never included as a mandatory question in the English census. In 1851 religious persuasion was asked during the census but there was no requirement that this question be answered under the law and the data thus gathered was published separately from the rest of the census. It can only be assumed that the government felt that it would not be politically expedient to include this question as an integral part of the census.

In any case, among the recommendations forwarded to the government with regard to the British census of 1871, there was once again a call for a question on the matter of religion. Once again this recommendation was rejected by the government. Interestingly, as with the Irish, the government had no qualms about including religious questions on the Indian census. Perhaps the most valid explanation of this apparent contradiction is that both the Irish and the Indians were conquered people and as such did not have the political power to affectively raise any complaint against the asking of religious questions in the census. If this was indeed the case, another piece of evidence has definitely come to the fore in favour of treating the history of the Irish as part of the greater history of the British Empire.

As subjugated as any other people and obviously just as desirous of independence. This question, however, is outside the scope of the present paper. In India, the British found themselves governing a greater number of people than anywhere else in the Empire. Amazement and disbelief at the shear number of people can be found throughout the writings of the British of the period. In part, the illusion of numbers was caused by the physical lay out of the towns and cities of India. Unlike their European counterparts, Indian urban areas did not display wide streets and thoroughfares in there business or market districts. Rather, there was a propensity for building narrow lanes and pathways which were surrounded by two and three story buildings.

This created a feeling of crowding and led to the perception that the population of these towns was much higher than was, in fact, the case. This is not meant to imply that the population of India was not high during the 19th century, it was. But due to the visual effect of the urban centres the British tended to overestimate. Benares, for example, was estimated to have a population of 582,000 in 1801 while later censuses showed that the figure was probably more like 152,000. This type of error was, in part, also due to the method used in many of these early censuses. A count was made of the number of houses and this was multiplied by an assumed figure of seven inhabitants per house. The problem was that defining what constituted a house was difficult, which resulted in shops being counted as houses, and that the number of people per house was greatly over estimated. The point is that the British came to believe that they ruled over a far greater population than was in fact the case.

To make matters worse, these early estimates were perpetuated by their use in later estimates and consequent compounding of the original errors. In any case, the British administrators were, understandably overwhelmed by these figures and felt obliged to find a way to compartmentalize chunks of population into manageable groups. The most obvious way to do so was through the use of India's unique caste system. The caste system had been a fascination of the British since their arrival in India. Coming from a society that was divided by class, the British attempted to equate the caste system to the class system. As late as 1937 Professor T. C. Hodson stated that: "Class and caste stand to each other in the relation of family to species. The general classification is by classes, the detailed one by castes. The former represents the external, the latter the internal view of the social organization."

The difficulty with definitions such as this is that class is based on political and economic factors, caste is not. In fairness to Professor Hodson, by the time of his writing, caste had taken on many of the characteristics that he ascribed to it and that his predecessors had ascribed to it but during the 19th century caste was not what the British believed it to be. It did not constitute a rigid description of the occupation and social level of a given group and it did not bear any real resemblance to the class system. However, this will be dealt with later in this essay. At present, the main concern is that the British saw caste as a way to deal with a huge population by breaking it down into discrete chunks with specific characteristics. Moreover, as will be seen later in this paper, it appears that the caste system extant in the late 19th and early 20th century has been altered as a result of British actions so that it increasingly took on the characteristics that were ascribed to by the British.

One of the main tools used in the British attempt to understand the Indian population was the census. Attempts were made as early as the beginning of the 19th century to estimate populations in various regions of the country but these, as earlier noted, were methodologically flawed and led to grossly erroneous conclusions. It was not until 1872 that a planned comprehensive census was attempted. This was done under the direction of Henry Beverely, Inspector General of Registration in Bengal. The primary purpose given for the taking of the census that of governmental preparedness to deal with disaster situations, was both laudable and logical. However, the census went well beyond counting heads or even enquiring into sex ratios or general living conditions.

Among the many questions were enquiries regarding nationality, race, tribe, religion and caste. Certainly none of these things were relevant to emergency measures responses by the government. Further, neither the notion of curiosity nor planned subterfuge on the part of the administration suffices to explain their inclusion in the census. On the question of race or nationality it could be argued that these figures were needed to allow analyses of the various areas in an attempt to predict internal unrest. However, there does not appear to have been any use made of the figures from that perspective. With regard to the information on religion and caste, the same claim could be made but once again there does not appear to have been any analyses done with the thought of internal disturbance in mind.

Obviously there had to be some purpose to the gathering of this data since due to the size of both the population and the territory to be covered, extraneous questions would not have been included due to time factors. Therefore, there must have been a reason of some sort for their inclusion. That reason was, quite simply, the British belief that caste was the key to understanding the people of India. Caste was seen as the essence of Indian society, the system through which it was possible to classify all of the various groups of indigenous people according to their ability, as reflected by caste, to be of service to the British.

Caste was seen as an indicator of occupation, social standing, and intellectual ability. It was, therefore necessary to include it in the census if the census was to serve the purpose of giving the government the information it needed in order to make optimum use of the people under its administration. Moreover, it becomes obvious that British conceptions of racial purity were interwoven with these judgements of people based on caste when reactions to censuses are examined. Beverly concluded that a group of Muslims were in fact converted low caste Hindus. This raised howls of protest from representatives of the group as late as 1895 since it was felt that this was a slander and a lie.H. H. Risely, Commissioner of the 1901 census, also showed British beliefs in an 1886 publication which stated that race sentiment, far from being:

Here is a prime example of the racial purity theories that had been developing throughout the 19th century. Here also is the plainest explanation for the inclusion of the questions on race, caste and religion being included with the censuses. Thus far this essay has dwelt almost entirely with British actions to the exclusion of any mention of Indian actions and reactions. This should not be taken to mean that the Indians were passive or without input into the process. Any change within a society requires the participation of all thc groups if it is to have any lasting effect. The Indian people had a very profound effect on the formulation of the census and their analysis.

However, Indian actions and reaction must be considered within the context of Indian history and Indian culture in the same way that British actions must be considered within British cultural context. For this reason, it has been necessary to postpone consideration of Indian reactions and contributions to the British activities until the next section of this essay which will then be followed by a more in depth examination of the development of British attitudes. Finally, the results of the combination of both Indian and British beliefs will be examined with a view to reaching a consensus on how they affected the compilation of and conclusions reached through the censuses.

The word caste is not a word that is indigenous to India. It originates in the Portuguese word casta which means race, breed, race or lineage. However, during the 19th century, the term caste increasingly took on the connotations of the word race. Thus, from the very beginning of western contact with the subcontinent European constructions have been imposed on Indian systems and institutions. To fully appreciate the caste system one must step away from the definitions imposed by Europeans and look at the system as a whole, including the religious beliefs that are an integral part of it.

To the British, viewing the caste system from the outside and on a very superficial level, it appeared to be a static system of social ordering that allowed the ruling class or Brahmins, to maintain their power over the other classes. What the British failed to realize was that Hindus existed in a different cosmological frame than did the British. The concern of the true Hindu was not his ranking economically within society but rather his ability to regenerate on a higher plane of existence during each successive life. Perhaps the plainest verbalization of this attitude was stated by a 20th century Hindu of one of the lower castes who stated: "Everything lies in the hands of God. We hope to go to the top, but our Karma (Action) binds us to this level." If not for the concept of reincarnation, this would be a totally fatalistic attitude but if one takes into account the notion that one's present life is simply one of many, then this fatalistic component is limited if not eliminated.

Therefore, for the Hindu, acceptance of present status and the taking of ritual actions to improve status in the next life is not terribly different in theory to the attitudes of the poor in western society. The aim of the poor in the west is to improve their lot in the space of a single life time. The aim of the lower castes in India is to improve their position over the space of many lifetimes. It should also be borne in mind that an entire caste could raise through the use of conquest or through service to rulers.Thus, it may be seen that within traditional Indian society the caste system was not static either within the material or metaphysical plane of existence. With the introduction of European and particulary British systems to India, the caste system began to modify.

This was a natural reaction of Indians attempting to adjust to the new regime and to make the most of whatever opportunities may have been presented to them. Moreover, with the apparent dominance exhibited by British science and medicine there were movements that attempted to adapt traditional social systems to fit with the new technology. Men such as Ram Mohan Roy, Swami Dayananda, and Ramkrishna started movements that, to one degree or another, attempted to explore new paths that would allow them and their people to live more equitably within British India. Roy in particular sits this description with his notion that the recognition of human rights was consistent with Hindu thought and the Hinduism could welcome external influences so long as they were not contrary to reason. While it is granted that the present paper is not the appropriate venue to explore such movements, they must be noted so that an impression of Indian submissiveness in the face of British intrusion may be avoided. There was a dynamic interplay between the British and Indians that had a profound effect on both societies. More appropriate to the task at hand, however, are the reactions of various groups within India to the census itself.

Unlike its predecessors in England, the census of India attempted not only to count, but to define and explain. As a result, the census became not simply an accounting of what existed but an active participant in the creation and modification of the society. As a result, Indians of many levels of society reacted to the census in attempts to gain or maintain status. In 1895, Fazl-i-Rabb wrote a book that attacked H. Beverly, Census Commissioner of Bengal for the 1871-72 censuses for stating that the Muslims of Bengal were converted low caste Hindus. It was Fazl-i- Rabb's belief that Muslims were being held up to ridicule by this report and that this was a grievous wrong that should be corrected. Whether this accusation was true or false is irrelevant for the present purposes.

What is important is the fact that more than twenty years after the 1871-72 censuses, the documents associated with that census were still having an effect on people within India. Group identity was based on a perception of the group's heritage and history and any threat to that perception was a threat to the very identity of the group itself. This identity appears to have had a much deeper significance for the group members than heritage had or has for people in the west. While individuals or families in the west may take pride in knowing the histories of their ancestors or in the case of the British, may have used family histories to claim certain privileges, in India there seems to be a much stronger and deeper meaning.

In fact, it is not uncommon for people in the west to take a certain pride in coming from humble or even notorious ancestry. It is interesting to note that this complaint is coming from a Muslim group since Muslims, theoretically, should not be concerned with their ancestry to any greater or lesser degree than Christians. However, in this case they certainly appear to have taken great umbrage at the statements made by Beverly twenty years earlier. One cannot help but wonder whether this was caused by their long association and cohabitation with Hinduism. Rabb's demands reinforce this suspicion when he states that the British Government should:

This is virtually a call for a public enquiry into what most westerners would consider a relatively minor matter of very limited concern.

A further example of Indian reaction to judgements made within the censuses becomes apparent from the claims of castes that they should have higher ranking following the census of 1901.One claim in particular that of the Mahtons, is of particular interest for the present paper. The Mahtons claimed that they should be granted the status of Rajputs because of both history and the fact that they followed Rajput customs. Therefore, since they had not received this status in the 1901 census, they requested the change to be affected in the 1911 census. Their request was rejected, not on the basis of any existing impediment but on the basis of the 1881 census which stated that the Mahtons were an offshoot of the Mahtams who were hunter/scavengers. Thus, it appears that the census system had become self reinforcing. However, after further debate the Mahton were reclassified as Mahton Rajput on the basis that they had separated themselves from the Mahtams and now acted in the manner of Rajputs.

Interestingly, it was at this point that the reasoning behind the claim became evident. Some of the Mahton wanted join an army regiment and this would only be possible if they had Rajput status. The Mahton, a rural agricultural group, were fully aware that the change of status would allow their members to obtain direct benefits. In and of itself, this definitely shows that the actions of the British in classifying and enumerating castes within the census had heightened indigenous awareness of the caste system and had added an economic aspect that the Indian people were willing and anxious to exploit.

With this in mind, it is interesting to note that in doing the censuses, Indians were used as both census takers and as advisors regarding the caste system of hierarchy. Since it is very likely that individual census takers filled out most of the data themselves, without consulting each individual in the area, the possibilities for self serving activity was immeasurable. Moreover, those Indians who were used as advisors certainly had more than ample opportunity to act in a manner that suited their own or their group's agenda since precedent was based on interpretations of the writings of the various Hindu holy texts. To even a marginally cynical mind this would suggest immense possibilities for graft and corruption. This, in turn, suggests the possibility that the

British were manipulated, at least to some degree, by their mainly Brahman informants.

Contrary to what the British appear to have believed, it seems doubtful that the Brahmans were dominant within the material world in pre colonial Indian society. A cursory examination of any of the ruling families quickly shows a dearth family of the Brahmin caste. Rather, one finds that the majority, though by no means all, of rulers were Kshytria and occasionally Vashnia. This suggests that although the Brahmin caste had power in spiritual matters, their power and control within the material world was limited to the amount of influence that they could gain with individual rulers. No doubt there were instances when this was quite considerable but there is also little doubt that there were times when Brahman influence was very weak and insignificant.

With this in mind, it is not difficult to imagine a situation where, Brahmans, seeing the ascendancy of British power, allied themselves to this perceived new ruling class and attempted to gain influence through it. By establishing themselves as authorities on the caste system they could then tell the British what they believed the British wanted to hear and also what would most enhance their own position. The British would then take this information, received through the filter of the Brahmans, and interpret it based on their own experience and their own cultural concepts. Thus, information was filtered at least twice before publication.

Therefore, it seems certain that the information that was finally published was filled with conceptions that would seem to be downright deceitful to those about whom the information was written. The flood of petitions protesting caste rankings following the 1901 census would appear to bear witness to this. To fully understand how the British arrived at their understanding of Indian society it will now be necessary to look at where British society was during the 19th century in both its concepts of self and of other. At the beginning of the 19th century, society in Britain was still attempting to come to terms with the social structure that had developed within the British Isles. Symptomatic of this phenomenon was the variation in terminology with reference to levels of societal existence that was extant at this time.

Phrases such as "gentlemen of wealth and property" and "the lower ranks from labour to thinking" were used to describe levels within society. While this is not meant to suggest that the British did not recognize that there were stratifications within there society, it seems to indicate that there was an absence of the modern notion of class and class structure. Instead, there appears to have been a linguistic shift occurring in which the various levels of society were being described in a variety of ways. Even within the two short phrases quoted above, there is description of three different attributes; social standing, economics and intelligence. This may be seen as a reflection of the mobility that was being experienced within Georgian society itself as non aristocratic, non landed groups moved up in the social order through the increase in industrialization. The use of the word "rank" itself indicates that the language had not entirely rid itself of feudal notions of high and low birth. It is also interesting to note that the connection between social status and mental ability had been made at this point in time.

This tends to point toward the determinism that would later be seen in the works of phrenologists such as Spurzheim in which the inheritance of a given skull shapes determined the entire character and ability of both individuals and nations. In turn, this deterministic attitude meshed well with later statistical ideas that human behaviour was caused and controlled by unvarying social laws and that free will was of little or no consequence in the grand scheme of human progress.Therefore, it can be seen that as the British became increasingly entrenched in India, three distinct but inter-related intellectual movements converged to provide the basis for British extrapolations and interpretations of Indian society. In this way, the British construction of Indian society was as much a reflection of their own attempts to understand their own society as it was an attempt to reach an understanding about another society. The main key in the evolution of all of this was the use of statistics.

Statistics was initially used as a tool to understanding the present state of European society so that power structures could make optimum use of resources during times of crisis and, in the case of Britain, as an attempt to avoid the societal unrest that dominated Europe during the first half of the 19th century. "Statistics, by their very name, are defined to be the observations necessary to the social and moral sciences, to the sciences of the statist, to whom the statesman and the legislator must resort for the principles on which to legislate and govern." Thus, at the turn of the century, statistics were used to accommodate manpower demands for the armies to fight the continental war against Napoleon and later during the 1830s, as a part of an attempt to control the population and avoid the turmoil that had engulfed the European mainland. Initially, statisticians confined their activities to the collection of raw data that was then used by others to form or confirm social theories. However, there was a desire on the part of statists to go further and to ground there new science on the same sort of constant that the universal law of gravity had provided for astronomy. This inspired the French statistician Quetelet to formulate a model of probability that he believed would give social scientists that same grounding.

Henry Thomas Buckle took this idea one step further. He believed that it was possible to gain access to the rules that operate the human mind through the use of statistics. Moreover, it was Buckle's belief that all human behaviour was caused by unvarying social laws and that moral causes were inherent to the nation, not to individuals. Buckles concept of mankind was shaped by the belief that there was no place for chance or supernatural intervention in accounting for the history and progress of mankind. All of history was the result of the universality of law. Within this viewpoint, Buckle saw corporate entities such as the church or political institutions, as interfering with the function of universal law and causing disfunction within society.

This was because they attempted to direct society for their own ends rather than allowing the laws of human activity to play themselves out naturally. Buckle pointed to the fact that no matter what any corporate entities did within society the suicide rate remained constant. He also pointed out that when Charles III of Spain attempted to emancipate his people from the oppressions of the Spanish clergy, the people turned on him because they were not enlightened enough to appreciate what he was trying to do. All of this led Buckle to the belief that:

In one sense this way of thinking totally disempowered all of mankind. If history was controlled by universal laws, as indicated the regularities of statistics, then the actions of individuals or corporate entities were of little consequence. Moreover, according to Quetlet and Buckle, the fact that social scientists could not give a detailed prediction of individual behaviour was of no consequence since the laws of probability would even out all individual actions over the long term. This challenged the entire concept of human free will however, and by the late 19th century the notion of randomness was introduced in order to bring free will back into the equations.

In considering the theories that were promoted by both Quetlet and Buckle, it must be remembered that they were not accepted without challenge and were, in fact, subjects of controversy throughout the 19th century. However, notwithstanding this caveat, these theories did have an effect on the way that the British viewed mankind as a whole. The social sciences were the only avenue available to the administration that offered any options for social control other than brute force. Since force was always expensive, it seems reasonable that administrators would attempt to control society without its use to the largest degree possible. Notions that the behaviour of large groups of people could be predicted through the use of statistics would have been particularly attractive to the British in India where they were faced with the task of ruling millions.

Moreover, these millions were very foreign in their ways of conceiving the world and for this reason posed a far greater problem of control than would an equal number of Europeans. Some kind of an overarching understanding of their newly acquired subjects was necessary. The most obvious, widespread feature that was available to the British was the institution of caste. However, this institution in and of itself, was outside of British experience. Therefore it was necessary, if this key was to be used, that an understanding of caste be attained. The tools at hand were the social sciences and the apparent key to the social sciences was statistics.

Among the social sciences that were popular in the 19th century were phrenology, physical anthropology and later, sociology and eugenics. Each of these areas of study had effects on each other and each of them, to some degree, affected the development of colonial policy as it referred to the control and maintenance of populations. However, due to the relatively late arrival of both eugenics and sociology, the present paper will concentrate on the effects of phrenology and anthropology. In the same way that astrology is related to astronomy, phrenology is related to anthropology. Both dealt with skull shapes and physiognomy and many of the same people who worked in anthropology also worked in phrenology from the beginning of the 19th century to the 1840s.

By the end of the 1840s phrenology had waned because of its failure to find a second generation of devotees but many of the collections that phrenologists had assembled were subsequently used by anthropologists. However, at the height of its popularity, phrenology had sixteen societies in

Scotland, six in England and two in Ireland. Throughout Europe there were more than thirty societies, about half of which met regularly, had good attendance and were financially solvent. The presence of sixteen societies in Scotland is particularly striking since this was a major center of intellectual thought during the period. This would give credence to the notion that there was a good deal of attention paid to phrenology in intellectual circles though it is granted that this attention was not always favourable. Further, it seems notable that the British Isles had a relatively large number of societies in comparison with other areas of Europe.

Phrenology attempted to define the potential of both individuals and nations based on the shape of skulls. It was contended that the outer shape of the human skull was a reflection of the configuration of the mind that it housed and that various parts of the mind affected the abilities and temperament of the individual. Moreover, it was believed that national and racial characteristics could be discerned from the study of a large number of skulls from any given race or nationality. Each area of the brain was believed to control a specific part of the personality or intellectual ability and the development of the skull in the corresponding areas was thought to indicate the development of the underlying brain. Thus, by simply examining the exterior of the head it was believed that the character and potential of the individual could be ascertained. This appears to have been a real concern of phrenologists as shown by the following except from the Phrenological Journal in 1825:

In examining this theory in relation to colonialism in India, it must be remembered that castes were often considered to be divisions based on race. Therefore, it is quite possible that these theories had an affect on the conceptual construct of the British in India with regard to their attitudes toward Indians of various castes. It is also interesting to note that Quetlet, one of the founders of statistics, while cautiously sceptical about phrenology, wrote Sur lhomme et le developpemment de ses facultes in 1835 in which he described the "average man" physically and intellectually on the basis of cranial measurements. Since Quetlet was very influential in the development of statistical thinking, the possibility that he spread these theories to statisticians is very strong.

As with all intellectual movements however, one must question how wide spread the ideas of phrenology became in the popular sense. Perhaps the best way to gauge this is to examine the amount of printed material that was available on the subject and whether there was any mention of the field in the press. On both accounts, the evidence indicates that there was a wide dissemination of phreno-logical information. There were journals in Britain, the United States and Germany and by 1836 there were 64000 volumes of writings devoted to phrenology. Further, there appears to have been regular mention of phrenology in the popular press. On this basis it should be safe to assume that phrenological theories were well spread outside of intellectual circles.

When phrenology faded in the late 1840s anthropology took up many of the underlying beliefs that phrenology had promoted. This can be seen by the continued belief that races could be classified and their societal development explained on the basis of the shape of their skulls. While this was primarily seen in the study of Negroid skulls, the theories were equally applicable to all non European groups. In the 1860s James Hunt, a noted anthropologist of the day, stated:

This statement shows that there was a belief in not only the superiority of the white races but that the inferiority of other races was believed to be caused by innate physiological attributes that could be observed and quantified. Belief in the innate inferiority of others and in the notion that this inferiority had physical, measurable manifestations was an old European tradition as shown by the following quote from le Comte de Buffon in 1749 as stated in L'histoire naturelle de l'homme in describing Laplanders:

This long standing deterministic fatalism was, therefore,

the same as that expressed by both phrenologists and statisticians. This attitude was legislatively expressed in India by the passing of the Criminal Tribes Act of 1871, the same year as the first full Indian census was being planned. In explanation of the Act it was stated that:

This statement clearly destined large groups of people to be condemned as criminals by birth. Further, it articulates the notion that caste is an ahistorical system that contributes to what the British perceived as a static Indian society. Criminals were not criminals for socio-economic reasons. They were criminals because of the caste into which they had been born. In observing this it should be recalled that caste was also believed to have been responsible for the maintenance of racial types in India. Therefore, there is an intimate connection between caste and race based on which castes intermarried and which did not. Herbert Risley, Commissioner for the 1901 census states that:

It therefore becomes plain that the British and in this case an influential official, saw caste as being motivated by the principle of race purity. From this point it is a very short intellectual leap for the British to equate cast and race. That is, caste as a system created a system that preserved race purity and therefore castes represent that preserved purity. This notion is further confirmed by Hodson in 1937 when he states that class, racial and linguistic groups may be visually differentiated.Moreover, Hodson goes on to define caste as: "mutually exclusive aggregates, the members of which are forbidden by an inexorable social law to marry outside the group to which they themselves belong."

On the basis of this definition and measurements of heads, noses and heights obtained from: "51 racial groups from all parts of India" Hodson goes on to claim that the caste system has created "pure lines". In fact this is simply an echo of what Risley had said in had said in 1915. In 22 years, very little had changed in the way that the British envisioned both the function and the form of caste. For evidence that the British believed that race was the supreme determinate of human activity one need look no further than Disraeli who wrote in 1844 that: "All is race, there is no other truth" and in 1880 that: "Race is the key to history".

What seems, however, to have confused the British, was the fact that when they asked Indians to identify the caste, tribe or race for census purposes, they received a bewildering variety of responses. Often the respondents gave the name of a religious sect, a sub-caste, an exogamous sept or section a hypergamous group, titular designation, occupation or the name of the region he came from. Obviously Indian self identifying concepts were quite different from those concepts that the British expected. In response to this problem, those in charge of the census data took it upon themselves to: "begin a laborious and most difficult process of sorting, referencing, cross-referencing, and corresponding with local authorities, which ultimately results in the compilation of a table showing the distribution of the inhabitants of India by Caste, Tribe, Race, or Nationality."

Certainly this leaves a great deal of room for error. It also virtually ignores the fact that many Indians, when questioned, did not identify themselves in the way that the British expected. Rather than ask themselves why this was, the British appear to have assumed that either the respondents did not understand the question or that they were incapable of correctly answering the question. It never seems to have occurred to any one involved with the census that the British may have been asking the type of question that had a variety of correct answers depending upon the circumstances in which the question was asked.

It is interesting to note that when modern sociologists posed the same type of question to Indians in the 1960s, they too received a wide variety of responses. The simplest explanation for this is that on a day to day basis caste may not be the most important factor in the life of a Hindu. While it is granted that extremely low groups such as the untouchables who suffer under a constant burden of being ritually polluting were very conscious of their caste and that Brahmins were also very caste conscious, it is questionable whether the majority of the Indian people actually concerned themselves with caste on a daily basis.

This notion is given support by a handbill that was distributed by Arya Samaj in Lahore just prior to the 1931 census:

While it is granted that the group distributing this handbill had a definite political agenda, it should also be borne in mind that they believed that the distribution of this information would influence the manner in which the people answered. Therefore, consideration of answering "Nil" to caste must not have been beyond the realm of possibility for a large number of people. This would tend to indicate that attachment to and self identification by caste was not crucial to the self concept of at least a portion of the population. Moreover, it clearly indicates that this group has identified caste as a means of British control over the Indian people.

This may also be coupled with the notion that the British, having constructed their own image of the caste system and forced the people to adhere to that construct through continual identification and extrapolation within the censuses, were now more the owners of the caste system than were the people of India. Moreover, by dismissing the idea of caste as non essential to Indian self identification, Arya Samaj's action may be seen as indicating that they believed that caste was essential to prolonging British abilities to rule India. Thus, the very institution of caste was now being seen as a tool of British rule rather than as an indigenous system of social organization.

The answers recommended for the questions of sect and races were also clearly designed to frustrate British attempts to continue to rule through their monopoly on knowledge. Arya Samajist would not have fit into British schemes of sect and caste and Aryan was not a specific enough term for race to satisfy their classification systems. This entire action could easily be interpreted as an attempt by Arya Samaj to win back the knowledge that they believed the British were using to maintain their hold over India. Indeed, there is ample evidence to show that the British viewed themselves as the source of knowledge for the Indian people and regarded the Indians in the same way as a scientist regards the subjects he studies.

Risely wrote that: "the caste system itself, with its singularly perfect communal organization, is a machinery admirably fitted for the diffusion of new ideas; that castes may in course of time group themselves into classes representing the different strata of society; and that India may thus attain, by the agency of these indigenous corporations, the results that have been arrived at elsewhere through the fusion of individual types." In making this statement Risley exposes the British agenda of creating a society that conformed to British ideals through the use of a British interpreted caste system. It is also interesting to note that Risley juxtaposes "individual types" with castes in such a way that it seems that he believed that there was a dearth of individuality within Indian society which could be compensated for through the substitution of caste structures.

To Risley caste was not only the essence of Indian society, it was the essence of Indians. The entire meaning of the individual was embodied in caste. Risley's paternalistic disdain for the Indian people was further illustrated by his belief that: "the factors of nationality in India are two - the common usage of the English language for certain purposes and the common employment of Indians in English administration." India's salvation, its only hope of becoming a nation, was through the language and tutelage of the British, according to Risley's brand of liberal paternalism.

In examining the writings of Edward Dalton, Commissioner of Chutia Nagpur, the nomenclature alone is enough to indicate that the Indian people were regarded as less than human in at least some regard. People are referred to as "specimens" and the only fear expressed over the possibility of bringing various "specimen" together for a display was that: "... if specimens of the more independent tribes fell sick and died in Calcutta or on the journey, it might lead to inconvenient political complications." It is also in these writings that one sees the type of classification of ability that the British in India have become so notoriously famous for. In considering Rajputs Dalton states that:

Needless to say, this description is far from flattering. However, what is more important is the contention that one can determine the character of people based on their physical appearance. This extended, as well, to the type of work that individuals were seen as being fit for under British rule. Thus Kayasths were seen as being natural clerks and scribes and Rajputs were natural for the military and as a local upper class. However, census data sometimes went beyond attributing occupational abilities to physical build and insisted on the maintenance of "traditional" occupations being listed with the caste groupings in the census.

Such was the case during the census of 1891. In an effort to arrange various castes in order of precedence: "... functional grouping is based less on the occupation that prevails in each case in the present day than on that which is traditional with it, or which gave rise to its differentiation from the rest of the community." This action virtually removed Indians from the progress of history and condemned them to an unchanging position and place in time. In one sense, it is rather ironic that the British, who continually accused the Indian people of having a static society, should then impose a construct that denied progress. In ways such as this, it is possible to see how the census began to increase the rigidity of the caste system, particulary when one considers the fact that one of the primary ways that a caste could traditionally raise its status was to change its occupation.

Once again, the British appear to be creating the situation where their interpretation of Indian society is validated through their own actions. In a similar way, Beverley's analysis of the 1872 census sought to prove continuity with the past by attempting to identify purity and impurity of race in ways that would fit with British theories of Indian history and British notions of group abilities and temperaments. As stated above, the British perceived India as being filled with a wide variety of races which had been preserved to greater and lesser degrees by the institution of caste. Therefore, it was quite logical within this construct for Beverley to state that: "A Bengali may, on the one hand, be of the purest Aryan type, or, on the other, he may scarcely differ in ethnic characteristics from the lowest aboriginal."

However, what is not logical is the immediately following statement that: "Speaking generally, they are not a robust or muscular race, yet are capable of greater fatigue and endurance than their purely vegetable diet and moist habitat would lead one to suppose. In active pursuits they are timid and indolent, but in intellect keen and subtle."Given the prevailing attitude of the linkages between caste and race and race and ability, this statement seems to be at odds with the internal logic of the argument. In this case Beverley has moved away from caste and toward region as the defining factor of the group. He clearly states that: "Bengal proper is inhabited by a heterogeneous race of mixed Aryan and aboriginal extraction, in every possible stage of development." If this is indeed so, how can any conclusions, even "generally speaking", be made about Bengalis as a whole? However, in typical British fashion, Beverley forged ahead with his analysis of the Bengalis and in spite of all obstacles made them fit into the popular stereotype that had been attributed to them. In examining "Hinduised aborigines", Hindus and Hinduism as a whole, Beverley encounters similar problem of internal logic.

After describing the "non-Aryan tribes" of Bengal and describing their interaction with the invading Aryan Hindus, Beverley then admits:

In spite of this admission of ignorance, Beverley goes on to describe the actions and interaction of the Aryans and the tribes that they encountered, and how these interactions have resulted in the variety of levels of civilization that were extant in Bengal. Moreover, he attributes the differences between the Hinduism of the Vedas and that which is presently before him in Bengal as the result of "contamination from aboriginal sources". It never seems to occur to him that changes in Hinduism could have come from within rather than from without. Thus, Beverley places Hinduism outside of history in a very similar way as the analysis of the 1891 census would place the Indian people outside of history. In essence, India, its people and their religion are portrayed as unchanging except as they are affected by external forces. This justifies the British belief that their role in India is to raise the society to a higher level of civilization and that without their influence India would be doomed to stagnation. Any concept of internal innovation appears to be dismissed without a thought. Even the manner in which Beverley envisions the history of the Aryan invasions betrays his inability to envision change occurring in any other way than that experienced in British history.

In the seventh or eighth centuries of our own era, England, as I imagine, presented a very similar appearance, from an ethnic point of view, to that which we find at the present day in Bengal. The Anglo-Saxon invaders spread themselves over the land, and gave their language, their manners and customs, to the aboriginal Welsh whom they had conquered. Some of these Welsh took refuge in the mountains and fastnesses of Strath-Clyde, Wales and Cornwall, where they still preserved their independence and their native speech. But the vast majorities were doubtless absorbed by the victorious Saxons into the English nation. Particular tribes lost their individuality, their differences being merged in one common stream, wide enough and deep enough to embrace all. So in Bengal the aboriginal tribes which remained in the plains are fast losing all traces of their origin, being gradually absorbed in the nationality, if I may use the term, of their Aryan conquerors. Only in the hills and in those primeval forests which proved inaccessible to Hindu and Mahommedan invader alike, do we now find the remnants of those tribes which formerly peopled the whole face of the country. That the great bulk of them have been swallowed up and merged into the nationality of their conquerors, sufficient traces remain to leave no room for doubt.

Within this statement is hidden a need for India's history to be like that of England. Further, there is a need to equate the original inhabitants with the same qualities as were believed to be in the conquered groups within England. By doing this, Beverley legitimates Britain's present position within Britain in the same way as the British justified their dominance over various ethnic groups within the British Isles. This allows the vision of the great march of progress, led naturally enough by the British.

Dalton also uses cherished British imagery to describe the Rajput landlords of Western Bengal. In this case it is the myth of the country gentry and the happy peasantry that intrudes on the history of India. The long established landowning Rajputs are described as:

This passage virtually exudes the long cherished belief of jolly old England and all the mythology that the landed gentry surrounded them with. One can almost see the emergence of the "sturdy yeomanry". However, it is doubtful whether Dalton ever actually consulted any of these "contented" peasants to enquire as to their position on all of this, any more than anyone ever asked the English peasantry how they felt about their overlords. But this myth was deeply held by the British gentry and they then projected it onto the Indian people during their attempt to understand Indian society. The conceptual framework within which Indian society was being understood was becoming British rather than Indian. This allowed the British to expropriate the basic concepts of Indian society and Anglicize it in such a way that only they would have the ability to interpret it within the new construct. A major factor in allowing this expropriation was the census system.

The censuses forced the Indian social system into a written schematic in a way that had never been experienced in the past. While the Mughals had issued written decrees on the status of individual castes, there had never been a formal systematic attempt to organize and schedule all of the castes in an official document until the advent of the British censuses. The data was compiled on the basis of British understanding of India. This understanding was deeply affected by British concepts of their own past, and by British notions of race and the importance of race in relation to the human condition.

Further, the intellectual framework, such as that provided by anthropology and phrenology, that was used to help create the ideas surrounding the concept of race, was foreign to the intellectual traditions of India. These concepts endured well into the 20th century and affected the analysis of the censuses throughout this period. Risley, for example, used anthropometric measurements, which were directly descended from anthropological and phrenological methodology, in his ordering of castes following the census of 1901.

These same notions led to a classification of intelligence and abilities based on physical attributes, and this in turn led to employment opportunities being limited to certain caste groupings that displayed the appropriate attributes. Indians attempted to incorporate themselves into this evolving system by organizing caste sabhas with the purpose of attaining improved status within the system. This ran contrary to traditional views of the purpose of the caste system and imposed an economic basis. With this, the relevance and importance of the spiritual, non material rational for caste was degraded and caste took on a far more material meaning. In this way, caste began to intrude more pervasively into daily life and status became even more coveted and rigid. In a sense, caste became politicized as decisions regarding rank increasingly fell into the political rather than the spiritual sphere of influence. With this politicization, caste moved closer to class in connotation. The actions of the Indian people that contributed to this process were not so an much acquiescence to the British construction as they were pragmatic reactions to the necessities of material life. In expropriating the knowledge base of Indian society, the British had forced Indian society and the caste system to execute adjustments in order to prosper within the rubric of the British regime.

In and of themselves, the physical taking of the censuses did not greatly affect Indian society. The census takers received slighter higher status and prestige within their own communities because of their employment and new found position of authority, but most, if not all of these individuals would have had high status before the censuses in any case. However, the analysis of Indian society that the censuses made possible did have a very strong affect. Without the basic information contained within the censuses the British would not have been able to justify their concepts of Indian society.

This would have handicapped their ability to rationalize their presence within India once simple economic reasoning had ceased to suffice. For the Indian people, the censuses acted as a catalyst for an increased consciousness of caste as caste status became an increasingly significant factor in attaining material status. While the original intent may have been to gather data to assist governments in dealing with natural disaster and famine relief, the effect of the analysis of that data went far beyond these goals. Ultimately, the census provided data that allowed the British to have a much deeper effect on Indian society than might otherwise have been possible.

Rel…
the N…

When …
consisted of …
assets. Even …
monks, it is …
but it is a …
even outside …
do the mo…
at once th…
conversion …
parlance, it …
better Hin…
Christian …
to the …
or the other …
different …
essence …
but the …
any system …
is much …

In all …
and under…
much at …

5

Religious Change through the Ramakrishna Movement

When it started in 1897, the Ramakrishna Order consisted of a dozen monks or so and had practically no assets. Even now, with its 160 centres and barely a thousand monks, it is small compared with the Christian organizations, but it is a name that commands respect all over India and even outside. What is the secret behind this? What exactly do the monks do in India and abroad? It must be made clear at once that the Ramakrishna Mission does not believe in conversion in the sense of the word as understood in common parlance. If anything, these monks try to make 'a Hindu a better Hindu, a Moslem a better Moslem, a Christian a better Christian' and so on. In other words, they ask people to go to the root of religion, which is trying to reach God somehow or the other and not merely talking of Him. They quote different prophets and different scriptures to show how in essence they preach the same thing. Their language differs, but their purpose is the same. They do not want to replace any system but want to draw attention to the fact that there is much in common between one system and another.

In all matters of religion, their approach is one of respect and understanding. Because of this approach, they feel as much at home among non-Hindus as among Hindus.

Because of this approach, non-Hindus also feel at home in their company; as a matter of fact they like these monks and often invite them to their services. Today ecumenism has become an attractive force in the Christian world. It must not be forgotten that long before Pope John gave official blessings to this, Sri Ramakrishna had preached and practiced it. His ecumenism was much broader though, for it embraced not some denominations but all denominations of religions.

Today, the Ramakrishna movement has become a great power for peace and happiness in this country as well as outside. In India where different sects and communities live, the idea of tolerance and brotherly feelings towards each other has great relevance. Another factor which contributes much to its popularity is the rational approach it brings to bear upon every vital problem of life. People who are influenced by Sri Ramakrishna believe religion to be a kind of science open to study and investigation. They do not agree that religious truths are to be accepted on trust; they rather declare that nothing need be accepted as final unless it has been tested and found true. Experience, personal and immediate, is the only acceptable proof of religion.

The fact that the Movement lays great stress on selfless service as a means of God-realization also attracts many people. The service it gives is open to all, irrespective of caste or creed or language. Not only the Ramakrishna Mission but hundreds of institutions which have sprung up all over the country today give this kind of service. Since the time of the Buddha, this is almost without parallel in India. What is significant is that most of them bear the name of Ramakrishna and draw inspiration from him.

As time passes, the Ramakrishna Movement is growing from strength to strength. People all over the country want the Mission to open more branch centres - schools, colleges, hospitals, orphanages, etc. for they know that the quality of services they will get from the Mission will be better than what they may get elsewhere. Their requests are almost always accompanied by offers of money, land, and buildings but the Mission proceeds cautiously and avoids proliferation unless there is a compelling reason in its favour. Apart from the fact that it suffers from shortage of manpower, it prefers that people themselves come forward to start such institutions, imbued with the spirit of selfless service. Happily, the present trend clearly shows that this spirit is fast spreading.

As the movement spreads, the attitude of the common people towards religion is also changing. Previously, religion was equated with rituals, but now people realize that religion is essentially a science of 'being and becoming something', something that concerns man's inner nature. The habit of prayer is good but if this is not accompanied by a corresponding improvement in one's nature, it is not worth much. Another change that is noticeable today is respect for religions other than one's own. There was once much arrogance in the attitude of people towards the religions of others, but there is now humility and a spirit of enquiry if not also reverence.

Ruskin once said "An idea is more powerful than an army". There must be much truth in this, else it is difficult to explain the influence Sri Ramakrishna and the Order of monks bearing his name have had over people all over the world. The strength of Ramakrishna Movement is not in money, men or organization, but the ideas it tries to present. These ideas are fast spreading, and wherever they are spreading, they are producing a great impact. Silently but inevitably, they are changing the minds of the people who come under their influence. They act like a catalytic agent transforming their personalities.

Ramakrishna Mission

The Mission is a registered Society laying emphasis on rendering welfare services undertaken with a spiritual outlook. The service activities are rendered looking upon all as veritable manifestation of the Divine. The Motto of the organisation is Atmano Mokshartham Jagad-hitaya Cha. Translated from Sanskrit it means For one's own salvation and for the good of the world. Swami Vivekananda met with thundering applause for his speech at the Parliament of Religions at Chicago (USA) in 1893 that reverberated throughout the world. When he returned, his countrymen recognized him as their undisputed cultural leader.

His message: "Nations like individuals must help themselves. Every nation, every man and every women, must work out his or her own salvation," gave concrete shape for the foundation of a new organization `Ramakrishna Mission` on May 5, 1897 a service wing of the monastery. Though he passed away at an early age of 39, his institutions still flourish.

He was chief disciple of Ramkrishna Parmahamsa .The Mission follows the inspiration of Ramakrishna Paramahamsa (1834-86), whose spiritual experience included Bhakti, Tantra, and Advaita Vedanta, as well as visionary realizations in Hinduism, Islam, and Christianity, and from these experiences he claimed that all religions lead to the same divine realization. Swami Vivekananda spread Ramakrishna's gospel to the world, said "Do not care for doctrines, do not care for dogmas...they count for little compared with the essence of existence in each man which is spirituality, and the more that this is developed in a man, the more powerful he is for good."

Although Ramakrishna is believed to have said that there are as many paths to salvation as there are points of view, some of his followers today advocate a quite definite path. Ramakrishna's experience was that the truth of all religions is a manifestation of the Shakti, or Divine Mother, and that this divine power is at work with everyone, including the poor, and thus inspiring the Mission's social service.

Ramakrishna, the God-man of modern India, was born as Gadadhar Chattopadhyaya in the Bengal village of Kamarpukur in 1836. His father was a dedicated Brahmin who the previous year on a pilgrimage to a shrine at a footprint of Vishnu at Gaya had a vision in which Vishnu promised to be born as his son. As a small boy Gadadhar loved to listen to recitals of Hindu myths and epics, afterwards telling them from memory to the villagers. He had his first religious ecstasy at the age of six. Gadadhar never went to school and stayed illiterate all his life. When he was sixteen he went to Calcutta to help his brother, a local teacher. Gadadhar after skillfully mending a Krishna image from one of the other shrines was put in charge after the priest who broke the image was dismissed in a 'Kali temple'. The widow's son-in-law suggested the young priest should be called Ramakrishna.

After Ramkumar, his brother, then priest of the temple died in 1856, Ramakrishna became priest of the Kali temple. He developed a special attachment to the devotion of this awesome goddess, whom he spoke of as "Mother." His devotion to her and continued meditation and religious ecstasies to gain a vision of the goddess's cosmic form attracted disciples and followers. His cousin looked after the temple while Ramakrishna was in frequent trances, which worried his family and they arranged for his marriage. Because of the poverty of the family it was difficult to find a bride; Ramakrishna himself indicated where she would be found. She was only five years when they got married. Ramakrishna saw the goddess in his wife and named her Sarada Devi.

For the rest of his life Ramakrishna oscillated between the Absolute and the Relative on the threshold of Absolute Consciousness. He explored other religions and the paths of different Hindu sects. He realized his identity with Christ as he had done with Kali. From about 1880 a group of young men from high-caste families in Calcutta, including Narendranath Datta, gathered around him and just before his death Ramakrishna initiated them as monks. Once Narendranath touched Ramakrishna in samadhi and immediately saw God himself. Two months after the death of Ramakrishna in 1886 his chosen disciple Narendranath established the Math (monastery) near Calcutta.

On Vaishakhi Purnima, the day of the birth, enlightenment, and passing away of the Buddha, Vows of celibacy and non-possession as well as formal initiation into sannnyas, total renunciation, used to take place. This required names to be changed and Narendranath became Vivekananda. After wandering for some years as a mendicant, Vivekananda represented Hinduism at the World's Parliament of Religions at Chicago. This gave Vivekananda an insight into the immense value of Indian thought to the West, and he saw clearly the vision of his life and he launched the Ramakrishna Mission in 1897 in India. This was part of the Ramakrishna Movement, which played an important part in the renaissance of Hinduism and inspired the early Indian nationalist movement.

The Monastry moved to Alambazar in 1891 and to Belur in 1898, a suburban village near Calcutta. From January 1899 this became the home and headquarters of the Ramakrishna Mission. In 1954 the Ramakrishna Sarada Math was founded as a division of the Ramakrishna Mission. Inspired by Sarada Devi, wife of Ramakrishna, this was for the training of an order of women mission workers.

Symbol

Monks of the Ramakrishna Order profess Advaita, Vedanta and Shankara, worshipping the Supreme through symbols or icons for the religiously small-minded. But there is a place for ritual in Advaita and the Ramakrishna monks has an elaborate ritual for daily aarti services. The icon becomes a photograph or bust of Ramakrishna, as with the marble statue of him in the Belur temple sitting in lotus posture on a lotus. The simplicity of the temple is similar to the interior of Jain temples.

Incense is used together with the handbell, flowers, oil lamps, and the shell symbolizing water and infinity, and some other symbols. Symbols are reinterpreted in an Advaitic context, so that the five basic elements - a flower for earth, a shell for water, an oil lamp for fire, a fly-whisk for air, and a folded napkin cupped in the hand for space - represent not an offering to a god but the fundamental unity of the person - the microcosm - and the macrocosm of being.

Management

The Ramakrishna Mission acquired a legal status when it was registered in 1909 under Act XXI of 1860. Its management is vested in a Governing Body. Though the Mission with its branches is a distinct legal entity it is closely related to the Ramakrishna Math. The Trustees of the Math are simultaneously the members of the Governing Body. The administrative work of the Mission is mostly in the hands of the monks of Math. The Mission has its own separate funds, for which it keeps detailed accounts, audited annually by chartered accountants. The Math and the Mission both have their Headquarters at Belur Math.

Controversies

To a large extent, the Ramakrishna Mission has avoided controversies through its policy of non-involvement in politics. However, in a move that was highly controversial within its own ranks, the Ramakrishna Mission went to the courts in the 1980s in order to have the organization and movement declared as a non-Hindu minority religion. According to the leadership, the mission did this purely as a matter of political necessity: there was a danger that the local government would take control of its charitable schools unless it could invoke the extra protection the Indian constitution accords to minority religions.

The Supreme Court of India ruled against the Mission, citing many pages of evidence that it had all the characteristics of a Hindu organization. The wisdom of the attempt by the Mission's leadership to characterize the Mission as non-Hindu was widely questioned within the membership of the organization itself, and the leadership today embraces the Mission's status as both a Hindu organization and as an organization that emphasizes the harmony of all faiths. Most members - and even monks - of the Ramakrishna mission consider themselves Hindus, and the Mission's founding figures, such as Swami Vivekananda never disavowed Hinduism.

This episode highlights the legal and constitutional discriminations in India against the Hindu majority, most urgently those in education and temple management. The constitutional bedrock of these discriminations is Article 30, which accords to the minorities the right to set up and administer their own schools and colleges, preserving their communal identity (through the course contents and by selectively recruiting teachers and students), all while receiving state subsidies. This same right is not guaranteed to the majority.

Sri Ramakrishna Paramahamsa, born Gadadhar Chattopadhyay, is a famous mystic of 19th-century India. His religious school of thought led to the formation of the Ramakrishna Mission by his chief disciple Swami Vivekananda—both were influential figures in the Bengali Renaissance and the Hindu renaissance during 19th and 20th century. He was considered an avatar or incarnation of God by many of his disciples, and is considered as such by many of his devotees today.

Ramakrishna was born in a poor Brahmin Vaishnava family in rural Bengal. He became a priest of the Dakshineswar Kali Temple, dedicated to goddess Kali, which had the influence of the main strands of Bengali bhakti tradition. His first spiritual teacher was an ascetic woman skilled in Tantra and Vaishnava bhakti. Later an Advaita Vedantin ascetic taught him non-dual meditation, and according to Ramakrishna, he experienced Nirvikalpa Samadhi under his guidance. Ramakrishna also experimented with other religions, notably Islam and Christianity, and said that they all lead to the same God.

Though conventionally uneducated, he attracted attention of the Bengali intelligentsia and middle class. The Ramakrishna movement was brought to the West by Swami Vivekananda. The Ramakrishna movement has been termed as one of the revitalization movements of India.

Birth and Childhood

The family shrine is on the left, birthplace temple on the right. Ramakrishna was born in 1836, in the village of Kamarpukur, in the Hooghly district of West Bengal, into a very poor but pious, orthodox Brahmin family. His parents were Khudiram Chattopâdhyây a, and Chandramani Devî. According to traditional accounts, Ramakrishna's parents experienced supernatural incidents, visions before his birth. His father Khudiram had a dream in Gaya in which Lord Gadadhara (a form of god Vishnu), said that he would be born as his son. Chandramani Devi is said to have had a vision of light entering her womb from Shiva's temple.

Ramakrishna was a popular figure in the village, with a natural gift for fine arts. Though he attended a village school with some regularity for 12 years, he later rejected the traditional schooling saying that he was not interested in "bread-winning education". Kamarpukur being a transit-point in well-established pilgrimage routes to Puri, brought him with contact to the renunciates and holy men. He became well-versed in the Puranas, the Ramayana, the Mahabharata, and the Bhagavata Purana, hearing them from wandering monks and the Kathaks—a class of men in ancient India who preached and sang the Purânas. He could read and write in Bengali.

Ramakrishna describes about his first spiritual ecstasy at the age of six, while walking along the paddy fields, a flock of white cranes flying against a backdrop of dark thunder-clouds caught his vision. He reportedly became so absorbed by this scenery that he lost outward consciousness and experienced indescribable joy in that state. Ramakrishna reportedly had experiences of similar nature a few other times in his childhood—while worshipping the goddess Vishalakshi, and portraying god Shiva in a drama during Shivaratri festival.

From his tenth or eleventh year on, the trances became common. Ramakrishna's father died in 1843, after which the responsibilities fell on his elder brother Ramkumar. This loss drew him closer to his mother, and he spent his time in household activities, daily worship of the household deities and became more involved in contemplative activities such as reading the sacred epics.When Ramakrishna was into his teens, the family's financial position worsened. Ramkumar started a Sanskrit school in Calcutta and also served as a priest. Ramakrishna moved to Calcutta in 1852 with Ramkumar to assist in the priestly work.

Priest at Dakshineswar Kali Temple

In 1855 Ramkumar was appointed as the priest of Dakshineswar Kali Temple, built by Rani Rashmoni—a rich woman of Calcutta who belonged to the kaivarta community. Ramakrishna, along with his nephew Hriday, became assistants to Ramkumar, with Ramakrishna given the task of decorating the deity. When Ramkumar passed away in 1856, Ramakrishna took his place as the priest of the Kali temple.The name Ramakrishna is said to have been given him by Mathur Babu, the son-in-law of Rani Rashmoni. After Ramkumar's death Ramakrishna became more contemplative. He began to look upon the image of the goddess Kali as his mother and the mother of the universe.

He became seized by a desire to have a darshana (vision) of Kali—a direct realization of her reality—and believed the stone image to be living and breathing and taking food out of his hand. At times he would weep bitterly and cry out loudly while worshipping, and would not be comforted, because he could not see his mother Kali as perfectly as he wished. People became divided in their opinions—some held Ramakrishna to be mad, and some took him to be a great lover of God.

One day, brought to the point of suicide by this longing, he had the experience of goddess Kali as the universal Mother,which he described as "... houses, doors, temples and everything else vanished altogether; as if there was nothing anywhere! And what I saw was an infinite shoreless sea of light; a sea that was consciousness. However, far and in whatever direction I looked, I saw shining waves, one after another, coming towards me."

Marriage

Rumors spread to Kamarpukur that Ramakrishna had become unstable as a result of his spiritual exercises at Dakshineswar. Ramakrishna's mother and his elder brother Rameswar decided to get Ramakrishna married, thinking that marriage would be a good steadying influence upon him—by forcing him to accept responsibility and to keep his attention on normal affairs rather than being obsessed with his spiritual practices and visions.

Far from objecting to the marriage, Ramakrishna mentioned that they could find the bride at the house of Ramchandra Mukherjee in Jayrambati, three miles to the north-west of Kamarpukur. The five-year-old bride, Saradamani Mukhopadhyaya was found and the marriage was duly solemnised in 1859. Ramakrishna was 23 at this point, but the age difference was typical for 19th century rural Bengal. After the marriage, Sarada stayed at Jayrambati and joined Ramakrishna in Dakshineswar at the age of 18.

Religious Practices and Teachers

After his marriage Ramakrishna returned to Calcutta and resumed the charges of the temple again, but instead of toning down, his spiritual fervour and devotion only increased. To cultivate humility and eliminatc the distinction between his own high Brahmin caste and pariahs belonging of low caste he would clean their quarters with his own hands and long hair.

He would take gold and silver coins, and mixing them with rubbish, repeat "money is rubbish, money is rubbish". He later said that "I lost all perception of difference between the two in my mind, and threw them both into the Ganges. No wonder people took me for mad." According to Swami Vivekananda, his hatred for money became so instinctive that his body would shrink back convulsively if were touched with a coin, even when asleep.

Bhairavi Brahmani and Tantra

In 1861, Bhairavi Brahmani, an orange robed, middle-aged female ascetic appeared at Dakshineshwar. She carried with her the Raghuvir Shila, a stone icon representing Ram and all Vaishnava deities. She was throughly conversant with the texts of Gaudiya Vaishnavism and practiced Tantra.According to the Bhairavi, Ramakrishna was experiencing phenomena that accompany mahabhava—the supreme attitude of loving devotion towards the divine and quoting from the bhakti shastras, she said that other religious figures like Radha and Chaitanya had similar experiences.

The Bhairavi initiated Ramakrishna into Tantra. Tantrism focuses on the worhip of shakti and the object of Tantric training is to transcend the barriers between the holy and unholy as a means of achieving liberation and to see all aspects of the natural world as manifestations of the divine shakti.Under her guidance, he went through a full course of sixty four major tantric sadhanas which were completed in 1863. He began with mantra rituals such as japa and purascarana and many other rituals designed to purify the mind and establish self-control. He later proceeded towards tantric sadhanas, which generally include a set of heterodox practices called vamachara (left-hand path), which utilize as a means of liberation, activities like eating of parched grain, fish and meat along with drinking of wine and sexual intercourse.

According to Ramakrishna and his biographers, Ramakrishna did not directly participate in the last two of those activities, all that he needed was a suggestion of them to produce the desired result. Ramakrishna acknowledged the left-hand tantric path, though it had "undesirable features", as one of the "valid roads to God-realization", he consistently cautioned his devotees and disciples against associating with it. Ramakrishna took the attitude of a son towards the Bhairavi.

The Bhairavi on the other hand looked upon Ramakrishna as an avatara, or incarnation of the divine, and was the first person to openly declare that Ramakrishna was an avatara.The Bhairavi also taught Ramakrishna the kumari-puja, a form of ritual in which the Virgin Goddess is worshiped symbolically in the form of a young girl. Under the tutelage of the Bhairavi, Ramakrishna also became an adept at Kundalini Yoga. The Bhairavi, with the yogic techniques and the tantra played an important part in the initial spiritual development of Ramakrishna.

Vaishnava Bhakti

The Vaishnava Bhakti traditions speak of five different affective essences, referred to as bhâvas—different attitudes that a devotee can take up to express his love for the God. They are: úânta, the serene attitude; dâsya, the attitude of a servant; sakhya, the attitude of a friend; vâtsalya, the attitude of a mother toward her child; and madhura, the attitude of a woman towards her lover.

At some point in the period between his vision of Kali and his marriage, Ramakrishna practiced dâsya bhâva. He started worshiping Rama in the attitude of Hanuman, the monkey-god, who is considered to be the ideal devotee and servant of Rama. According to Ramakrishna, towards the end of this sạdhana, he had a vision of Sita, the consort of Rama, merging into his body. In 1864, Ramakrishna practiced vâtsalya bhâva under a Vaishnava guru Jatadhari. During this period, he worshipped a metal image of Ramlâlâ (Rama as a child) in the attitude of a mother. According to Ramakrishna, he could feel the presence of child Rama as a living God in the metal image.

Ramakrishna later engaged in the practice of madhura bhâva— the attitude of Gopis and Radha towards Krishna. During the practise of this bhava, Ramakrishna dressed himself in women's attire for several days and regarded himself as one of the Gopis of Vrindavan. According to the Ramakrishna, madhura bhava is practised to root out the idea of sex, which is seen as an impediment in spiritual life.According to Ramakrishna, towards the end of this sadhana, he attained savikalpa samadhi—vision and union with Krishna.

Ramakrishna visited Nadia, the home of Chaitanya and Nityananda, the 15th-century founders of Bengali Gaudiya Vaishnava bhakti. According to Ramakrishna, he had an intense vision of two young boys merging into his body.Earlier, after his vision of Kali, he is said to have cultivated the Santa bhava—the passive "peaceful" attitude — towards Kali.

Totapuri and Vedanta

The mud hut has been replaced by a brick one. In 1865, Ramakrishna was initiated into sanyassa by Tota Puri, an itinerant monk who trained Ramakrishna in Advaita Vedanta , the Hindu philosophy which emphasizes non-dualism. Totapuri first guided Ramakrishna through the rites of sannyasa—renunciation of all ties to the world. Then he instructed him in the teaching of advaita—that "Brahman alone is real, and the world is illusory; I have no separate existence; I am that Brahman alone."Under the guidance of Totapuri, Ramakrishna reportedly experienced Nirvikalpa Samadhi which is considered to be the highest state in spiritual realisation.

Totapuri stayed with Ramakrishna for nearly eleven months and instructed him further in the teachings of advaita. After the departure of Totapuri, Ramakrishna reportedly remained for six months in a state of absolute contemplation. Ramakrishna said that this period of nirvikalpa samadhi came to an end when he received a command from the Mother Kali to "remain in Bhavamukha; for the enlightenment of the people". Bhavamukha being a state of existence intermediate between samâdhi and normal consciousness.

Islam and Christianity

In 1866, Govinda Roy, a Hindu guru who practiced Sufism, initiated Ramakrishna into Islam. Ramakrishna said that he "devoutly repeated the name of Allah, wore a cloth like the Arab Moslems, said their prayer five times daily, and felt disinclined even to see images of the Hindu gods and goddesses, much less worship them—for the Hindu way of thinking had disappeared altogether from my mind." According to Ramakrishna, after three days of practice he had a vision of a "radiant personage with grave countenance and white beard resembling the Prophet and merging with his body".

At the end of 1873 he started the practice of Christianity, when his devotee Shambu Charan Mallik read the Bible to him. Ramakrishna said that for several days he was filled with Christian thoughts and no longer thought of going to the Kali temple. According to Ramakrishna, one day when he saw the picture of Madonna and Child Jesus, he felt that the figures became alive and had a vision in which Jesus merged with his body. In his own room amongst other divine pictures was one of Christ, and he burnt incense before it morning and evening. There was also a picture showing Jesus Christ saving St.Peter from drowning in the water.

Arrival of followers

Ramakrishna in samadhi at the house of Keshab Chandra Sen. He is seen supported by his nephew Hriday and surrounded by brahmo devotees. In 1875, Ramakrishna met the influential Brahmo Samaj leader Keshab Chandra Sen. Keshab had accepted Christianity, and had separated from the Adi Brahmo Samaj. Formerly, Keshab had rejected idolatry, but under the influence of Ramakrishna he accepted Hindu polytheism and established the "New Dispensation" (Nava Vidhan) religious movement, based on Ramakrishna's principles—"Worship of God as Mother", "All religions as true" and "Assimilation of Hindu polytheism into Brahmoism".

Keshab also publicized Ramakrishna's teachings in the journals of New Dispensation over a period of several years, which was instrumental in bringing Ramakrishna to the attention of a wider audience, especially the Bhadralok (English-educated classes of Bengal) and the Europeans residing in India. Following Keshab, other Brahmos such as Vijaykrishna Goswami started to admire Ramakrishna, propagate his ideals and reorient their socio-religious outlook. Many prominent people of Calcutta—Pratap Chandra Mazumdar, Shivanath Shastri and Trailokyanath Sanyal—began visiting him during this time (1871-1885).

Mozoomdar wrote the first English biography of Ramakrishna, entitled The Hindu Saint in the Theistic Quarterly Review (1879), which played a vital role in introducing Ramakrishna to Westerners like the German indologist Max Muller. Newspapers reported that Ramakrishna was spreading "Love" and "Devotion" among the educated classes of Calcutta and that he had succeeded in reforming the character of some youths whose morals had been corrupt. Ramakrishna also had interactions with Debendranath Tagore, the father of Rabindranath Tagore, and Ishwar Chandra Vidyasagar, a renowned social worker. He had also met Swami Dayananda.

Ramakrishna is considered as one of the main contributors to the Bengali Renaissance. However, some Brahmos like Upadhyay Brahma-bandhab disapproved of his avatarahood, ascetic renunciation and considered Ramakrishna's Samadhi as a nervous malady. Among the Europeans who were influenced by Ramakrishna was Principal Dr. W.W. Hastie of the Scottish Church College, Calcutta. In the course of explaining the word trance in the poem The Excursion by William Wordsworth, Hastie told his students that if they wanted to know its "real meaning", they should go to "Ramakrishna of Dakshineswar." This prompted some of his students, including Narendranath Dutta (later Swami Vivekananda), to visit Ramakrishna.

Sarada Devi

At the age of eighteen Sarada Devi joined Ramakrishna at Dakshineswar. By the time his bride joined him, Ramakrishna had already embraced the monastic life of a sannyasin; as a result, the marriage was never consummated. As a priest Ramakrishna performed the ritual ceremony—the Shodashi Puja where Sarada Devi was made to sit in the seat of goddess Kali, and worshiped as the Divine mother. Ramakrishna regarded Sarada as the Divine Mother in person, addressing her as the Holy Mother and it was by this name that she was known to Ramakrishna's disciples. Sarada Devi outlived Ramakrishna by 34 years and played an important role in the nascent religious movement.

Teachings

Ramakrishna's teachings were imparted in rustic Bengali, using stories and parables. Ramakrishna's teachings made a powerful impact on the Calcutta's intellectuals, despite the fact that his preachings were far removed from issues of modernism or national independence. His spiritual movement indirectly aided nationalism, as it rejected caste distinctions and religious prejudices. Ramakrishna emphasised God-realisation as the supreme goal of all living beings.

Ramakrishna taught that kamini-kanchana is an obstacle to God-realization. Kamini-kanchan literally translates to "women and gold." Carl T. Jackson interprets kamini-kanchana to refer to the idea of sex and the idea of money as delusions which prevent people from realizing God.Jeffrey Kripal translates the phrase as "lover-and-gold" and associates it with Ramakrishna's alleged disgust for women as lovers.

Ramakrishna looked upon the world as Maya and he explained that avidya maya represents dark forces of creation (e.g. sensual desire, evil passions, greed, lust and cruelty), which keep people on lower planes of consciousness. These forces are responsible for human entrapment in the cycle of birth and death, and they must be fought and vanquished. Vidya maya, on the other hand, represents higher forces of creation (e.g. spiritual virtues, enlightening qualities, kindness, purity, love, and devotion), which elevate human beings to the higher planes of consciousness.

Ramakrishna practised several religions, including Islam and Christianity, and recognized that in spite of the differences, all religions are valid and true and they lead to the same ultimate goal—God. Ramakrishna's proclaimed that jatra jiv tatra Shiv (wherever there is a living being, there is Shiva) which stemmed from his Advaitic perception of Reality. His teaching, "Jive daya noy, Shiv gyane jiv seba" (not kindness to living beings, but serving the living being as Shiva Himself) is considered as the inspiration for the philanthropic work carried out by his chief disciple Vivekananda.

Impact

Several organizations have been established in the name of Ramakrishna.The Ramakrishna Math and Mission is one of the main organizations founded by Swami Vivekananda in 1897. The Mission conducts extensive work in health care, disaster relief, rural management, tribal welfare, elementary and higher education. The movement is considered as one of the revitalization movements of India.

Other organizations include the Ramakrishna-Vedanta Society founded by Swami Abhedananda in 1923, the Ramakrishna Vivekananda Mission formed by Swami Nityananda in 1976, and the Sri Sarada Math and Ramakrishna Sarada Mission founded in 1959 as a sister organization by the Ramakrishna Math and Mission. Ramakrishna was born during a period of social upheaval in Bengal in particular and India in general. During Ramakrishna's time, Hinduism faced a significant intellectual challenge from Westerners and Indians alike.

The Hindu practice of Idol worship came under attack especially in Bengal, and many had denounced Hinduism and embraced Christianity or atheism. Ramakrishna and his movement, the Ramakrishna Mission, played a leading role in the modern revival of Hinduism in India, and on modern Indian history. His life and teachings were an important part of the renaissance that Bengal, and later India, experienced in the 19th century. Many great thinkers including Max Muller, Mahatma Gandhi, Jawaharlal Nehru, Sri Aurobindo, Leo Tolstoy have acknowledged Ramakrishna's contribution to humanity. Ramakrishna's influence is also seen in the works of the artists like Franz Dvorak (1862–1927), and Philip Glass.

6

Basic Presuppositions of the Divine Life Society

The Divine Life Society is a shining example of the creative aspect of the Divinity within man. It is a remarkable achievement of the Founder, His Holiness Sri Swami Sivananda, who from the year 1936, has built up the wonderful mansion of 'Divine Life' brick by brick, on the firm foundations of purity, integrity, nobility and magnanimity. The ideals of the Society are lofty, most practicable and within the reach of every human being, irrespective of position, caste, colour, country and creed. The Institution caters to the cultural needs of all ranks of people, to whatever class they may belong. Each one can tap whatever suits him the best according to his stature and intellectual or spiritual attainments. The holy river Ganga flows by the side of the Ashram, coming down from the icy regions of the Himalayas, carrying with her the message of seers and sages of the past and the present, thus in a way keeping intact the connection between the ancient and the modern and nourishing the body and the mind of the wearied soul in its earthly sojourn.

There is also available a Jnana Ganga (river of knowledge) emanating from the prolific pen of the Great Master Sri Swami Sivananda and his direct disciples, whom the Master has chiselled and moulded into his own pattern with the laudable idea of enabling them to continue and further the cause of his lofty mission. The lofty ideal of 'Divine Life' has its humble beginning in the building of a true human being, even as the fine superstructure has its small start in the foundation. Just as the strength of a building depends on its foundation which remains silent and invisible, so is the achievement of the Divine dependent on the strenuous preparation of man, to annihilate the animal in him, to develop the human nature and to allow it to blossom into Godliness. Thus there is no Divine Life without one being, or trying to become, human first, and one cannot claim to be a human being merely because he walks on two legs and talks with his tongue. It is our attitude, our behaviour and our dealings with others that go to decide whether we are humans, sub-humans or superhumans.

What is our attitude to our fellow-beings, to ourselves and to the Creator? This will decide what we are. Hence the noble Mission of Sri Swami Sivanandaji Maharaj was to bring about the needed transformation in man, to gradually eradicate the animal in him and to unfold the Divinity within to its perfection. This transformation is needed by everyone, irrespective of caste, creed, colour, country, sex, position high or low, and the Society therefore attracts seeking souls from all walks of life and from every country. The Divine Life Society carries out its object of a world-wide revival of spirituality through publication of books, pamphlets and magazines dealing scientifically with all the aspects of Yoga and Vedanta, universal religion and philosophy, and ancient medicine; holding and arranging cultural and spiritual conferences and discourses; establishing training centres for the practice of Yoga and the revival of true culture; and taking such other steps from time to time as may be necessary for bringing about a quick moral and spiritual regeneration in the world.

This institution serves as a place of preservation of the

ancient traditions and cultural practices that has come down as a time-honoured heritage. It has been built up to serve as a model of many-sided, altruistic activity, an ideal to copy, intended to bring about a complete unfoldment of the human personality, and to reveal the essential blending together of all sides of human nature. The Society also functions as an ideal place of spiritual retreat for the educated citizens of the world, wherein he can renew himself and recreate and refresh his being, physically, mentally, morally and spiritually.

Location

Sivananda Ashram, the Headquarters of The Divine Life Society, is housed at Shivanandanagar, on the right bank of the Ganga, at a distance of 3 kilometres from Rishikesh Town, (Distt. Tehri-Garhwal, U.P., India) and is served by 3-wheeler Autos and taxis. Rishikesh is about 24 kilometres from the renowned pilgrim centre, Haridwar, and is linked by rail and road. Regular buses and taxis are available throughout the day, at any time. Haridwar is situated on the banks of the river Ganga at a distance of 263 kilometres to the north of Delhi (Capital of India), and is served by rail and road. Haridwar Railway Station is on Delhi-Dehra Dun line.

Here labour a band of Sannyasins (renunciates) and Sadhaks (spiritual practitioners), whose life are entirely dedicated to the service of humanity, to learn and put into practice the Yoga of Synthesis and to function actively as dynamic centres of spirituality. The Society has as its aim the awakening of humanity to the true and lofty purpose of life, enlightening them on the various means and methods of attaining the Goal of life, and inspiring them and urging them to strive for its attainment.

Visitors to the Ashram

The Sivananda Ashram,-the Headquarters of the

international organisation, the Divine Life Society,-is situated in sylvan surroundings, with multihued hills all around and the beautiful and holy Ganga flowing majestically by its side. The setting is so alluring and capturing that all physical and mental ailments are forgotten for a moment, and there appears to be a standing invitation by the hills and dales and the sacred Ganga for periodical visits by people from all countries and from all strata of society for recoupment and conditioning of both body and mind. Added to this is the healing balm of the generous reception accorded by the Ashram to the visitors from all parts of the world, and to the travellers proceeding to the sacred Himalayan shrines, viz., Badrinath, Kedarnath, Gangotri and Yamunotri, who intend to make a brief halt at the foot of the Himalayas, which takes one to sublime heights of exhilaration.

The Aims and Objects

The Divine Life Society has been established:

1. To Disseminate Spiritual Knowledge:
   a. By publication of books, pamphlets and magazines dealing with ancient, oriental and occidental philosophy, religion and medicine in the modern scientific manner, and their distribution on such terms as may appear expedient to the Board of Trustees;
   b. By propagating the Name of the Lord, and by holding and arranging spiritual discourses and conferences and frequent Sankirtans (singing the Lords name) or spiritual gathering for singing and glorifying the Name of the Lord;
   c. By establishing training centres or societies for the practice of Yoga, for moral and spiritual Sadhanas (spiritual practices) and the revival of true culture, to enable aspirants to achieve regeneration through worship, devotion, wisdom, right action and higher meditation with systematic training in asanas

(postures), pranayama (breathing exercise), dharana (concentration), dhyana (meditation) and samadhi (superconscious state); and

d. By doing all such acts and things as may be necessary and conducive to the moral, spiritual and cultural uplift of mankind in general and to the attainment of the above-mentioned objects in Bharatavarsha (India) in particular;

2. *To Establish and Run Educational Institutions:* On modern lines and on right basic principles and to help deserving students by granting them refundable and non-refundable scholarships for doing research work in the various branches of existing scriptures and comparative religion, as also to train them to disseminate spiritual knowledge in the most effective manner;
3. *To Help Deserving Orphans and Destitutes:* By rendering them such assistance as the Society may deem proper, whether in any individual case or in any particular class of cases;
4. *To Establish and Run Medical Organizations:* Or any other medical institutions and hospitals or dispensaries for the treatment of diseases and dispensing medicines and performing surgical operations, etc., to the poor in particular and to the other public in general, on such terms and in such manner as may be deemed expedient by the Board of Trustees;
5. *To Take Such Other Steps from Time to Time:* As may be necessary for effecting a quick and effective moral and spiritual regeneration in the world and in Bharatavarsha in particular. The Society was registered as a Trust in the year 1936 and has been actively functioning since then to fulfill the above aims and objects in the world.

Swami Chidananda

Born in South India in 1916, the eldest son of an orthodox Brahmin family, Swami Chidananda was inspired at an early age by devotional songs and stories from the Hindu scriptures. During his college years, the lives and teachings of modern saints such as Sri Ramakrishna, Swami Vivekananda, Ramana Maharshi and Swami Ramdas awakened in him a fiery aspiration for spiritual life. In 1943 he joined the ashram of the world-renowned saint and sage Swami Sivananda, the founder of the Divine Life Society, whose passionate spiritual writings had long attracted him. Sivananda ashram, which then consisted of only a few buildings, was located on the banks of the Ganges River in the foothills of the Himalayas near Rishikesh, India.

During this period of his life, Swami Chidananda, among other activities, gave lectures, attended to ashram guests, and served the sick, expressing what would become a lifelong concern for the welfare of the lepers. Late in 1959 he was sent on a two-year world teaching tour by Swami Sivananda and eventually succeeded him as president of the Divine Life Society after Swami Sivananda passed away in 1963. Swami Chidananda's life since has been one of almost continuous travel, both in India and abroad, in the cause of the central objective of the Divine Life Society: the dissemination of spiritual knowledge.

When Andrew Cohen phoned from Australia and asked us if we could interview Swami Chidananda on the role of celibacy in the spiritual life, our first reaction was: "How will Swamiji ever find the time?" But our second reaction was that if there was anyone in the world who had a practical understanding of celibacy, it was Swamiji, and therefore we should make the request. So when Swamiji returned to the ashram a few days later for the five days of the Navaratri worship, our written request was given to him. That night, after satsang [a gathering with a spiritual teacher], he turned to me and said that while it would not be possible to find time during the next few days, if we didn't mind a little inconvenience, we could join him in a couple of weeks near Delhi.

The location was a new country home that he had been

requested to officially open and bless, and where we would then spend a few days resting. We readily agreed, and so toward the end of October, over four full days, we not only had some informal time with him, but we also managed to record five hours of dialogue relating to the subject of this issue of What Is Enlightenment? Our interview was supposed to start late morning of the first day, but Swamiji was exhausted, and so the first we saw of him was when he joined us for a walk at dusk.

As we were slowly walking along the country road we came upon a watchman guarding a gate. Swamiji stopped and carried on a fifteen-minute conversation. We didn't understand most of the Hindi, but we knew he was inquiring about the man's family and where he lived. As we moved on, we saw that another life had been touched by one who still remains at heart a simple monk, whose aim in life is to do as much good as possible for as many people as possible. When we returned from the walk and were climbing the steps, Swamiji turned to us and said, "The subject of brahmacharya, or celibacy or self-restraint, does not necessarily have, in Hindu society, any connection at all with the spiritual life, or sadhana [spiritual practice], or with Self-realization.

It is not normally discussed or recommended only with a view to promote spiritual life." After we had climbed the stairs and joined him in his room, Swamiji continued, describing traditional Hindu social life and how it relates to the subject of brahmacharya and sexual life, so that we would understand the broader context in which brahmacharya is viewed in the Hindu tradition. In ancient India, he explained, a person's life was reckoned as one hundred years, divided into four stages. The first stage was the student stage, or brahmacharya stage, where young people were expected to study hard, build a good physique, and in all ways prepare themselves for their adult lives to come. During this stage they were expected to observe strict celibacy.

The second stage was the householder stage, where the

exercise of the sexual faculty was taken for granted and recognized as a legitimate part of human life; it was regarded as a fundamental duty of a family to offer progeny to form the next generation. Swamiji continued: "Of course, its exercise was not meant to be unrestrained; otherwise it would be degrading. But it was given the full sanction of society. "The third stage of life was the retired stage, when the couple turned the burdens of earning a living over to the children and turned their minds to higher things," Swamiji explained. Here again they begin to practice brahmacharya as part of their sadhana.

"Then, during the fourth stage, one's entire life was to be devoted to God. One became a sannyasin, or monk, and then, of course, celibacy was automatic. So you see, the concept of brahmacharya was part and parcel of the Indian-Hindu social tradition. In its narrowest sense brahmacharya meant complete celibacy, but in its broader sense, as it could be applied to the life of a householder, it meant self-restraint, not abusing the sex function and strict fidelity to one's partner." Our conversation then turned to the role of spiritual practices and how they help to lift the consciousness by fostering the higher tendencies within us.

"The vast majority of human beings are human animals only," Swamiji said. "They are totally rooted in body consciousness. They have no idea of being something else, something other. Even their mental function is instinctive. It's all a reaction to whatever happens to them, not a purposeful independent exercise of their mental faculty. They have no time for it. From the moment they get up, they are absorbed by their daily activities.

"And the whole of the spiritual life," he continued, "is a gradual elimination, eradication, of the animal within, and the refinement or purification and education of the entire human nature so that it loses its movement in all other directions and starts taking on an ascending vertical direction. Once the human nature is given an upward turn, one simultaneously starts awakening the sleeping Divinity with the help of all one's spiritual practices. If one knows that the spiritual process, the spiritual life, is the elimination of the animal, the refining and directing upward of the human, and the awakening and unfoldment of the Divine, then all spiritual practices, including the role that brahmacharya plays, fall into their right place."

Swamiji seemed to have enjoyed our first conversation. He smiled and said, "So we must thank Andrew Cohen for this, for ultimately he is at the back of it, the root of it. Tomorrow we will start discussing the questions one by one." Our dialogues over the next few days revealed a side of Swamiji that is not often visible. Normally one sees in him what one would expect of a saint—holiness, sweetness, joy, constant consideration for others, beauty of movement, and a presence that makes itself subtly felt in the hearts of those who cross his path. The following interview shows the stuff a saint is really made of. It helps to complete the picture.

The Functions of the Divine Life Society

The spiritual institution is a place of training for suitably equipped temperaments and mature minds towards the acquisition of the higher knowledge of human life. This specialised knowledge is not like one of the sciences or the arts taught in modern colleges or universities, among which a student can prefer anyone to the exclusion of others, but it is the central art and science which enables one to recognise the true meaning of life in general. Spiritual life is not one of the ways of living or even one of the stages of life, but that general background of motive and understanding which vitalises all stages and gives life and meaning to every way of thinking and mode of activity.

One cannot live wisely and successfully in the world without adopting the spiritual perspective of the Universe. Spirituality is not worship of the deity in a temple, performance of rituals, following any code of behaviour or conduct, or even the practice of any cult, creed or religion. It is not even faith in God merely, for it rises above even this concept. Spirituality is that comprehensive understanding and envisagement of values, by which the Universe is taken in its totality not in bits or parts by which its unity is recognised. Not merely this; the aim of spiritual life is the recognition and realisation of this totality of the Universe as a single omnipresent, omniscient and omnipotent Self, or Atman. Obviously, this is a solution to all human ills, and all problems in creation.

The spiritual philosophy makes one the best of any kind, a farmer becomes the best farmer, a gardener the best gardener, a driver the best driver, a clerk the best clerk, an official the best official, a teacher the best teacher, and so on. The noblest element in a person is brought out by the technique of spiritual living. It is, thus, not a question of option left to people or a theme to be discussed as to whether it is necessary or unnecessary, for it is the only meaning of all existence. The Institutions that teach this science and art of life are the spiritual organisations of the world and their existence is naturally a must for the benefit and the peace, plenty and prosperity of mankind.

Anyone devoted to the ideals of truth, non-violence and purity can become a member of the Divine Life Society which is a non-sectarian Institution, embodying in its wide perspective the common fundamental principles of all the religions of the world, and of spiritual life in general. The Society accords equal place of honour to all faiths and religious traditions, and its members recognise no distinction or disruptive sentiment on account of each others different traditional background, or religious affiliation, all which the principles and the philosophy and teachings of the Society do integrate.

Through the pages of the various books and journals of the Society, what is endeavoured is to reveal the secret of spiritual action, namely that it lies in the Knowledge of the true Self and in the effacement and transcendence of the ego; and to present Sri Swami Sivanandas profound teachings that each soul is potentially divine and that everyones goal is to strive to manifest this divinity within by controlling the internal and external nature by being good and doing good. Anyone with the above ideals is welcome to become a member of the Divine Life Society. The Divine Life Society has been a pioneer in advocating and popularising health, culture and physical fitness through daily practice of yoga asanas and surya-namaskara among the students and youth of India.

This health-building work it has been doing through the length and breadth of India, from Rishikesh to Kanyakumari, and from Assam to the Punjab, since the past about forty years. The Founder Swami Sivanandaji Maharaj had commenced this valuable yoga work even before. His world-wide yoga practice movement was one of the earliest movements in this direction. The organisation and spiritual work of this Society being entirely non-sectarian, non-denominational and fully tolerant in its nature, it has been a cementing factor amongst the people of this country. The Ashram has drawn its residents from all provinces in India. Its Branch Centres are to be found throughout the country and their spiritual work fosters tolerance and encourages national unity.

The Institution propagates unity of religions and good-will among the communities. Almost all its annual Conferences, at State level as well as All-India level, feature one or two sessions as All-Religions-Meet or Sarva-Dharma-Sammelana. Thus, its work is intended to function as a constructive force promoting goodwill and harmony and peaceful relationship in Indian society.

These Societys spiritual teachers in foreign countries have been welcomed everywhere as the countrys cultural and spiritual ambassadors of goodwill, who have endeared themselves to countless people by their sincerity and their service in the field of yoga. The vast goodwill thus earned for India and its spiritual science (adhyatma-vidya) is an invisible and yet a tangible asset whose value cannot be easily estimated. This good work is spreading progressively all over the world.

Even long before any of our present-day teachers had started to go abroad, Swami Sivanandas spiritual teachings and yoga literature had made such a powerful impact in other countries during this recent era that it had raised the name and the prestige of our nation and its culture to very great heights in the eyes of the educated peoples of numerous foreign countries the world over. His books on yoga were very eagerly translated into French, German, Latvian, Estonian, Italian, Danish and Spanish languages, with the earnest objective of bringing about the widest possible spread of our countrys most precious spiritual heritage. The dignity and eagerness of the countrys cultural heritage has obviously risen high in the eyes of the peoples of other nations by this Institutions work.

A perusal of the spiritual teachings and a careful examination of the work of the Institution can make it evident that it has been propagating practices and indirectly working for targets for which the Government itself is now working and striving through various means and methods. Aims and goals such as national health and physical fitness, integrity of character, dutifulness and discipline, avoidance of wastage, limitation of family size, simplicity and thrift have been directly propagated and taught to people by this Institution from the time of its most revered Founder, who was known throughout India as one of the foremost spiritual leaders of his time and an illustrious well-wisher of the country, its people and its culture.

About a hundred or more deserving students of Uttar Pradesh, most of them from the very poor and backward District of Tehri-Garhwal, are receiving regular educational aid from the Institution for their school and college studies. In addition to their fees, the Institution helps them for their textbooks as well as for their school uniforms and clothes. Besides this, the Ashram sometimes gives aid to poor and deserving schools nearby to help them out of their monetary problems and difficulties. On the health and medical side, the Society, besides its regular year-round free medical service rendered to the public through the Ashrams Hospital, has conducted (a) twenty Eye Camps for free surgical and medical treatment of the public; (b) twenty Annual Women and Childrens Medical Treatment Camps; (c) three First Aid Training Courses; and (d) a few Child and Maternity Welfare (prenatal) Camps and food and nutrition education exhibitions. Such medical relief and service activities are carried on by a number of its Branches in different parts of India.

The Divine Life Society has reclaimed from the streets a large number of leper beggars and is providing for their maintenance in their own settlements. These leprosy patients have thus stopped begging on the streets since some years past and improved their general health. Medical care is provided to them. Also periodical repairs to their hutments and supply of clothes are made to them. In addition to this humanitarian Social Welfare project, the Society also bears a major part of the financial burden of running another leprosy colony of more than 120 leprosy patients since the past many years. The Institution has been a regular and unfailing participator in a number of national schemes by contributing appreciably towards Small Savings Fund, National Savings Certificates, Defence Bonds and collection drives undertaken by the Government. It also contributes its share in times of natural calamities like famines, epidemics, floods, etc.

As a centre of revival, propagating and perpetuating the countrys invaluable cultural heritage, the Institutions yeoman service is very well known throughout this nation over the past three decades. The Headquarters Ashram has ever tried to be a haven of refuge for persons in distress, disappointment, grief, dejection, friendlessness and despair.

The grieving and the sorrowful, the agitated and the confused come here for peace and solace. Such people rest and recover in this place and return in a better condition to face their problems and situations. No distressed person is ever turned away without assistance. No hungry person is ever refused a meal at the Ashrams kitchen. No shelterless person is ever turned away without night's shelter here.

Through the year's men and women, old and young, high and low, all come to this Institution on the banks of the Ganga by the highway to the Himalayan shrines, seeking to fulfil some inner want, some indefinable need. In the name of the Almighty, the Institution strives to fulfil in some measure the inner need of countless persons. The value and importance to their lives of what they find and receive here is only known to them and can be assessed only by them. The Divine Life Society has been not only helping and supporting the imparting of education by normal schooling but also imparting education by correspondence. The Society is conducting classes on yoga, Vedanta and Indian Culture in general, including classes in Sanskrit language, music, physical culture etc., regularly, throughout the year.

Postal correspondence work is also done on spiritual and cultural subjects, as well as themes of humanitarian service. Further, at periodical intervals, trained instructors from our Society are invited by the National Academy of Administration in Mussoorie and the Officers Training School, Nainital, to give training in yoga for the benefit of the officer trainees of the Academy. Thus, I.A.S. Probationers attending the foundational course as well as senior officers attending Advance Management Development and Planning course conducted at the National Academy of Administration have undergone training under the able Instructors deputed by the Society. Similar such training courses are conducted in different parts of the country in places like factories, industrial townships, universities like the Pantnagar

University, the Delhi University, the Jawaharlal Nehru University, New Delhi, etc.

The Divine Life Societys Library contains a very good collection of valuable books on Indian culture, philosophy and religion not only in English and other Indian languages but also in foreign languages. The Library is available for free use by all and a number of students and scholars are regularly visiting the Library and making use of the facilities. The aim of the Yoga-Vedanta Forest Academy of this Society is not merely an academic equipment of students, but a providing of the requisite training to enable them in their endeavour to blossom into truly humane, serviceful, integrated personalities, so that they succeed, at least in an appreciable measure, in living a life of goodness and wholeness personally, and of dedication, unselfish cooperation and constructive work socially.

It needs no special mention that this achievement in ones own person and in society is obviously rooted in the extent to which ones practical life is attuned to the Ultimate Reality of the Universe. Philosophical discipline, thus, is the precondition to leading a perfectly sociable, ethical and progressive life of an onward expansion towards the realisation of the Supreme Goal of existence. The teachers of the Academy will strive to hold aloft this objective set before the students, and are not just instructors in the well-known intellectual sciences. The basic spiritual foundation of all life is the principal motive governing the curriculum of the Academy, and students with this elevated spirit of quest seek admission. Every year the Society also conducts intensive training camps in which people from all walks of life from every region, irrespective of caste, colour or creed, take part.

During this period intensive training on yogasanas, pranayama and meditation is given to the participants. During the morning and evening sessions, instructive and illuminating discourses on the theory and practice of leading a spiritual life with a view to develop the integrated personality of man even while attending to the normal duties in ones respective walks in life are given. The printing and publication section is only intended for carrying out the educational programme in building character and all-round development of the personality so as to bring out the nobler qualities inherent in all human beings. A substantial output of the publication section is distributed free to those who are interested in undergoing physical as well as mental discipline and extending the frontiers of their knowledge.

By way of medical relief, the Society is running (1) an Allopathic Section, (2) an Ayurvedic Section, and (3) a Leprosy Relief Section, and also arranging free medical relief camps in and around Rishikesh, the Headquarters of the Society. The Allopathic Section is equipped with a clinical laboratory, X-ray machine and the Physiotherapy Section has facilities for ultra-short wave diathermy, infra-red and ultra-violet therapy. The hospital has 20 beds and more than 30,000 patients are treated on an average every year. Treatment in all departments is free to all, irrespective of caste or religion. In the Ayurvedic Section, medicines are prepared strictly according to the injunctions contained in the science of Ayurveda and such medicines are distributed free at the dispensary to patients who seek treatment.

It should not be difficult to appreciate that all charitable activities and service to humanity, particularly service to the poor and the sick, flow from the conviction in a Transcendent Presence which holds humanity together as a single fraternity. In India, as in other parts of the world, all true charitable activities are carried on with a spiritual zeal which oversteps the boundaries of classes, creeds and cults. The Divine Life Society is religious if by religion we are to understand the grounding of ones life in the structure of a Cosmic Reality. But, no one, definitely, we hope, would be prepared to abrogate the need for such a religion, if religion is the name we prefer to give to it. It is, rather, the Science of Life, on whose basis this Society has always been working ever since its inception. It attempts to make man human to enable him to live at peace with himself and the Society at large. It lays emphasis on the brotherhood of man to regulate his conduct with his fellow beings and to promote a sense of unity among things.

The Divine Life Society is essentially a Charitable Institution and its main object is education, spread of knowledge, and promotion of cultural progress, medical relief and relief of the poor. The fact that the workers engaged in carrying out the objectives of the Society have faith in a Super-Power that guides the destinies of men and believe that the ultimate goal of human endeavour should be to realise and experience oneness with that Power, would only adumbrate the integral approach of the Society as a whole. Religion, to the Divine Life Society, does not mean any particular faith, creed or cult, or any ism in the sense it is usually construed with relevance to the organised, the traditional or the accepted religions of the world.

To this Institution, and to all its followers, religion means that consciousness or that conduct which manifests in practical life as well as personal demeanour the laws that are supposed to operate behind the working system of the universe. Thus, religion becomes a scientific principle, a philosophical necessity and a spiritual ideal which regulates human life in every field of its activity, personal, social, national or international. Thus, again, religion becomes an inviolable law of the world as a whole, by which individuals are united into a fraternity or brotherhood in the light of a total culture of humanity which may be said to be directed towards the achievement of the purpose of human life as such, without any distinction characteristic of the ordinary religions. This feature exemplifies the universal nature of the activities and the aims and objects of the Society.

The following are the principal departments of The Divine Life Society:

The Yoga-Vedanta Forest Academy trains seekers in the knowledge of Indias Culture and in the practice of yoga as a general discipline for personal integration as well as human welfare. The Yoga-Vedanta Forest Academy Press prints the cultural and spiritual books as well as the journals and other literature of the Society. The Sivananda Publication League caters to the public demand for this valuable literature. The Free Literature Section distributes freely books and other literature to deserving seekers and aspirants the world over. The Sivananda Ayurvedic Pharmaceutical Works manufactures genuine Ayurvedic medicines from pure Himalayan herbs. The Charitable Hospital renders free medical service to the public and conducts periodical medical relief camps freely. The Annapurna Annakshetra, which is the common kitchen of the Ashram, feeds about 250 permanent residents as well as the daily visiting sadhakas and guests and pilgrims in varying numbers.

The Guest House looks to the needs of the many visitors and guests (visiting sadhakas) that come to the Ashram for spiritual guidance and yoga training. The Temples of worship hold prayers for the peace of the world conduct regular worship and continue the recitation of the Divine Name throughout the 24 hours of the day, for the welfare of mankind. The Library contains some of the most precious books in philosophy, yoga and culture. The Correspondence Section provides proper replies to countless queries that come from seekers all over the world in various walks of life. The daily satsanga held in the Ashram is a perennial source of inspiration to the souls that seek communion with inner peace. Yoga courses held in other parts of India, outside the Headquarters, in other Institutions and Organisations, are, again, channels of the much-needed inspiration to students, officials and people in general, which work the Society carries on through its Yoga Instructors who travel for this purpose.

The Divine Life Conferences held in different places in India have become effective means of mustering in the moral and cultural forces of people and bringing them together for the purpose of achieving individual and social solidarity. The Cultural Tours conducted by the senior swamis of the Ashram have become a by-word to anxious seekers in India as well as in other countries, who are benefited immensely by the teachings, lectures and personal guidance provided by the swamis travelling for this purpose. The Personal Guidance which the senior swamis at the Headquarters render in a paternal way to hundreds of people coming to the Ashram from the various countries in the world has been ever giving a healing touch to the tension-ridden personalities in society.

The Daily Meditation sessions are a practical mobilisation of mental and soul-force for a reconstruction of the human personality towards the various noble purposes in life. The Annual Sadhana Weeks are Spiritual Camps held in the Ashram, to which hundreds flock in eagerness for cultural and spiritual rejuvenation of their minds and hearts. The Educational Activities of the Society consist in helping poor students, about a hundred in number, right from the primary standard to the post-graduate level, by providing them with the requisite facilities in their studies, as a free gesture of the Ashrams goodwill towards the welfare of people. The Leprosy Relief Work of the Society is so well-known that it has always been regarded as part and parcel of the love extended by the Society to some 200 or more leper-patients who are rehabilitated and taken care of in a suitable manner.

The Social Service Wing attends to such services as medical aid to the poor and needy, contribution towards different relief works in the country, and such other gestures of charity as would relieve the sufferings of people, in some measure, from poverty, disease and ignorance. These services and activities of the Ashram are so conceived and conducted that they form a vehicle for the expression of the spiritual aspirations of seekers and become a venue for manifesting in practical life the broad-based inclusive ideal of the Oneness of God, the brotherhood of creation and the immortality of the soul.

The fundamental aims and objects of The Divine Life Society, as a whole, are purely spiritual and cultural, entirely non-sectarian, universally applicable and perfectly tolerant. The Society offers a peaceful haven wherein is provided ample opportunity and actual help for the restoration of peace to the troubled, conflict-ridden and psychologically traumatised personality of the modern man.

"You have come to this earth to attain spiritual perfection. You have come here to attain supreme and unalloyed bliss. The purpose of this human birth is the achievement of divine consciousness. The goal of life is Self-realization." Swami Sivananda.

Swami Sivananda is most definitely one of the great spiritual saints of India. His books on yoga and the multifaceted scriptures of India are some of the best books I have ever read on the subject. He writes with an electrifying nature that is filled with devotion and very useful, practical, spiritual information. Swami Sivananda was born on September 8, 1887, in South India. He was born into a family of devotees, saints and philosophers, who worshipped Shiva. As a boy he showed signs of a desire for a life of renunciation and love for his fellowman. In high school he was scholastically at the top of his class and won prizes every year in this regard.

The professional path he chose to follow in life was that of becoming a medical doctor. In his first year in medical school he could answer papers that even students in their final year of medical school could not answer. Again he topped his class in all subjects. Needless to say, Swami Sivananda had an absolutely brilliant mind and his entire life had more energy and enthusiasm for living than any saint I have ever studied. He is literally a Master of all spiritual paths and spiritual texts of Eastern religions. He not only understood them, but was clearly able to teach them in his lectures and writings.

While in medical school he started a medical journal called "Ambrosia", which gained great popularity. He was not only absolutely brilliant, but this brilliance was blended with an ingrained spirituality and desire for selfless service. After graduating medical school he traveled to Malaya and served the poor as medical doctor there for ten years. God came to Swami Sivananda as an all consuming aspiration to realize Him as the Self of all. God came to Swami Sivananda in the form of the sick and suffering in Malaya.

While there he was put in charge of an entire estate hospital. His integrity, positive disposition and hard work won him praise and promotion at every turn. It was while in Malaya that a wandering sadhu gave him a book by Swami Satchidananda on the soul's path to God. This ignited the last vestiges of his dormant spirituality. He began to intensively study the teachings of Sankara, Theosophical movement, the Bible, and the vast Indian scriptures, such as the Vedas, Bhagavad Gita, and the Ramayana.

He left Malaya in search of a life of renunciation as a sanyasin. He traveled to many different religious centers and studied with many great yogis, mahatmas, and spiritual teachers. He finally found his guru Paramahansa Viswananda Saraswathi, who gave him initiation on the banks of the Ganges River of June 1st, 1924. His guru named him Swami Sivananda Saraswathi. Swami Sivananda had a brilliant mind, and an unbelievably intense devotion to God. He practiced all the various yogic paths and studied the scriptures, unceasingly until he finally achieved nirvakalpa samadhi. Besides his continuing and ongoing spiritual practices, he decided to open a medical dispensary to help the poor, the sick, the devotees and mahatmas.

People began to come to him in large numbers for his spiritual teachings as well as for medical help. He began teaching classes and holding meetings for the singing of bhagvans (devotional songs). One time he did this in the ashram of Sri Ramana Maharshi and His devotees. It was in 1936 that Swami Sivananda started the Divine Life Society on the right bank of the Ganges River. This small organization was to eventually grow into a world wide organization with branches all over the world. The steady flow of free spiritual literature that was given out attracted a steady stream of devotees to Swami Sivananda. Swami Sivananda has actually written over 300 books. His teachings are totally universalistic, with the highest regards for all religions and all spiritual paths that lead to God. He calls his type of yoga the "Yoga of Synthesis".

As time went on after the initial opening of the Divine Life Society, Swami Sivananda traveled extensively throughout India and Ceylon for two months disseminating spiritual knowledge. He went to schools, colleges, universities, public meetings, cities, towns and villages teaching his universalistic, eclectic, spiritual knowledge. He was a fiery and dynamic speaker and was well received wherever he went. He never accepted any money from the organizers but instead asked them to print large numbers of pamphlets in different languages for wide circulation.

Swami Sivananda was a spiritual teacher par excellence. He never attempted to be anyone's guru and never accepted titles of sadguru or avatar. He never attempted to be famous, but his profound devotion to God, humility and service of humanity through his teachings, center, ashram and books has made him so. There are over 300 branches of the Divine Life Society throughout the world. He initiated thousands of students into the order of Sanyasins (renunciates). He began there also, a Yoga-Vedanta Forest University. He also began the Sivananda General Hospital. He opened a temple of all faiths. His ashram eventually grew into what might be called a spiritual colony.

His message was to carry the message of the sages and saints of all religions, to help humanity achieve peace, bliss, and liberation. He taught how all people could realize God regardless of their station in life, and whether they were single or a householder. The central core of his was the path of yoga and Vedanta. He acknowledged one of his main teachers to be the great Avatar Sri Sankara, who revolutionized the teachings of Hinduism. Also established in the ashram was a university press for the printing of all his books and pamphlets.

The basis of this movement was the adherence to the ideals of truth, non violence and purity. It is a path of the essence of all yogas and the essence of all religions and spiritual paths. The ashram also publishes a monthly journal called the "Divine Life", which began in 1938. During World War II Swami Sivananda started a non-stop chanting for world peace, and a three time a day regular worship service. He also opened a Sivananda Ayurvedic pharmacy with Ayurvedic herbal preparations from the Himalayas.

In 1957 the Sivananda Eye Hospital was formerly opened. Even after the Swami Sivananda achieved Maha-samadhi in 1963, the entire ashram with all its services has continued to serve to this very day. Senior monks now run the facility under the directorship of the president, Sri Swami Chidananda. The Divine Life gospel can be summed in six words of Swami Sivananda: "Serve, love, give, purify, meditate, and realize."

The essence of the teachings is to help seekers to realize their true self and to transcend ego. That each soul is potentially divine and that everyone's goal is to manifest this divinity by controlling the internal and external nature by being good and doing well. Anyone who is compatible with these goals is welcome to be a member. In Swami Sivananda's autobiography his message to individual aspirants and branches of the Divine Life Society reads as follows: "You have come to this earth to attain spiritual perfection. You have come here to attain supreme and unalloyed bliss. The purpose of this human birth is the achievement of divine consciousness. The goal of life is self realization."

"Man is not a sensual animal. Man, in his essential nature, is an ever free, ever pure, even perfect, immortal, spiritual being. Feel this. Feel that you are the immortal self, that you are satchidananda. Remember the words; "Ajo nityah saswatogam puranah - You are the unborn, the eternal, the imperishable and ancient." To live in this exalted consciousness is to experience indescribable joy every moment of your life, to experience a limitless freedom in the spirit. This is your birthright. This is the aim of your life. This is the goal. To realize this through a life of truth, purity, service and devotion is the chief purpose of the Divine Life Society.

"Fear dominates in this era of nuclear weapons for mass destruction. Hatred rules the policies of vast sections of the so-called enlightened and civilized mankind. This age of advancement has been exposed to be, in reality, an age of degeneracy in the views and values, the ideals and morals, of the greater masses of mankind. At this juncture in time, cultured men and women all over the world look to the sacred land, India, for light and knowledge. It is your noble task to spread this light of spiritual knowledge and spiritual idealism to all corners of the globe."

The message of divine life, according to Swami Sivananda, is; "See God in all faces. Serve all. Love all. Be kind to all. Be compassionate. Feel everyone to be your own. Serve your fellow beings in the spirit of worship offered to the divine which indwells them. Service of man is truly the worship of God." He goes on to say: "Know well that the heart of the Vedas, the heart of the Bible, the holy Koran, the sacred Gathas, and all the world's scriptures are, in truth, one, and sing in unison the sweet message of love and concord, goodness and kindness, service and worship." "Discard the barriers of name and form. Seek the oneness at the heart of all beings. Include within your spiritual embrace the entire humanity. Live for peace. Live for universal love. Live the life divine."

Later in his autobiography Swami Sivananda gave "his creed" for living. "To behold the Atman or the Self in every being or form; To feel the Brahmic consciousness everywhere, at all times and in all conditions of life; To see, hear, taste, smell and feel everything as the Atman. This is my creed. To live in Brahman, to melt in Him, and to merge and dissolve in Him is my creed. Whilst dwelling in union with Brahman, to utilize the hands, mind, and senses and the body for the service of humanity; to sing the Lord's name for elevating devotees of God; To give instructions to sincere aspirants; And to disseminate knowledge far and wide through books, pamphlets, leaflets, magazines and platform lectures. This is my creed."

In a later section he speaks on the purification of the inner nature. "Purify your mind. Develop sattwic (harmonious) qualities such as nobility, courage, magnanimity, generosity, love, straight forwardness and truthfulness. Eradicate all evil qualities such as lust, greed, anger, avarice, likes and dislikes, and other negative traits which stand in the way of ethical perfection and Self-realization. Ethical perfection is a prerequisite to self-realization. No amount of practice can be of any value to the aspirant if he ignores this side of sadhana (spiritual practice). Love all. Prostrate yourself before everybody. Become humble. Talk loving, sweet endearing words. Give up selfishness, pride, egoism, and hypocrisy. Regenerate your lower nature.

On spiritual development in his autobiography, he states: "The one Brahman or the Supreme Self appears as the divine universe in all the planes or degrees of its manifestation and therefore, the aspirant has to pay his homage to the lower manifestation before he steps into the higher. Sound health, clear understanding, deep knowledge, powerful will and moral integrity are all parts of the process of realizing the ideal preached by Vedanta.

I insist on all-round discipline of the lower self. The teachings of Vedanta are not in conflict with Hatha, Bhakti (devotional yoga), Raja (yoga of mind), or Karma yoga (selfless service). All these are blended together as elements constituting a whole. On how to convert the nature of man, this is what Swami Sivananda has to say. "Honor those who are bad characters. Serve the rogue first. Treat him as a future saint, as a saint himself. This is the way to purify your heart and to elevate him also. I take special delight in serving such people carefully. I always keep around me any number of people who would abuse me, vilify me, insult me, and even try to injure me. I want to serve them, educate them, elevate them, and transform them. I address them in the most respectful terms. Acclaim the rogue or the thief as a saint and publicly honor him. He would be ashamed to continue his evil doings."

7

Islam in India

Islamization of India did not occur as a result of mass conversions. The process took several centuries. Though the province of Sindh was conquered in early 8th century it was not until the incursions of Mahmud of Ghazni and Muhammad of Ghor that serious settlement of the subcontinent with Muslims took place. Even then contrary to belief it was not the forced conversions that increased the number of Muslims in India. Of course, the unfair taxes called jizya of all non-Muslims had an effect. Many Hindus were forced to convert to Islam to escape from the punishing taxes. The invading sultans like Qutb ud-din Aibak and Ala-ud-din Khilji often offered clemency to the enemy after their defeat if they converted to Islam. Many of these local rulers switched back to Hinduism as soon as the sultans turned their backs and returned to Delhi.

The major reason for mass settlement of India by Muslims was the invasion of Mongols into central Asia. Genghis Khan, his grandsons and later Timurlane wreaked havoc in the Central Asian countries causing migration of countless number of people seeking refuge in the relative safety of India. Just how disastrous Muslim conquest was for India and how much resistance had been offered to preserve its heritage by Hindu rulers are controversial subjects. Much of the history was written by Muslim historians and could be biased. The little history documented by Indians was also written with an eye towards glorifying their kings. These as well could be simply exaggerations. Hindu writers write about countless accounts of heroism by their warrior, some of them mere boys in their teens. Some of the fiercest resistance probably came from lesser tribes and simply went undocumented. However, it is clear that the Muslim conquest of India took several centuries. Idolatry was condemned but many sultans simply ignored the practice by the Hindus and did not impose Islam on them forcibly.

Better results were obtained by imposing taxes on non-Muslims, although the Brahmins and some Buddhists were exempt form it until the rule of Feroz Shah Tughlaq in the latter half of 14th century. When the Mughals established their empire, the whole of India was almost completely under the Muslim rule, especially during the rule of Aurangazeb. Religious fanaticism of Aurangazeb, unlike his ancestor Mughals finally led to the cessation of Muslim control of India. As a consequence of his intolerance, the Mughal Empire weakened precipitously after his death and steadily shrank in size over the next century and a half, to finally be taken over by another foreign force in the nineteenth century, the British. What Akbar had achieved with tolerance and reconciliation was reversed by Aurangzeb's zeal to force Islam on Hindus.

The religion of Islam stormed into India in a similar manner as it did in the Arabian countries. Powerful regimes succumbed to the religion at a remarkably fast pace as evidenced by the fact that within a century after its inception, it had spread to the entire Middle East and Northern Africa. But in India, Islam had a more difficult time to insinuate into the Hindu and Buddhist societies. Even then, Islamization of India took several centuries and was never complete. The barbaric nature of the sultanates rule and the invasion of Mongols may have had a negative effect on the Hindu practitioners. The earlier Mughals had breeched the division somewhat, but Aurangzeb in his zeal to turn India into an Islamic nation alienated all other religions. From then onward moderate Muslim rule was an oxymoron. It is also apparent that the Hindus revered their idols much more than the Muslim conquerors estimated. A sweep of India never occurred and India remained predominantly Hindu, with only about twenty percent of its population as Muslims, at any given time in its history.

Greater India once included Pakistan and Afghanistan. Gandhara (Kandahar) is mentioned in Mahabharata epic (Gandhari, wife of Drtarashtra hailed from Gandhara). Ashoka and Kanishka ruled Afghanistan and it was an integral part of India until it was lost to Islam. Afghanistan had been lost to India for many centuries until Babur, the founder of the Mughal Empire, united it with India. Lost to Shah of Persia by Humayun, Akbar had re established the sovereignty in Afghanistan by conquering both Kabul valley and Kandahar. Then Jahangir and Shah Jahan lost Kandahar forever to the Shah of Iran, never to be regained though Kabul remained in Mughal hands until the reign of Aurangzeb. Even the British in the nineteenth century were unable to re-conquer it. India lost further territory when Pakistan and Bangladesh were lost to India in the modern era, in the middle of twentieth century.

As you read this article it will surely dispel the myth that the Mughals were more detrimental to Hindu dominance of India than any other dynasty. If destruction of Hindu temples is any measure the Sultans of Delhi did far worse damage than the Mughals (except Aurangzeb). The marauders like the Mahmud of Ghazni, Muhammad of Ghor, Timurlane, Nadir Shah and Ahmad Shah Abdali did loot and destroy idols in the temples all over the North, but the rulers like Aibak, Iltumish, Khilji and Feroz Shah Tughlaq, continued to do the desecration of temples in the name of cleansing the religion of Hindus and Buddhists over a long period of time in a sustained way. A large library of Buddhist literature was set ablaze by Khilji in Odantapuri, even before knowing what they contained.

The emergence of Islam in the region is concurrent with the Turko-Muslim invasion of medieval India (which includes large parts of present day Pakistan and the Republic of India), where these rulers took over the administration of large parts of India. Since its introduction into India, Islam has made significant religious, artistic, philosophical, cultural, social and political influences to Indian history. Contrary to popular belief, Islam came to South Asia prior to Muslim invasions of India. Islamic influence first came to be felt in the early 7th century with the advent of Arab traders. Trade relations between Arabia and the subcontinent are very ancient. Arab traders used to visit the Malabar region, which was a link between them and ports of South East Asia, to trade even before Islam had been established in Arabia.

According to Historians Elliot and Dowson in their book The History of India as told by its own Historians, the first ship bearing Muslim travelers was seen on the Indian coast as early as 630 AD. H.G. Rawlinson, in his book: Ancient and Medieval History of India claims the first Arab Muslims settled on the Indian coast in the last part of the 7th century AD. Shaykh Zainuddin Makhdum's "Tuhfat al-Mujahidin" also is a reliable work.This fact is corroborated, by J. Sturrock in his South Kanara and Madras Districts Manuals, and also by Haridas Bhattacharya in Cultural Heritage of India Vol. IV.It was with the advent of Islam that the Arabs became a prominent cultural force in the world. The Arab merchants and traders became the carriers of the new religion and they propagated it wherever they went.

The first Indian mosque was built in 629 A.D, at the behest of Cheraman Perumal, during the life time of Muhammad (c. 571–632) in Kodungallur by Malik Bin Deenar. In Malabar, the Mappilas may have been the first community to convert to Islam because they were more closely connected with the Arabs than others. Intensive missionary activities were carried out along the coast and a number of natives also embraced Islam. These new converts were now added to the Mappila community. Thus among the Mapilas, we find, both the descendants of the Arabs through local women and the converts from among the local people.

In the 8th century, the province of Sindh (Pakistan) was conquered by an Arab army led by Muhammad bin Qasim. Sindh became the easternmost province of the Umayyad Caliphate. In the first half of the 10th century, Mahmud of Ghazni added the Punjab to the Ghaznavid Empire and conducted several raids deeper into modern day India. A more successful invasion came at the end of the 12th century by Muhammad of Ghor. This eventually led to the formation of the Delhi Sultanate.

Arab-Indian Interactions

There is much evidence in history to show that Arabs and Muslims interacted with India and Indians from the very early days of Islam, if not before the arrival of Islam in Arabia.

Many Sanskrit books were translated into Arabic as early as the Eighth century. George Saliba writes in his book 'Islamic Science and the Making of the European Renaissance' that "some major Sanskrit texts began to be translated during the reign of the second Abbasid caliph al-Mansur, if not before; some texts on logic even before that, and it has been generally accepted that the Persian and Sanskrit texts, few as they were, were indeed the first to be translated."

Spread of Sufi Islam

Sufis (Islamic mystics) played an important role in the spread of Islam in India. They were very successful in spreading Islam, as many aspects of Sufi belief systems and practices had their parallels in Indian philosophical literature, in particular nonviolence and monism. The Sufis' unorthodox approach towards Islam made it easier for Hindus to practice. Hazrat Khawaja Muin-ud-din Chisti, Qutub-Ud-Din Bakhtiyar Kaki, Nizam-ud-din Auliya, Shah Jalal, Amir Khusro, Sarkar Sabir Pak, Shekh Alla-ul-Haq Pandwi, Makhdoom Ashraf Simnani, and Waris Pak trained Sufi groups for the propagation of Islam in different parts of India.

Once the Islamic Empire was established in India, Sufis invariably provided a touch of colour and beauty to what might have otherwise been rather cold and stark reigns. The Sufi movement also attracted followers from the artisan and untouchable communities; they played a crucial role in bridging the distance between Islam and the indigenous traditions. However there is also evidence of fanatical and violent conversions carried out by Sufi Muslims. Ahmad Sirhindi, a prominent member of the Naqshbandi Sufi advocated the peaceful conversion of Hindus to Islam. Imam Ahmed Rida Khan contributed a lot by defending traditional and orthodox Islam in India by his famous work Fatawa Razvia.

Islam in Modern India

Muslim influx and influence in India started almost at the inception of the religion. The traders from Arabia were frequent visitors to the Indian subcontinent even before Prophet Muhammad revealed the Koran. They brought the word of Muhammad to India in the 7th century and this resulted in some peaceful conversions of Hindus to Islam. Following this, Mohammad-ibn-Quasim in the year 712 A.D conquered the Province of Sindh. However, this event in history does not seem to have influenced India as much as expected. Beginning with the invasion of Mohammad of Ghazni in the 10th century, followed by a barrage of invaders from Persia, Turkey and Afghanistan in the 11th and 12th centuries, a full force of Islam was thrust upon India.

Forcible conversions of people of other faiths with inducements as well as unfair taxation resulted in spread of the Islam in Hindustan. The British conquest in India that started insidiously with the establishment of the East India Company, eventually usurped the Muslim stronghold of India, in the 18th century. Today there are more than a quarter of a billion Muslims living in the Indian subcontinent (India, Pakistan and Bangla desh). This amounts to more than a quarter of the total Muslim population of the world. Muslims form about fifteen percent of the Indian population. It is unique that the Muslim population of India has been influenced by the Hindu religion throughout history. Sufism, for example is an adaptation of Vedanta.

Over many centuries, Islam in India has undergone several attempts at reforms, some towards modernization and some leaning more towards fundamentalism. The Muslims in India are categorized into two distinct classes based on their origins. This is similar to the caste system of Hinduism (so called Varnashrama). Muslims are broadly divided into two groups, namely, Ashraf and Ajlaf. Ashraf are again grouped as Sayyeds, Sheikhs, Mugahls and Pathans. The Sayyeds are said to be descendents of the Prophet and regarded in high esteem. The Sheikhs are of Arab descent and are next in line in prestige. The Mughals are descendents of the greatest Muslim rulers of India, the Mughals and occupy third place. Pathans including Sepahis hail from the northwestern regions including Afghanistan and form the last group of Ashraf.

The Ajlaf on the other hand are the Indian converts and are considered to be of common ancestry. They are considered to be of inferior class when compared to the Ashraf. Nineteenth century India saw great socio-religious reform in Hinduism. The reform movements of Rajaram Mohan Roy in 1827 first started the abolishing of Sati and recognition of widow marriage as well as education of women by founding of his Brahmo Samaj in Bengal. Many reform movements followed this, significantly the Prarthana Samaj started by Keshab Chandra Sen in 1867 (later popularized by G.M.Ranade and Bhandarkar), Arya Samaj established in 1875 by Dayananda Saraswati and Ramakrishna Mission of Vivekananda.

The Theosophical Society of Colonel Cleott popularized by Annie Besant in 1886 in Madras, the Rehnumai Mazdayasan Sabha of the Parsees established by Dadabhai Navaroji in 1851 in Bombay and the Sri Narayan Dharma Paripalan Yogam started by Sri Narayana Guru in 1903 in Travancore were some other reform movements of late 19th century. All these reforms were attempts at steering the Hindu religion towards Vedanta, which is the backbone of its philosophy. Unlike Hinduism, which is flexible and amenable to reform, Islam is rigid and difficult to change. Criticism of old archaic practices is shunned and viewed as anti- Muslim rhetoric. Modernization is seen as a threat to the way of life of a Muslim. In the face of such persistent orthodoxy all the reforms of the 19th century generally have been reverting to more fundamentalism rather than modernization. Two such reforms were the Wahabis and Tabligis.

The Wahabis

The Wahabi movement started in Saudi Arabia in the 18th century by Muhammad ibn-Abd-al-Wahab (17031792) regards all other religions as heretical and thus intolerant towards them. The Indian Wahabi movement was founded by Syed Ahmed Brelavi (1789-1831) belonging to Rai Baraili. When he saw Islam drifting towards superstitions and exaggerated veneration of saints and prophets, he steered Islam to its more fundamental roots similar to the Arabian Wahabi movement. However, the Brelavi Wahabis had no direct contact with their counterparts in Arabia. Its aim was to establish Muslim sovereignty in India or a Dar-ul-Islam.

Though the Wahabis took part in fighting the British, the basic tenet of the movement did not change, that is to establish Muslim supremacy over all of India. Influenced by the Wahabi movement, two other fundamentalist movements came into existence. Shariatullah started Fairazi movement in attempt to aid the poor peasants in Bengal against the oppressive zamindars. Soon this became an anti-Hindu movement as well. More significant was the second movement called the Deoband. They established the Muslim schools for education, the model of which is still followed in the madrassahs around the Muslim world.

These Deoband faction attracted students from all over the Muslim world. Financed by the rich Muslim Arab nations, fundamentalism was institutionalized in these schools. In India there is an undercurrent of discord between the Deoband faction and the Brelavi Wahabis, mainly due to the financial disparity. In course of time the movements started as reform of Muslims shifted course and has been preoccupied with power and control of the populous.

The Tabligis

Dayananda Saraswatis Arya Samaj targeted Muslim converts and attempted a purification drive (shuddhikaran). As a response Maulana Iliyas of Mewat in Rajastan started the Tabligi movement in 1927. The Hindu converts were practicing a mixed form of Islam as they were culturally more Hindu than Muslim. Maulana Iliyas started his movement to transform these converts into complete Muslims and put forward the slogan, Aye Musalmano! Musalman bano (O Muslims! Be Muslims). True Islamic teachings and practices were taught in an uncompromising way. Initially localized to Mewat, the movement caught on and spread rapidly after the death of the Maulana.

The Tabligis follow strict codes of the Islamic law. They are bound by the religious dogma, dressing patterns, detailed methods of religious practices. Meetings of thousands of Muslim gatherings (Jamaat) are held where minute details of the religious practices are taught for

Muslims to follow. Half the populations of Muslims in the subcontinent are now adherents of this movement. Though apolitical in its organization, they have a capacity of mobilizing a large number of Muslims at short notice to gather. More moderate reforms of the Islamic religion also occurred simultaneously. The adherents of such reforms are much less in number today. The Aligarh and the Ahmedia movements are the two main moderate attempts at reform.

The Aligarh Movement

Sir Syed Ahmed Khan (1817-1891) attempted a social upsurge amongst the Indian Muslims with his so-called Aligarh movement. His main contribution was to enhance education with starting of many schools and colleges. Much importance was given to Urdu language. He undertook reconciliation between Islam and Christianity and he pointedly showed the similarities between the two religions. He even published a sympathetic study of the Bible. Urdu translation of books on western arts and sciences were done by a translation society founded by him. Despite all the successful launching of social reforms, Sir Syed failed to bring about much needed moderation of the religion such as womens education and the purdah system for oppressed women. Only the education of upper and middle class and has been criticized for not going far enough with his reforms of the entire Muslim society.

The Ahmedias

Founded in 1889 by Mirza Ghulam Ahmed, the movement was based on universal religion of all communities. It spread western liberal education among Muslims by starting a number of schools and colleges. It was opposed to Jihad but at the same time infused vigorous religious spirit among Muslims. It is the most closely knit and organized group of Muslims in the country. Its perceived mysticism was its downfall.

The Aga Khans Flock

Apart from the Sunnis (the followers of Omar, the Caliph) and Shiites, (followers of Ali, Prophes son in law) there is another sect in Indian subcontinent called the Aga Khanis. It is the Nizari Ismaili community with Aga Khan as their Imam. It originated as a splinter group of Shiite sect, when they accepted Ismail as the seventh Imam instead of his brother. They trace an unbroken line of Imams up to the current day Aga Khan (Prince Karim), who is 49th in succession. Many Shiite sects refused to accept any Imams after the eleventh Imam died without an heir.

In this way the Nizari Ismailis are different. Thirteen generation after Ali, the Shiite sect further divided between followers of Nizar and his brother (later came to be known as Bohra community). Nizari Ismailis follow Aga Khan as their leader and celebrate his birthday as a holy day rather than the Muharram, which most of the Shiites celebrate as a holy day because of the death anniversary of Hussein, son of Ali. Followers of Aga Khan are more westernized than any other Muslim community. Most of the recent Aga Khans have been educated in England. Thousand years ago they were rivals of the caliphate of Baghdad and ruled as the Fatimid caliphate of Cairo. After the decline of their influence in Egypt and Asia, they remained in Persia until 1840, when the 46th Imam was forced to leave Persia. They then moved to India and Pakistan where they formed an amicable relationship with the British. They were not accepted into Mecca and did not undertake pilgrimage.

In 1866 their interpretation of the Koran resulted in dissension among its followers and many left the faith and reverted to some other form of Shiite sect. The Aga Khans were also accused of mishandling the Nizari finances in 1905 though they won a court battle in this regard. However, the modernization of the religion by the Aga Khans did not sit well in the Muslim world. The Nizari Ismailis of Gujarat are called Khojas. During the 16th and 17th centuries, for example, Indian Nizaris often deemed it necessary to consult Hindu texts as well as The Holy Koran (which is of course their primary Book); in fact even today a fair number of Aga-Khanis enjoy and derive some inspiration from the Bhagavad-Gita. Unlike other Muslims, they sometimes sing hymns during their services, usually in an Indian language such as Gujarati. In addition, many Nizaris believe that reincarnation of souls is possible under certain circumstances.

Mostly these are Muslims who embrace Sufism. An attempt was once made to categorize Hazrat Ali as the tenth avatar of Vishnu by Aga Khan though they no longer believe this. As a result of the rift between the reformers and the orthodox sections of the religion, many deserted and joined other Shiite sect, thus becoming indistinguishable from them. It was thought that only about four million Muslims remained faithful to Aga Khan. However, after the breakup of the Soviet Union and birth of independent countries like Uzbekistan, Turkmenistan and Tajikistan where many Aga Khanis were found to be followers of the faith. Now it is believed that there are about 20 million followers.

Other Attempts

Other attempts have been made to modernize the religious practices with varying effects. Shibli Numani attempted Muslims to adopt a more flexible attitude towards Hindus and accept new ideas, but failed. Barruddin Tyebji (1844-1906) attempted to do away with the Purdah in Bombay. Moves toward re-interpretation of scriptures, history and behavior have been attempted by Hali and more recently by Maulana Vahiddudin Khan. Traditional Muslim forces are too strong to allow any radical changes in the socio-religious front. Unlike Hindu reforms, real radical reforms of Islam have remained a dream of certain individuals over the course of history.

Phadke wrote in 1989 that so tight has been the hold of orthodoxy on the Muslim mind that nowhere in India has Muslim society been so far able to support a vocal group of liberal Muslims committed to modern values. There has been no serious attempt of a thorough critical appraisal of their heritage. After Indian Independence the reform of the Islam has become even more difficult as any attempt is viewed with suspicion because of the minority status of the Muslims. Another moderate Muslim movement attempting to reform is the Bohra Reformist Group. Bohras are mainly business people mostly in the hardware and gun smithy. This is a modern movement attempting to soften the authority of the religious leaders on the religion. Started by Engineer, Contractor and Poonawala they have even attempted to interpret Koran in the perspective of a Christian liberal theology.

In the 1970's a reformist named Hamid Dalwai made a serious attempt at modernizing Islam in India. He proposed abandonment of purdah and more freedom to women among the Maharashtra Sunni Muslim community. For this effort he was branded as heretic and his movement did not survive after his death. Dalwais movement was called Muslim Satayshodhak Mandal (MSM). Many more similar attempts have so far failed to produce significant results in reforming the socio-religious aspect of Islam in India. The fundamentalism is readily accepted whereas the moderate reforms are shunned.

The Future

Any attempt to bring the religion in par with the modern scientific world is perceived as a threat to Islamic identity. Religion is law in Islam and any change is thought to be breech of faith and belief. Sir Syed (Aligarh Movement) was called a kafir or infidel for his attempts and Dalwai (MSM) was branded as munafique or a heretic. Religion forms an integral part of the day-to-day practice of Islam that any reform devoid of religion is bound to fail. At the same time the injudicious reliance on religion can result in extreme fundamentalism like the Wahabi or directionless organization of the Tablig Jamaat.

Being a minority status in India has resulted in any attempt at modernization to be called as an attempt at Hindu-isation of Islam. Even the purdah system is defended as a religious identity, discarding the humanitarian aspect and discrimination. Somehow a middle ground has to be sought both by the minority Muslims and the majority Hindus in India. There has to be an exchange of moderate ideas in a non-religious context that does not cross the line of infuriating the religious faction. From a distance this looks like an impossible feat as both sides have vowed not to give an inch. This rigidity has made the clash of two of the great religions all the more difficult to avoid. The divergent paths followed by both in their philosophy and theosophy seem to be drifting apart at a rapid pace.

New Steps In Madrasa Reform

Madrasas were originally intended as institutions for the preservation and transmission of the Islamic religious tradition as a whole. In contemporary India, however, they focus largely, although not exclusively, on the teaching of fiqh or Islamic jurisprudence. Most Indian Muslims adhere to the Hanafi School of jurisprudence and so most madrasas in the country restrict themselves to the teaching of the books of Hanafi fiqh. Almost all these books were written between the ninth and the fourteenth centuries, in a context very different from that of India today. Most of their authors lived and worked in Central Asia, Iran and parts of the Arab world. Consequently, their understanding of fiqh was shaped by the particular environment in which they lived.

The questions that they raised and the answers that they provided were a product of the concerns of their own times. Not surprisingly, their books do not deal with many issues of contemporaryconcern and relevance. Despite this, most Indian madrasas continue to employ these texts, and, consequently, the teaching of fiqh has been gradually distanced from real-world concerns. An interesting and innovative experiment to reform the teaching and understanding of fiqh is the work undertaken by Delhi-based Islamic Fiqh Academy (IFA). Following the example of similar academies in some Arab countries, Europe and North America, the IFA believes that ijtihad, or the creative, context-sensitive interpretation of fiqh, is absolutely essential in order to provide islamically suitable answers to issues of contemporary relevance, issues on which the corpus of traditional fiqh is silent or else irrelevant. Thus, it questions the widely held assumption of taqlid or blind imitation of the earlier jurisprudents or fuqaha, stressing instead the inherent dynamism of Islamic law.

In contrast to past precedent, it believes that ijtihad on many issues is no longer possible on the part of a single scholar or 'alim. Because many questions of contemporary concern involve a range of disciplines, it argues for what it calls 'collective ijtihad', bringing together 'ulama trained in the traditional Islamic sciences as well as experts in various fields of modern knowledge to deliberate on various issues and provide islamically acceptable solutions. Interestingly, and in contrast to many traditional 'ulama, the IFA does not identify itself with any particular school of thought (maktab-i fikr). It stands for tolerance and respect of differences between the different Sunni mazhabs or schools of fiqh. The IFA's activities are wide-ranging, including publishing books, organising lectures and training programmes and holding seminars.

It has produced several texts on a variety of contemporary issues, from insurance and birth control to modern commercial transactions and organ transplants, offering opinions on these based on collective ijtihad. It has held a number of seminars in different parts of the country, in which 'ulama and modern scholars have participated to collectively discuss various issues which the traditional books of fiqh are silent on, but which Muslims have increasingly to face today. A major focus of the IFA's work has been the promotion of new understandings of fiqh in the Islamic madrasas in the country. One of the most successful of its initiatives in this regard was its madrasa training programme, which, however, has since been discontinued. The concept of the programme emerged at the IFA's annual seminar at Bangalore in 1990.

The next year, it sent out letters to various madrasas in the country, offering to arrange, at its own expense, for extension lectures by university lecturers in their campuses on various modern subjects. The lectures would cover a range of disciplines, including the social and natural sciences, modern medicine, philosophy, comparative religion and so on, but presented in a suitable Islamic form and located within the contemporary Indian context. It proposed that these lectures should later be collected and published as textbooks, which could then be incorporated into the madrasa syllabus. It saw this initiative as helping to bridge the gap between madrasa-trained and university-educated Muslims, and to dispel what it saw as the wrong, though widely-held, notion of 'religious' (dini) learning as being somehow distinct from 'worldly' (duniyavi) knowledge.

Between 1991 and 1993, the IFA organised training camps at some 40 madrasas in different parts of India to acquaint students and teachers with issues of contemporary relevance. At the camps, professors of different subjects from various universities, including the Aligarh Muslim University, Jami'a Millia Islamia and Lucknow University, in addition to some leading 'ulama, spoke to and interacted with students and teachers of the madrasas on a range of issues. Although most madrasa students who attended the lectures responded enthusiastically, some madrasas, says IFA's secretary Amin 'Usmani, were not very welcoming, fearing that this might 'divert' the attention of the students from their religious studies. Unfortunately, the programme was discontinued two years after it was launched, primarily because of shortage of funds.

Usmani opines that unless the teaching of fiqh in the madrasas is reformed, madrasas can play little role in enabling the Muslims to deal with the challenges of modernity. He suggests major curricular reforms in this regard. He argues that the focus of the teaching must be on the 'usul (basic principles) of the Qur'an and the Hadith, rather than, as at present, on the furu' or minor details of fiqh. He argues that while madrasas generally place great stress on the teaching of intricate details of ritual purity, the nitty-gritty of marital relations and the minute intricacies of divorce and so on, they tend to neglect what he sees as the 'basic spirit' of the Qur'an and the Hadith. 'Usmani also stresses that the teaching of fiqh must take the contemporary Indian context seriously. He suggests that madrasas should equip their students with the knowledge and skills needed to operate in a modern religiously plural society.

For this, he stresses the need for madrasas to introduce the teaching of other religions from a non-polemical perspective so that Muslims and people of other faiths can understand each other in a more sympathetic way. He advocates the introduction of what he calls 'Peace Studies' as a regular subject in the madrasas, through which the students could be taught the importance of peace and ways of working for it in accordance with the Qur'an and the Hadith. 'Usmani places his hopes on the younger generation of madrasa students, who, he feels, are more open to alternate views and willing to critically engage with issues of contemporary concern so as to develop more relevant, and, therefore, more authentic understandings of Islam, including of fiqh. Older generation 'ulama, he laments, seem to be either hostile or indifferent to voices such as his that are today calling for the reform of the madrasa.

Barelwi Ulama Movement

The Barelwi Ulama Movement is a reform movement of Sunni Sufism in British India that was founded by

Ahmed Raza Khan of Bareilly, Rohilkhand India. Barelvis are an extensive portion of the Hanafi Muslim communities in India, Pakistan, Bangladesh, South Africa and also the United Kingdom. This community also has its presence in other places around the world. Ahmad Raza Khan was the pivotal figure around which the Barelwi Ulama Movement was promoted in the Indian subcontinent between the 19th and 20th centuries and thus earned numerous followers and opponents. The name Barelvi came into use to indicate the followers of Ahmad Raza Khan. The terms Nuri and Barkati depict the Sufi Tariqa associated with Ahmed Raza Khan. The term "razavi" depicts those people who have been initiated into the Qadri Sufi Tariqa via the heredity of Ahmed Raza Khan. Supporters of Ahmad Raza Khan in India are mainly Hanafi by Madhab, which is the School of jurisprudence, but accept the other three Sunni schools to be legitimate.

Beliefs of Barelwi Ulama Movement

Aqidah - Barelwi follow one of the Ashari or Maturidi schools of Aqidah, the Hanafi school of Fiqh. Other than Ashari, they also posses the Qadiri, Chisti, Naqshbandi or Suhrawardi Sufi orders. According to Barelwi Ulama Movement belief Muhammad had "knowledge of the unseen" and of the deeds of each and every Muslim and also had been given ample knowledge of all creations by Allah. It is also believed that he is created from Noor or "light".

Practices of Barelwi Ulama Movement

During Mawlid or the birthday of Muhammad, special recitations or Naats that have been written by scholars such as Ahmed Raza Khan are elaborately recited amidst grandeur. The salat o salam with Durood and Hamd o Naat is narrated after Fajr and Jumuah prayers, and are seen as a discriminating feature from others within Islam. The Miraj, Shaberat or Shab-e-Barat, Laylat al-Qadr and Gyarvi Sharif of Sheikh Abdul Qadir Jilani is also celebrated.

The supporters of Barelwi Ulama Movement have expanded their missionary activities in various countries of Asia, Europe, North America and South Africa through the organization Dawat-e-Islami, which was founded by Maulana Ilyas Attar Qadri in 1981. Dawat-e-Islami obtained certification from the Pakistani Defence Ministry as a non-terrorist organization. Their non-political and merely religious behavior has contributed to an optimistic picture of the Barelwi Movement.

While the Barelwi Ulama Movement operated in various regions of the countries, Deobandi and Salafi critics, among others, contended that the teachings of Ahmad Raza Khan Barelvi constitute bid'ah. As a result, the Salafi Permanent Committee for Islamic Research and Fataawa also issued a fatwa, declaring that their group should not pray with Barelwis due to practices which are considered to be as kufr and bid'ah; however, their bid'ah should be reacted with good manners.

The main opponents of Barelwi Ulama Movement remained as the Islamic movements that condemned many of the customs, defended by the Barelwis. Their position was then similar to movements of orthodox defence in other religions. Although acculturative socio-religious movements called for change, not all did so in an outwardly aggressive manner, as was exemplified by the Radha Soami Satsang of the Hindus with its inward orientation.

Tariqah-i-Muhammadiyah

An Islamic leader, Sayyid Ahmad Barelwi was the leader of the Revivalist Movement, called the Tariqah-i-Muhammadiyah. This movement preached of both a return to past purity and an open struggle, a jihad with non-Muslims. Sayyid Ahmad Barelwi had interpreted the fatwa of 'Abdul 'Aziz that declared British India dedar ul-harb (the house of war) as a territory ruled by non-Muslims. By the late 1820s one of Sayyid Ahmad Barelwi's disciples, Titu Mir

(1782-1831), started to preach in rural western Bengal. He expounded a fundamentalist policy that predestined elements of popular Islam as mistakes and called upon his followers to practice equality among their coreligionists, and to take on a unique appearance as an outward sign of their religious pledge.

Titu Mir opposed Hinduism and the landlord class and quickly won supporters among the peasants. His Revivalist Movement, however, ended in 1831 when he and his followers rose against the government. They briefly controlled three districts, but were restrained by British troops. In 1832, another disciple of Sayyid Ahmad, 'Inayat 'Ali, came to Bengal. He began traversing the rural areas and expounded to the Muslim peasants a sanitized Islamic doctrine. 'Inayat 'Ali traveled until 1840 and settled in the district of Jessore. Within four years another disciple of Sayyid Ahmad Barelwi reached Bengal. In 1835 Mawlana Karamat 'came to Bengal, where he remained an efficient proponent of Islam and Revivalist Movement until his death in 1873.

Karamat 'Ali sailed across the rivers of Bengal and Assam for nearly forty years in a flotilla that constituted a traveling-cum-residential college'. His Ta'aiyuni movement taught a purified Islam shared by the Tariqah-i-Muhammadiyah and other nineteenth-century Islamic movements. He met with Shari'at 'Ullah in 1836-7 and conflict between the two became public in 1839 at Bansal, the scene of a debate between Karamat 'Ali and the Fara'izis. The primary point of disagreement lay on the factor that whether or not congregational prayers could be legally held on Fridays and on the annual Id festivals. Below this rested the question of whether British India should be classed as dadar ul-harb or dadar ul-Islam (the house of Islam). Here the Muslims could and should practice their religious rituals.

Both the Tariqah-i-Muhammadiyah and the Fara'izis adopted the former interpretation, and based it on the fatwa of 'Abdul-'Aziz. Karamat 'Ali, however did not accept this view. Thus for the Ta'aiyunis these prayers were suitable and even required. Although the two movements mutually agreed on basic points of theology, such as an acceptance of the Hanafi School of law, a rejection of polytheism and erroneous innovations, and an emphasis on puritanical Islam, the doubt of prayers remained an hostile point of difference between them. Tariqah-i-Muhammadiyah and the Fara'izis clashed repeatedly and the tracts of defending each position were made public as this controversy came to symbolize personal dogmas. In general, the Ta'aiyunis were more modest than the Fara'izis or the Tariqah-i-Muhammadiyah.

Karamat 'AH, himself a Shi'ah, whole-heartedly accepted the pir-muridi system of religious teachers and their disciples that was never accepted by other movements. Not all Islamic movements publicly disagreed. The Ahl-i-Hadith, another successor of the Tariqah-i-Muhammadiyah came to Bengal. The Tariqah-i-Muhammadiyah too practised Jum'ah and 'Id prayers, but there is little indication of conflict between it and the Fara'izis. Internal Muslim discord was settled in the twentieth century by a strengthened intellect of common unity. The proponents of a purified Islam and the socio-religious movements they created produced serious changes among Bengali Muslims, particularly in the rural areas.

The sense of mutual identity of being a Muslim was clarified and made clear. Popular tracts, nasibat ndrnabs, written in Bengali, discussed all aspects of Muslim belief and life. This literature was intended to instruct ordinary Muslims in the basic tenets of Islam. It also described the proper life for all Muslims. The creation of extensive religious literature in Bengali inspired Muhammad Naimuddin's translation of the Qur'an into Bengali and completed in the years 1892-1908. Public religious debates popularized the basic concepts of Islam and became occasions of social enlistment and social assimilation as well.

Satnamis

Ghasi Das, the native of Bilaspur district founded a socio-religious movement in Chhattisgarh and called it the Satnamis. The founder of Satnamis was probably a Chamar by caste, an untouchable leather worker. He was a servant in the village of Girod of Raipur district. During the 1820s, Ghasi Das and his brother set out on a pilgrimage to the Vaishnava temple of Puri in Orissa. They did not complete this journey and after reaching Sarangarh, they returned joyously shouting 'sat naam', proclaiming the idea of a single 'true' god. Ghasi Das deserted his normal life and became a religious austere. He retired to the forest for contemplation and periodically reappeared in the locality making him available to individuals who sought spiritual inspiration and moral aid. Gradually his reputation grew and he had a group of disciples.

Although anyone could come to Ghasi Das yet almost all of his followers were from the Chamar caste. The religious career of Ghasi Das gradually moved to a new stage when he withdrew to the forest for six months and then returned to preach a new religious doctrine. Ghasi Das asked his followers to discard idol worship and all that it is demanding. He believed that all men were equal, thus stood against the system of caste. Ghasi Das also asked for a restructuring of nutritional practices. Meat along with liquor and anything that was associated to flesh or blood were restricted, tomatoes, lentils, and chillies were also banned. Beyond the issue of diet and basic belief, Ghasi Das taught his disciples to withdraw themselves from using cattle for ploughing after midday or from taking food out to the open fields.

The local Brahmins frowned upon the use of cattle for ploughing actions in the afternoons. Ghasi Das brought his untouchable disciples into conformity with upper-caste customs, through the dietary changes he advocated. Until his death in 1850, the Satnamis primarily focused on improving the status of the Chamars through adjustments within the untouchable community. Balak Das, Ghasi Das's eldest son, became the successor of the Satnamis. Balak Das was forceful and radical in his attitudes to caste discrimination. He started wearing the sacred thread that was only for the first three varnas. The twice-born Hindus were deeply insulted by what they considered his extreme arrogance. In the 1860s, a group of Rajputs retaliated by murdering Balak Das.

This murder sparked an element of social protest and rebellion against the upper castes of the Satnamis. Many refused to pay their land-taxes as the conflict escalated to include riots and further murders. Meanwhile, his son Sahib Das as leader of the Satnamis replaced Balak Das, although real power rested with Agar Das, a brother of the founder Ghasi Das. On the death of Sahib Das the line of succession went over to the two sons of Agar Das, Ajab Das and Agarman Das, who became high priests of the movement. They divided all property and the right to collect a rupee from each of the Satnami households. Leadership then passed down these two lines of descent accordingly. In addition to this formal dissection of authority, the Satnamis suffered an earlier crack over a ban on tobacco and smoking.

Popular among many Chamars and other inhabitants of the Central Provinces was the chunngi (leaf pipe). One section of the Satnamis maintained and propagated that Ghasi had taken away the ban before his death and broke away from the parent group. The new subsect was known as chungias and another subdivision of the Satnamis were the Jahorias, named so from the term jobar (essence), and composed of those Satnamis who took oaths of mendicancy. They ate only pulses and rice, never slept in a bed and wore only uncolored clothes. Eventually, the Satnamis were linked to the Hindu bhakti saint, Ramananda. It was claimed that Rohi Das, also a Chamar disciple of the great northern saint, was the real inspiration for the Satnamis. Those who accepted this story became his follower and adopted the name Rohidasi, rather than

Satnami. Chhattisgarh were an extension of the Ramanandi movements of the North and the area had been influenced by the teachings of Sant Kabir. By the first decade of the twentieth century the Kabir-panthis of this area had almost 685,672 members in their own movement.

In the same period the Satnamis had a group of around 477,360 members. Of this number only 2,000 or so were not members of the Chamar caste and within that community almost 52 per cent of the Chamars were Satnamis. Chhattisgarh remained the centre of this movement with 42 per cent of the Satnami residing within it. The Satnamis became a permanent subdivision of the Hindus of the Central Provinces. Lawrence Babb conducted field research among the Satnamis in 1966-7 and described them as essentially a single-caste movement with its own hierarchical system of priests, its holy centres and a special calendar of ritual events.

As an intermediary socio- religious movement the Chhattisgarh, Satnamis followed the well-established path of Ramanandi Hinduism, then for a short period of extreme prejudice tried to strike out against the caste system and society in general, but finally returned to an existence within that very system. This Satnami movement persisted as an untouchable form of Hinduism with its own priests, its hereditary control and its followers almost exclusively from one untouchable caste, with its area of impact limited to the Chhattisgarh plain. They were an extension of the religious and cultural developments within the Gangetic basin, a dimension that sets these two movements apart from Satya Mahima Dharma or the third intermediary movement.

8

Zoroastrian Religion in Modern India

Though the total number of Zoroastrians in Indian population is very less yet they continue to be one of the important religious communities of India. According to the 2001 census, there were around 70,000 members of the Zoroastrian faith in India. Most of the Parsis (Zoroastrians) live in Maharashtra (mainly in Mumbai) and the rest in Gujarat. Zoroastrians or Parsis are mainly the descendants of the tenth-century immigrants from Persia. Though the number of Zoroastrians in India is alarmingly low yet they wield great influence because of their financial position. The level of Zoroastrian population is ascribed to migration, low birth, late marriages, non-marriages, divorce and infertility.

In the beginning, the Parsis or Zoroastrians were engaged in shipbuilding and trade activities and were located in the ports and towns of Gujarat. Slowly and gradually their entrepreneurial skills saw them expanding and controlling trade and commerce. With colonial expansion they got more trading opportunities and substantial number of Parsis moved to Bombay. From then onwards Mumbai or Bombay served as a base for expanding their business activities throughout India and abroad. Sanjan, Nausari and Udvada towns in Gujarat are of great importance to Parsis as they served as community centers before the Zoroastrians or Parsis migrated to Bombay in the nineteenth century. The Zoroastrians enjoyed the benefit of Western commercial contacts and English-language education and expanded their commercial dominance rapidly and became the most cosmopolitan community in India during the British rule.

In modern India, Parsis are the most urban, elite, and wealthy of almost all the religious groups of India. Parsis have played an important role in the development of trade, industry, finance, and philanthropy, which has earned them an important place in the India's social and economic life. Many of the Parsis or Zoroastrians have earned accolades in government services and law. The religious book of the Parsis is called source the Avesta, which includes a number of sections in archaic language attributed to Zoroaster and which preserve the cult of the fire sacrifice as the focus of ritual life. The religious and ritual life of pious Parsis revolves around sacred fires.

The most important rite for most lay Parsis is the Navjote. It is performed when a person is between the age group of seven and fifteen. It initiates the young person into the adult community of the Parsis. The Navjote ceremony involves purifying bathing, reciting Avesta -based scriptures, and being invested with a sacred shirt and waist thread (kusti) that should always be worn after the ceremony. The dead Parsis are disposed of by exposure to vultures Dakhmas (or towers of silence).

Zoroastrianism in India

According to the 1991 census, there were 79,382 members of the Zoroastrian faith. Some 79 percent lived in Maharashtra (primarily in Bombay) and most of the rest in Gujarat. Zoroastrians are primarily descendants of tenth-century immigrants from Persia who preserved the religion of Zoroaster, a prophet of Iran who taught probably in the sixth century B.C. Although the number of Parsis steadily declined during the twentieth century as a result of emigration and low birth rates, their religion is significant because of the financial influence wielded by this mostly trading community and because they represent the world's largest surviving group of believers in this ancient faith.

Originally, the Parsis were shipbuilders and traders located in the ports and towns of Gujarat. Their freedom from food or occupational restrictions based on caste affiliation enabled them to take advantage of the numerous commercial opportunities that accompanied the colonial expansion of trade and control. Substantial numbers moved to Bombay, which served as a base for expanding their business activities throughout India and abroad. A combination of Western commercial contacts and English-language education during the colonial period made the Parsis arguably the most cosmopolitan community in India.

Socially, they were equally at home with Indians and Westerners; Parsi women enjoyed freedom of movement earlier than most high-caste Hindu or upper-class Muslim women. In contemporary India, Parsis are the most urban, elite, and wealthy of any of the nation's religious groups. Their role in the development of trade, industry, finance, and philanthropy has earned them an important place in the country's social and economic life, and several have achieved high rank in government. The source of Parsi religion is a body of texts called the *Avesta,* which includes a number of sections in archaic language attributed to Zoroaster himself, and which preserve the cult of the fire sacrifice as the focus of ritual life.

The supreme spirit is Ahura Mazda (or Ohrmazd), whose will is manifest in the world through the actions of bountiful immortals or good spiritual attributes that support life and love. Opposing the supreme spirit is the force of evil, Angra Mainyu (or Ahriman), which is the cause of all destruction and corruption in the world. Equipped with free will, humans can choose sides in this struggle and after death will appear at the bridge of judgment. People who choose to do good deeds go to heaven; those who commit evil go to hell. The opposed cosmic forces battle through the history of the universe, until at the end of time there will be a final judgment and a resurrection of the dead to a perfect world.

The extensive ritual life of devout Parsis revolves around sacred fires, of which there are three grades dependent on extensive ceremonial preparation. The highest two grades can only be maintained in fire temples by hereditary priests, who undergo extensive purificatory rites and wear special face masks to prevent polluting the flames with breath or saliva, while the third grade of fire can exist in the household. The most important rite for most lay people is the Navjote, which occurs between the seventh and fifteenth year of life, and initiates the young person into the adult community. The ceremony involves purifying bathing, reciting *Avesta* -based scriptures, and being invested with a sacred shirt (*sudrah*) and waist thread (*kusti*) that should always be worn thereafter.

Marriage is also an important rite, complete with scriptural recitations. At death, great care is taken to avoid pollution from the body, and funeral services usually take place within twenty-four hours. The dead are then disposed of by exposure to vultures on large, circular "towers of silence" (*dakhma*). Most rituals take place in the home or in special pavilions; congregational worship at fire temples is limited to spring and autumn festivals. The towns of Sanjan, Nausari, and Udvada in Gujarat are of prime importance to Parsis, having long served as community centers before mass migration to Bombay in the nineteenth century. Bombay is home to 70 percent of India's Parsis, where the management of Parsi affairs rests in the hands of a *panchayat*, the assembly that serves as a charitable and educational organization providing a comprehensive social welfare system at the local level.

Judaism in India

Trade contacts between the Mediterranean region and the west coast of India probably led to the presence of small Jewish settlements in India as long ago as the early first millennium B.C. In Kerala a community of Jews tracing its origin to the fall of Jerusalem in A.D. 70 has remained associated with the cities of Cranganore and Kochi (formerly known as Cochin) for at least 1,000 years. The Pardesi Synagogue in Kochi, rebuilt in 1568, is in the architectural style of Kerala but preserves the archaic ritual style of the Sephardic rite, with Babylonian and Yemenite influence as well. The Jews of Kochi, concentrated mostly in the old "Jew Town," were completely integrated into local culture, speaking Malayalam and taking local names while preserving their knowledge of Hebrew and contacts with Southwest Asia.

A separate community of Jews, called the Bene Israel, had lived along the Konkan Coast in and around Bombay, Pune, and Ahmadabad for almost 2,000 years. Unlike the Kochi Jews, they became a village-based society and maintained little contact with other Jewish communities. They always remained within the orthodox Jewish fold, practicing the Sephardic rite without rabbis, with the synagogue as the center of religious and cultural life. A third group of Jews immigrated to India, beginning at the end of the eighteenth century, following the trade contacts established by the British Empire. These Baghdad Jews came mostly from the area of modern Iraq and settled in Bombay and Calcutta, where many of them became wealthy and participated in the economic leadership of these growing cities.

The population of the Kochi Jews, always small, had decreased from 5,000 in 1951 to about fifty in the early 1990s. During the same period, the Bene Israel decreased from about 20,000 to 5,000, while the Baghdad Jews declined from 5,000 to 250. Emigration to Australia, Israel, Britain, and North America accounts for most of this decline. According to the 1981 Indian census, there were 5,618 Jews in India, down from 5,825 in 1971. The 1991 census showed a further decline to 5,271, most of whom lived in Maharashtra and Mizoram.

Parsi

A Parsi or Parsee is as member of the larger of the two Zoroastrian communities of the Indian subcontinent. According to tradition, the present-day Parsis descend from a group of Iranian Zoroastrians who immigrated to Western India over 1,000 years ago. The long presence in the region distinguishes the Parsis from the Iranis, who are more recent arrivals, and who represent the smaller of the two Indian-Zoroastrian communities. The term 'Parsi' is not attested in Indian Zoroastrian texts until the 17th century. Until that time, such texts consistently use Zarthoshti, "Zoroastrian" or Behdin, "[of] good nature" or " the good religion." The 12th century Sixteen Shlokas, a Sanskrit text in praise of the Parsis and apparently written by a Hindu, is the earliest attested use of the term as an identifier for the Indian Zoroastrians.

The first reference to the Parsis in a European language is from 1322, when a French monk, Jordanus, briefly refers to their presence in Thana and Broach. Subsequently, the term appears in the journals of many European travelers, first French and Portuguese, later English, all of whom use a Europeanized version of an apparently local language term. For instance, Portuguese physician Garcia d'Orta, who in 1563 observed that "there are merchants in the kingdom of Cambai known as Esparcis. We Portuguese call them Jews, but they are not so. They are Gentios." In an early 20th century legal ruling Justices Davar and Beaman asserted (1909:540) that 'Parsi' was also a term used in Iran to refer to Zoroastrians.notes that in much the same way as the word "Hindu" was used by the Iranians to refer to anyone from the Indian subcontinent, the term 'Parsi' was used by the Indians to refer to anyone from Greater Iran, irrespective of whether they were actually ethnic Persians or not.

In any case, the term 'Parsi' itself is "not necessarily an indication of their Iranian or 'Persian' origin, but rather as indicator — manifest as several properties — of ethnic identity". Moreover, (if heredity were the only factor in a determination of ethnicity) the Parsis — per Qissa — would count as Parthians. The term 'Parseeism' is attributed to Anquetil-Duperron, who in the 1750s, when the word 'Zoroastrianism' had yet to be coined, made the first detailed report of the Parsis and of Zoroastrianism, therein mistakenly assuming that the Parsis were the only remaining followers of the religion.

As an ethnic community

Although the Parsis originally emigrated from Persia, most Indian Parsis have lost social or familial ties to Persians. Many do not share language or recent history with them. Over the centuries since the first Zoroastrians arrived in India, the Parsis have integrated themselves into Indian society while simultaneously maintaining their own distinct customs and traditions (and thus ethnic identity). This in turn has given the Parsi community a rather peculiar standing: they are Indians in terms of national affiliation, language and history, but not typically Indian (constituting only 0.006% of the total population) in terms of consanguinity or cultural, behavioural and religious practices.

Genealogical DNA tests to determine purity of lineage have brought mixed results. One study supports the Parsi contention that they have maintained their Persian roots by avoiding intermarriage with local populations. In that 2002 study of the Y-chromosome (patrilineal) DNA of the Parsis of Pakistan, it was determined that Parsis are genetically closer to Iranians than to their neighbours. However, a 2004 study in which Parsi mitochondrial DNA (matrilineal) was compared with that of the Iranians and

Gujaratis determined that Parsis are genetically closer to Gujaratis than to Iranians.

Taking the 2002 study into account, the authors of the 2004 study suggested "a male-mediated migration of the ancestors of the present-day Parsi population, where they admixed with local females leading ultimately to the loss of mtDNA of Iranian origin." If we were to to name one minority community that has enriched India, educationally, industrially, economically and culturally, it is the Parsee (a.k.a Parsi) community or Zoroastrians. Parsis from Persia (present day Iran) have found a permanent homeland in India. Numbering today less than a hundred thousand among the one billion Indians, this highly educated and prosperous community is fast disintegrating due to religious and social reasons.

The ancient Persians were racially akin to Indo-Aryans. They worshipped the sun and other elements like earth, water, ether, air and fire (panchamahabhootas). They built temples and installed sacred fire. They are followers of Zarathushtra who lived 3000 years before Christ. Zarathushtra preached monotheism in the name of Ahurmazda who has no form shape, beginning or end. He however acknowledged archangels who protected the humanity through the sacred elements. Hence the purity of five elements was to be protected. Significantly it is fire god the purifier who symbolizes beginning of civilization. He is most sacred to Parsees.

The Parsis perform sacred-thread ceremony (Navajot) and some rituals are common with Hindus. But the entirely different custom is the disposal of the dead. Unlike cremation, they throw the dead bodies to vultures, allowing the nature for final rites. A human living or dead must be most useful to animal planet. Left to vultures, the soul gets purified for heavenly abode, getting rid of all earthly attachments. The fire worshippers led a peaceful and happy life in their native land and Zoroastrianism was quite popular in parts of Asia and Europe. But with the arrival of Islam in the 7th and 8th centuries, religious zealots invaded Persia and forcible conversions took place on a very large scale. People fled to different lands. Some came to India by sea, carrying the sacred fire with them.

Tradition declares that the flames were collected from potters, goldsmiths, brick makers, and shepherds etc, sixteen vocations undertaken by ancient Parsees. When the first immigrants landed on the swampy port of Navsari (Gujarat) and requested for shelter and patronage of the local ruler; he sent them a bowl of milk full to the brim, indicating that though they are welcome, his land is full of inhabitants. The Parsee high Priest asked for some sugar and put it in the bowl and sent it back. The milk did not overflow and sugar added the taste-suggesting merger as subjects and eternal help to the ruler by the refugee community.

The ruler was impressed. India thus became a second homeland to new comers like Jews, Syrian Christians, Central Asian and African communities. All were free to follow their own faith and take up different pursuits. The fair skinned, mild tempered, intelligent community adopted local language and some customs. They made a mark with the arrival of the British. Many adventurous Parsis had taken to oversees trade. Several had excelled in banking and commerce. With English education Parsee men and women shone in different fields. With prosperity came charity. Many charitable hospitals, schools, colleges, orphanages, choultries in Surat, Mumbai and Pune bear witness to the munificence of the community which reached all strata of society. They also excelled as lawyers, solicitors, doctors and administrators.

Many Parsis availed British patronage and started industries, a privilege enjoyed only by the ruling class. But some were great nationalists like Dadabhai Navroji (1825-1917) known as Grand old Man of Indian Nationalism, Sir Pherozshah Mehta and Madame Bhikaji Cama. Sir

Jamshedji Tata broke the monopoly of the Europeans in industry. Even today the Tatas are a leading industrial house in India. Wadias, Godrejs and scores of other Parsis have made India progressive. But the genetic stock of this highly intelligent section has become weak. A very conservative community as far as religious matters are concerned has never allowed conversions.

Any man or woman marrying an outsider is considered as an outcast. As a result of in-breeding, high incidence of genetic defects has set in. Asthma, heart and neurological problems, myopia, and depression have become hereditary. Many have become Christians and as a result are disowned by the sect. Thus the number is diminishing. The Parsee priesthood is hereditary. There is a twentieth generation priest in a Mumbai Fire Temple (Agyari). The clergy claim to have kept Zoroastrian race intact and pure. The oldest and biggest Fire Temple is at Udvada (Gujarat). Others are in Navsari, Surat, Mumbai and Pune, where there is concentration of the Parsis. Oldest sacred fire flame still burning today in Mumbai is thirteen centuries old.

The disposal of the dead (throwing the body to the vultures) is a hoary tribal practice of ancient Iran. The scavenger birds made the clean job in the past in the dokhmas or "towers of silence" where the dead were thrown earlier were situated outside the city with high walls. Mumbai metro has since grown beyond borders, and the towers are in the midst of the city. They are a health hazard. The shy vultures avoid crowd and have become almost extinct. Special efforts are on to breed carnivorous vultures. Many enlightened Parsis opt for cremation these days. Inter-religious marriages are taking place. These developments are causing concern to elders and religious heads of a fast diminishing community whose birth rate has fallen ominously down.

Like languages, Parsis adapted Indian costumes with their own designs. Women used to were long sleeved blouses and sarees with reverse pallu. Men wore trousers (not dhoti) with long coats and tall cornered black caps. Nowadays there is nothing special to distinguish them from other highly westernized Indians except their fair complexion and sharp features. Parsee cuisine with liberal use of egg base is very popular. Their vegetable, meat, pulse and rice potpourri (dhanshakh) and fish stuffed with spice rolled in banana leaves (patrani machchi) are a rage.

Zoroastrian Festivals of India

The Zoroastrian, or Parsi, community is the smallest major religious group in India. They number about 100,000, and are concentrated overwhelmingly in Mumbai city and in the state of Gujarat. That is one reason why Parsi festivals are not highly visible. Another, and equally important, reason is that Parsi festivals are not accompanied by public ceremonies and attendant features like music and celebrations. The Zoroastrian religion is founded on the three tenets of 'Good thoughts, good words, good deeds.' The Zoroastrians are fastidious and meticulous where their religion is concerned, and their festivals are also structured to reflect the chief aims of Zoroastrianism. Take into account that the Parsis are a very close-knit group, and you have festivals that are celebrated almost strictly within the community, and confined to the homes, community centres and temples.

The Parsi calendar is divided into 12 months of equal length and five festal days. The five festal days are presided over by guardian angels. So are each of the other days of the year. So, loosely, every day of the year could be considered special. The Zoroastrian year has six seasons, and there is one major festival in each season - feasts known as Gahambars, that later got associated with religion. The Zoroastrian feasts are elaborate affairs. Festivals are ritual-oriented, and temple-worship, feasting and community interaction are central to them. So does munificence. Charity plays an important role in a Zoroastrian's life. During festivals or sacred days, the Zoroastrians are instructed to be especially generous and rededicate themselves to their pledge of justice and charity.

In traditional Zoroastrian society, celebrations are closely communal and, as a rule, non-Parsis are not allowed into their places of worship. Zoroastrian festivals occur during different months of the year, depending on the calendar that is followed. There are three different calendars, and three sects of Zoroastrians based on the calendar they follow. However, most of the Zoroastrians in India follow the Shehanshahi, or Parsi, calendar, not the Iranian (Kadimi) or the Fasli calendar. According to this, the New Year, Pateti, falls sometime in August. The Kadimi new year is not officially recognised in India, though the Fasli New Year, Jamshed-E-Navroz, is.

The other important Zoroastrian festivals are Khordad Sal, the birthday of Zarathushtra; Muktad, All Souls' Day; Zardosht, the day commemorating the death of Zarathushtra; and Adar roj nu Parab, the birthday of fire. There are also festivals in homage to justice, water, the rains and fertility. Besides, specific rites are prescribed for the special occasions of a Zoroastrian's life, like birth, initiation (Navjote, the sacred shirt and thread ceremony) marriage (lagan) and death. In a closed community like the Zoroastrians', whose celebrations don't spill over into the streets or even out of their homes and temples, it can be very difficult to know what their religion and festivals are like, except from a source. But if you can get access to a traditional Zoroastrian home, you could get one side of the picture first-hand.

The Manav Dharma Sabha

Mehtaji Durgaram Manchharam, Dadoba Panderung Tarkhad and a few others founded Manav Dharma Sabha on 22 June 1844 in Surat. This Sabha was one of the earliest socio-religious reform movements in Gujarat and British India. The goals of the Manav Dharma Sabha were to expose the deceitful arts present in Christian, Muslim and Hindu religions. Although the Manav Dharma Sabha had a very short life span and ceased to exist as Dadoba left for Bombay in 1846 and Durgaram left for Rajkot in 1852, it acted as a secret society and is believed that the revelation of its survival compounded to its downfall. The British resided in Surat since the second decade of the seventeenth century; however, it was not until the 1840s that tensions arose through the introduction of western education and missionary activities.

Commencing in 1820, the Bombay government started a school in Surat and another in Broach. Within a decade other schools were added all across the cities of Gujarat. Their program comprised of English texts and translated them into the vernaculars. The teaching staffs arrived from local communities, but were often educated in Bombay, as was illustrated by the life and career of Mehtaji Durgaram Manchharam (1809-78). He was a Nagar Brahman, born in Surat and trained in Bombay. In 1830 he achieved the post of a headmaster in a Government School in Surat, an institution founded in 1826. Four years later when the Surat English School was opened, Durgaram took the position of headmaster. Mehtaji Durgaram Manchharam became a leading figure among the small group of cultured Gujaratis who came together in the 1830s as critics of contemporary society.

The prominent participants in this group were Dinmani Shankar, Dadoba Panderung Tarkhad, Dalpatram Bhagubai and Damodar Das. Advocates of cultural and religious amend were incited to action by the conversion of a Parsi student, Nasarwanji Manakji, and the consequential uproar amidst the Parsi and Hindu communities. The Manav Dharma Sabha had only a short career as an active organization. It began to shatter in 1846 when Dadoba Panderung went back to Bombay, and almost stopped to function in 1852 when Durgaram Manchharam left for

Rajkot. Although the life of Manav Dharma Sabha was severely limited, it was directly linked to later developments in Maharashtra and Gujarat as its members carried with them the ideals of the movement and became leaders in parallel organizations.

The Manav Dharma Sabha appealed to the small, sophisticated elite of Surat and began as a reaction to Christian conversions. For a short period this society appeared to be the groundwork of an acculturative socio-religious movement with a philosophy that spoke of the need for noteworthy change. Its ideas and programme however did not have the ability to generate strong commitment on the part of its followers, commitment of satisfactory strength to directly confront the leadership and domination of recognized religion. In spite of the short life span of Manav Dharma Sabha, the ideas that came out from the discussions were passed on to two direct descendants, one of which was the Paramahansa Mandali of Maharashtra. The absence of the Manav Dharma Sabha did not wash away its teachings, because they were deeply instilled in the minds of the participants.

9

Singh Sabha Movement in Punjab

The Singh Sabha intended to restore Sikhism to its past purity by publishing historical religious books, magazines and journals, to propagate knowledge using Punjabi, to return Sikh apostates to their original faith, and to involve highly placed Englishmen in the educational programme of the Sikhs. After the Nirankari and Namdhari movements of 19th Century, a fresh century was about to be started with a new movement called Singh Sabha. Nirankari and Namdhari movements could not encourage the Sikh people to a considerate point and because of the limited scope and schismatic character they acquired. Once Sardar Harbans Singh said that the Singh Sabha that followed them, had a much deeper effect and it influenced the entire Sikh Community and reoriented its attitude and spirit. Ever since the emergence of the Gurus nothing so important event had taken the effort to nurture the consciousness of the Sikhs.

The Singh Sabha by leavening the intellectual and cultural processes brought a new way of outlook to the personal life of the community and thus its heritage. Starting in the seventies of the last century, it marked a turning point in the history of the Sikhs. The Singh Sabha touched Sikhism to its very roots, and revived the religion once again. The incentive it provided has shaped the Sikhs' attitude and ambition for more than past one hundred years. The people who helped to establish the Singh Sabha were Kanwar Bikram Singh of Kapurthala, Sir Khem Singh Bedi, Giani Gian Singh and Thakur Singh Sandhawalia. Sandhawalia became its president and Giani Gian Singh its secretary, when it was formed. An Executive Committee consisting of the president and secretary plus a few members directed the Singh Sabha.

As the Sabha expanded, new officers were appointed, a vice-president, assistant secretary, a giant (scholar of the Sikh scriptures), an updeshak or preacher, a treasurer and a librarian. They were elected each year and there was the provision of re-election. Members had to be Sikhs with a strong belief in the teachings of the gurus. The members paid a monthly subscription and were asked to oath themselves to serve the community and to be loyal to Sikhism till death. All the original members were baptized Sikhs, although no obligation for this was written into the constitution of the Sabha. They held a meeting every two weeks and also held anniversary celebrations. They arranged special meetings on festival days or in response to specific challenges by other religious groups. The Sabha soon began to issue records of its decisions and also kept records of its earnings and expenditures, and produced annual reports.

The cause behind the success of the Singh Sabha was the motivation to search for Sikh individuality and self-assertion that we are not just another part of Hinduism. Earlier, Hindu philosophers thought Sikhs to be another sect of Hinduism and 2500 years ago, same thing was applicable for Buddhism. In those days, Buddha was believed to be as the re-embodiment of Vishnu by Brahmins, thus ending Buddhism in India. Singh Sabha remembered this and started their campaign of development for pastoral Khalsa that eventually came under the direct threat of Christian Missionaries, Muslim Maulalivis and Arya Samajis. Khalsa's ethical force and dynamic energy was rediscovered and Singh Sabha was inspired by its history and tradition with clear and self-judicious eye.

Everything that went against Gurus teaching was discarded. Rites and customs were regarded as regular and steady with Sikh principles and traditions were established. For some, legal sanction was kept secured through government rule. With this came the restructuring of Sikh Shrines. Later in 1920's Sikh Historic Shrines like Golden Temple, Nankana Sahib, TarnTaran Sahib, Punja Sahib and others were freed from the hold of traditional Mahants. These mahants used to practice rites and ritual conflicting with Sikhism, such as not letting people of "lower caste" enter the Gurdwaras, publicly smoking, idol worshipping of various Gods and Goddesses, and holding Shraddhas and other rituals that were strictly forbidden by the Sikh Gurus.

This period of the Singh Sabhas also witnessed the modern development and emergence of new cultural and political aspirations. The Sikhs properly achieved higher level of literacy. Famous Khalsa College at Amritsar and hundreds of Khalsa Schools were established all across Punjab. Many Sikhs went outside India at this period and settled at Malaysia, Canada, U.K, Africa and USA. The first anniversary of the Lahore Singh Sabha was on April 22, 1905. Singh Sabha movement not only reformed the Sikh institutions of the customs and rites like casteism but also ensured that in future, these rituals would not come back into the society.

The Singh Sabha was an idiom of the impulse of the Sikh community to clear itself of the base adulterations and accretions, which were draining away its energy, and to revive the foundations of its actual inspiration. Unlike other Indian reform movements of the period that were the creation of the privileged class, the Singh Sabha was a mass expansion. The Singh Sabha represented the leaders of the Sikh community. It was united by members of the landed gentry, the aristocracy, and by various types of temple servants. The Sabha prepared a calendar that had listed the correct dates of the births and deaths of the ten gurus. They embarked on the creation of an ultimate text of the Dassam Granth; however, this task proved so difficult that a separate organization, the Gurmat Granth Pracharak Sabha was also founded to complete it. The Singh Sabha published numerous tracts and books and in 1894 organized the Khalsa Tract Society to make the Punjabis popular, the Gurmukhi script, and to issue monthly publishing on the Sikh religion. Soon the Singh Sabha of Amritsar was followed by new organizations that also proved to be competitors for leadership within the Sikh community.

Sikhism

The word 'Sikh' means a disciple. So Sikhism is essentially the path of discipleship. The true Sikh remains unattached to worldly things just as the lotus keeps its blossom over and above the surface of water. The Sikh must do his duty to his family and to the community. The main thing is leading a pure and moral life, full of noble deeds and kind words. A Sikh does not regard fasting, austerities, pilgrimages, alms-giving and penance as important things. Bhagti: Those who know the importance of Bhagti feel like Guru Nanak Sahib that forgetting God is just like death and brooding upon His Name is life and joy. Without the nectar of God's name, the polgrim dies his misery. But Bhagti is possible after certain conditions are fulfilled:

1. Faith in God.
2. Following Truth.
3. Unattachment and desirelessness.
4. Control over throught, word and deed.
5. Association with holy men(Satsang)
6. Humanity and submission to Hukam.

Salvation/Mukti

The Guru says, "The man of God rejects salvation. He wants only love of God and nothing else. The joys of heaven are nothing as compared to the merging in the Divine Spirit. The ultimate goal of man is union with God. Man does not become God, only the spark merges in the fire. This is called self-identification." A man may have done many noble deeds but if he has not undertaken meditation on God, he cannot have any hope of Mukti. Guru Nanak Sahib says in Asa-di-Var: "That is true knowledge when the thruth is in the heart, when the dirt of falsehood vanishes and life is pure and clean. That is true living when one fixes one's love on truth and finds joy in the hearing of the Name."

Need of Guru: Almost all the great religions of the world emphasis the need of a preceptor or Guru or holy man for the attainment of salvation. The Vedas enumerate the qualities of a religious guide. Even Guru Nanak Sahib empha-sises that bliss can be obtained only through the grace of the Guru. Sikhism does not recognise either chosen prophets or chosen people. Guru Nanak Sahib did not insist on a physical Guru (Dehdari}. His own Guru was God Himself. What is important is not the person but the word- "The word is the Guru. The Guru is the word. If the devotee follows what the word says, surely the Guru will save him." That is why Guru Gobind Singh Sahib installed Sri Granth Sahib as Guru for all time.

We do not need any man as Guru because the word is now with us. Guru Arjan Sahib says, "Without a Guru, liberation cannot be won. The Guru is my boat, which will ferry me across the rough ocean of existance." The Guru destroys illusions and attachment to worldly objects. Guru Ramdas Sahib says, "The Guru is the Sikh and the Sikh who practices the Guru's word is equal to the Guru." Guru Gobind Singh Sahib says, "I live and have my being in the Khalsa." The Guru lives in the form of the Panth. He resides in the Sangat. All the Gurus are identical with Nanak. Guru Gobind Singh Sahib passed on the corporal succession to the Panth, which is regarded as the embodiment of the Guru.

The Panth represents the Guru and it is progressing, With the passage of time, the Panth is evolving. It is a dynamic and corporate personality with authority to make decisions (Gurmatas) binding on the Sikhs. In this way, there is a two-fold concept of Guru-dom, one permanent, the other progressive. The Word is the embodiment of eternal and changless truth, while the Panth is the progressive, collective personality of the Guru in Sikhs. Guru Granth Sahib is the living embodiment of the Ten Gurus. It is the living flame of the Name, which lights the lamp of the disciple.

There is no place for a living Guru in the Sikh religion, because Gurbani is Guru and Guru is Gurbani. After all, what the Guru does is to guide the disciple by means of words, in the same way Guru Granth Sahib guides the Sikh through its song-message. When a Sikh is in doubt about any principle of Sikhism, he refers the matter to the Panth for decision.

Reading of Scriptures

Many good thoughts and noble sayings are found in sacred books but mere reading cannot help much. It is only the first step. Guru Nanak Sahib says:"If a man reads books throughout his whole life, till breath leaves his body, only the Holy Name is valuable, all else is vanity of the self." Again, "the scholar is an idiot if he has greed, avarice and pride." What is important is the practice of the Name and the cultivation of virtue.

An ounce of practice is preferable to a ton of knowledge. Ethics and laws tell us what to believe and what to do; they are like signposts. But one has to do the walking oneself. One cannot reach God by books or by rituals. Scriptures are our guides for action. They cannot fill the disciple with divine love. The knowledge of Vedas does not bring liberation: "God is beyond the Vedas, beyond the holy books." He can be found within the self by digging inward.

The Doctrine of Grace

Guru Nanak Sahib tells us that God has chosen him as a bride out of a large number. This is the reward for the qualities of the bride- humility, loyalty, sweet words-which have won for her the grace of the Lord. Surrender to God is the highest virtue of freedom. Just as a faithful wife gets the utmost pleasure in her complete surrender to her good husband, in the same way, the devotee gets supreme bliss by surrendering himself to God. Self-surrender to God means the absence of earthly cravings and desires.

Grace and Karma: The modification of Karma by grace is an essential principle of Sikhism. Guru Nanak Sahib says:

Karma is the cause of birth in this world,

But salvation can be obtained by His Grace.

Good actions win not only public approbation but also divine favour. God does not interfere with man's choice, though as the Ruler of the universe, he controls the over-all destiny of individuals.

Caste and Sikhism

Sikhism does not inculcate belief in caste. No man is born great or low. Guru Amardas says, "All colours and forms are thine." Guru Arjan Sahib gives the simile of the potter. The clay has been moulded in different forms. All men are the vessels of God. People may follow different faiths or divide themselves under different labels, but essentially man is one and indivisible. Whoever meditates on God becomes as great as He. Look at Ravidas the cobbler, Sadhna the butcher, Saina the barber. They were raised to the pedestal of saintliness and honoured by all. Just as the philosopher's stone transmutes iron ore into gold, in the same way God's name changes a low-born person into a Bhagat. God's name cleanses and purifies. It burns away all impurity.

A person of high caste is worse than one of the lowest caste if he does not meditate on the Name. Moreover, caste is of no consequence in the next world. In God's Court, men shall be judged by their thoughts and deeds, and not by their family or pedigree. The Guru brought the four castes under one banner. And yet he taught us to be humble and poor in spirit, because without it, we cannot sublimate egoism (humai).

Place of miracles

Saints and prophets should not perform miracles to confirm the faith of people in them. Miracles should not be worked to prove the greatness or truth of a religion. In fact, it is a hindrance in the spiritual path. Guru Amardas says, "The desire to perform miracles is a worldly attachment and is an obstacle in the way of the Name residing in our hearts." Guru Nanak Sahib had no taste for miracle. The greatest miracle was not to perform a miracle, inspite of his capacity to do so. He said:

If I exercise supernatural powers
And can create wealth at pleasure,
Can appear and disappear at will,
And thus win popular respect,
These delude fools only,
Who have no God in their hearts.

When the Sidhs asked Guru Nanak Sahib to show them a miracle, he replied that he would not do so: "Except the True Name, I have no miracle." Guru Arjan Sahib and Guru Teg Bahadur underwent tortures but refused to perform miracles. Men of God do not like to engage in such tricks. Guru Hargobind rebuked his son Baba Atal for exhibiting supernatural powers for which the latter had to pay with his own life.

Renunciation of the world

Leaving one's home and family and living away from people is not favoured in Sikhism. Guru Nanak Sahib remonstrated the Yogis and the. Sidhs who lived in lonely and deserted places. The mind does not get peace in physical solitude. He writes in Sidh-Gosht:

Even when one is far away from cities,
The mind wanders away in sleep;

Live by all means in society,

But covet not another man's wife,

Through His Name, one gets self-control.

The Gurus regarded married life {Grahsta} as the best mode of life. Escapism from the realities of life is not saintliness. The house-hold is a school where self-love is transformed into service of others and where the need to make an honest living leads to elevation of character.Guru Arjan Sahib says:

Renunciation of lust, anger, and attachment is praise-worthy.

Guru Gobind Singh Sahib described renunciation thus: "o my soul, practise renunciation in this way; consider your house as a forest and yourself as an ascetic in it. Let continence be your matted hair and communion with God your ablutions; instead of growing long nails pray daily; exert for acquiring divine knowledge ; instead of rubbing ashes on the body repeat His Name." Guru Nanak Sahib says, "He who fixes the mind on God's feet, who remains desireless amid desires and is in love with the True One, is a real Sanyasi" Such a man is neither depressed by sorrow and misfortune nor elated by joy. He accepts happiness and sorrow with the same spirit."

Pilgrimage

According to Sikh religion, pilgrimage confers no spiritual benefit. Guru Nanak Sahib says, "Pilgrimage does not have the value of even a mustard seed. At places of pilgrimage people take bath in holy rivers or tanks. But outward washing does not cleanse the mind. Guru Nanak Sahib says:

Why wash the body from outside?

Wash the mind,

Clean it of the dirt of desire, '

And tread the path of salvation

All Gurus have tried to remove the wrong notion of the efficacy of pilgrimage. Guru Nanak Sahib says, "I would like to go to pilgrimage only if it pleased Him." Again he says, "My places of pilgrimage are the Word, contemplation and divine knowledge within me."

Fasting

Sikhism does not regard tasting as an act of religious merit. Fasting, in order to overcome disease or abnormality, is perfectly Icghnitaic. But fasting a aii austerity and ritual is hateful. Guru Nanak Sahib says, "Penance, fasting, austerity, alms-giving are inferior to truth; right action is superior to them all." To affirm that spirituality depends on the quality or quantity of food is absurd. One must take normal food. If a man cannot take it, there is something wrong with him. But to fast for the sake of fasting is futile.

Maya

Maya has been defined in various ways. According to some, this world is Maya an illusion. According to Sikhism, the universe being the creation of the Supreme Being, is the temple of Divinity. It is as embodiment of His Eternal Truth. The world is subject to the Divine Will; it has no independent existence of its own. In that sense, it is unreal or illusory; it is subject to decay: ''The universe is insubstantial as a shadow, fleeting like a dream, short-lived as a bubble," as compared with the Creator, the Eternal Truth, The Guru writes:

In a thousand water'pots
There is one sky reflected,
When the water-pots burst,
The sky remains as before.

Man is caught with the infatuation of desire. This lure of worldliness makes him regard worldly things as the goal of human life.

The Concept of Education in Sikhism

Sikhism includes a comprehensive system of self-education. The function of education is to prepare the aesthetic and emotional background in which the individual may pet an opportunity for self-growth. Besides this, Dharma must inspire all the instruction and atmosphere in educational institutions. It is the knowledge of the Hand, the knowledge of the Head and the knowledge of the Heart. The education of the Hand means the realization of the dignity of labour and the readiness of the individual to earn his living with manual work. It also includes the service of humanity with the hand. Guru Nanak Sahib says:

Those who earn their living
By the sweat of their brows,
And give it to the needy
Are the people who know?
The path of Truth and Virtue.

Education does not imply the acquisition of powers to rule over others or to exploit their simplicity or backwardness for selfish ends.

Make knowledge your merchandise,
Truth the horses you take to sell,
Tie up virtues as your travelling expenses,
Think not in your heart of the morrow,
When you reach the land of your love,
You shall obtain endless joy.

Guru Nanak Sahib gave a practical demonstration of this system of education by training his successor Sri Guru Angad Sahib. It was the training of the disciple through discipline. Man is to merge with the higher self, with Beauty. Truth and Goodness. This makes education both creative and purposeful.

Union with God

The feeling of unity of the individual with the Universal on the psychic plane is called liv. The man of God does not renounce the world. He lives in it and performs all his duties as a householder. But he does not feel attached to worldly desire. The apparent attachment of the mind with the world is lost; the mind remains in constant communion with Divinity. Such a man meditates or does well naturally and automatically. In tune with the infinite, the individual soul feels no pain or sorrw.

Union of Soul with God

Guru Arjan Sahib has mentioned five aspects of the actual experience of the union of the individual soul with the Universal Soul. Firstly, the darkness of ignorance disappears and the individual realises the wonder of God's universe. Secondly, there is an inner illumination, a kind of revelation - enlightenment, not of the intellect but of mystic exaltation. Thirdly, the individual gains equipoise, a state of indefinable peace and confidence, coming from the loss of the ego. This sense of tranquillity-shanti-is due to the identification of the self with Divinity. Fourthly, the individual begins to love the entire humanity and is filled with a great longing for the service of his fellow-men. Fifthly, the individual realises everything as emanating from God. His soul which had emanated from God is united with the Ultimate Source.

The True Yogi

A true yogi is not one who leaves his family and home, and wanders all over the country. A true yogi finds renunciation in the house itself. He does not regard llie house as his own but of the Lord, He renounces egoism. The true yogi is a friend of all: he is a servant of servants. He fixes his mind on Goit and remains desireless in the world.'" He remains indifferent to sorrow and happiness. He is free from cares, because he loves the only one God.

Guru Nanak Sahib rebuked the yogis for going to the houses of laity for begging. He denounced parasitism and recommended renunciation of desire and attachment in the midst of temporal life through the discipline of the Name.

The Concept of Woman

The Gurus held woman in high esteem. So with the rise of Sikhism, woman gained in dignity and social position. Some ancient scriptures denounced woman as unworthy of teaching or religious exercises. Woman was regarded as evil and unclean. Guru Nanak Sahib challenged this view: Why should we treat woman with contempt and cruelty? A woman is not to be condemned on the ground of her sex. Guru Granth Sahib says:

Of a woman we are conceived,

Of a woman we are born,

To a woman we are betrothed and married,

It is a woman who is a friend and partner of life,

It is a woman who keeps the race going,

Why should we consider women cursed and condemned,

When from woman are born leaders and rulers. (Rag Asa, I)

Religious gatherings and Kirtan were thrown open to women; they could participate on equal terms with men in temporal and secular observances. Bhai Gurdas ji, the veteran Sikh theologian affirmed: "Woman is man's other half, and as such, helps him in attaining to salvation." Guru Hargobind Sahib called woman "the conscience of man." Khande di Pahul (Amrit) is obligatory both for man and woman. The rules of conduct and the sphere of religious duties are identical both for man and woman. In religious meetings, men and women sing and lecture like equals. Guru Amardas Sahib condemned the practice of widow-burning (Sati): He said, "They are not satis who burn themselves with the dead bodies of their husbands. Those are real Satis who die of the mere shock of separation from their husbands." Thus the equality of sexes is emphasised in Sikhism.

Sikhism Twentieth Century Developments

The existence of the Khalsa creates a potential division within the Sikh community between those who have undergone the baptism ceremony and those who practice the system laid down in the *Guru Granth Sahib* but who do not adopt the distinctive life-style of the Khalsa. Among the latter is a sect of believers founded by Baba Dayal (d. 1853) named the Nirankaris, who concentrate on the formless quality of God and his revelation purely through the guru and the *Guru Granth Sahib*, and who accept the existence of a living, enlightened teacher as essential for spiritual development. The dominant tendency among the Sikhs since the late nineteenth century has been to stress the importance of the Khalsa and its outward signs.

Revivalist movements of the late nineteenth century centered on the activities of the Singh Sabha (Assembly of Lions), who successfully moved much of the Sikh community toward their own ritual systems and away from Hindu customs, and culminated in the Akali (eternal) mass movement in the 1920s to take control of *gurdwaras* away from Hindu managers and invest it in an organization representing the Sikhs. The result was passage of the Sikh Gurdwara Act of 1925, which established the Central Gurdwara Management Committee to manage all Sikh shrines in Punjab, Haryana, and Himachal Pradesh through an assembly of elected Sikhs. The combined revenues of hundreds of shrines, which collected regular contributions and income from endowments, gave the committee a large operating budget and considerable authority over the religious life of the community.

A simultaneous process led to the Akali Dal (Eternal Party), a political organization that originally coordinated nonviolent agitations to gain control over *gurdwaras*, then participated in the independence struggle, and since 1947 has competed for control over the Punjab state government. The ideology of the Akali Dal is simple—single-minded devotion to the guru and preservation of the Sikh faith through political power—and the party has served to mobilize a majority of Sikhs in Punjab around issues that stress Sikh separatism. There is no official priesthood within Sikhism or any widely accepted institutional mechanism for policy making for the entire faith. Instead, decisions are made by communities of believers (*sangat*) based on the *Guru Granth Sahib* —a tradition dating back to the eighteenth century when scattered bodies of believers had to fight against persecution and manage their own affairs.

Anyone may study the scriptures intensively and become a "knower" (*giani*) who is recognized by fellow believers, and there is a variety of training institutes with full-time students and teachers. Leaders of sects and sectarian training institutions may feel free to issue their own orders. When these orders are combined with the prestige and power of the Central Gurdwara Management Committee and the Akali Dal, which have explicitly narrow administrative goals and are often faction-ridden, a mixture of images and authority emerges that often leaves the religion as a whole without clear leadership.

Thus it became possible for Sant Jarnail Singh Bhindranwale, head of a training institution, to stand forth as a leading authority on the direction of Sikhism; initiate reforms of personal morality; participate in the persecution of Nirankaris; and take effective control of the holiest Sikh shrine, the Golden Temple in Amritsar, Punjab, in the early 1980s. His takeover of the Golden Temple led to a violent siege and culminated in the devastation of the shrine by the army in 1984. Later terrorist activities in Punjab, carried out in the name of Sikhism, were performed by a wide range of organizations claiming to represent an authoritative vision of the nature and direction of the community as a whole.

Sikhism in India

About 2% of India's populations are Sikhs. Even so, the Sikhs, because of their unique appearance sometimes stand for India. Traditionally the men keep their hair and do not shave their beard or moustache. They gather their head hair in a turban. Sikhism is comparatively a new religion in India. This religion was established by Guru Nanak. Nanak was born into a Hindu family in 1469 in the Punjab region. Since childhood he loved to travel, learn and preach humanity. In those days people who taught and preached were titled Guru meaning teacher, his followers became to be known as Sikhs meaning learners.

And so Guru Nanak developed a new religion and it also included beliefs from the two dominant religions in the Punjab region, Hinduism and Islam. Some claim that Guru Nanak tried to developed a new religion and included in it what he thought were the good beliefs of these two religions. Like in Islam the belief in the existence of one invisible God. Like in Hinduism the belief in Karma and reincarnation, meaning your actions in this life will decide your fate in the next incarnation. The Sikhs also cremate their dead ones as is done in Hinduism. The creators of Sikhism tried to abolish some of the Indian customs such as the caste system and Sati - burning of the widow. In Sikhism everyone has equal rights irrespective of caste, creed, color, race, sex or religion. Sikhism rejects pilgrimage, fasting, superstitions and other such rituals. Sikhism does not have a clergy class as it considers this as a gateway to corruption. However they have readers and singers in their temples.

A Sikh place of worship is called Gurdwara. Sikhism does not support pilgrimage to holy sites because according to Sikhism, God is everywhere and not in any certain place. But Sikhism has a few important sites, of which, the Hari Mandir, also known as the 'Golden Temple' in Amritsar in Punjab is the most important site and is considered the holiest shrine of Sikhism. Sikhism emphasis community services and helping the needy. One of the distinct features of Sikhism is the common kitchen called Langar. In every Gurdwara there is a Langar. Every Sikh is supposed to contribute in preparing the meals in the free kitchen. The meals are served to all and are eaten sitting on the floor and this is to emphasis the point that all are equals.

Sikhism does not believe in holding fasts for body is God's present to human being and therefore humans must foster, maintain and preserve it in good sound condition, unless fasting is done to foster the human body like healthy diets. Guru Nanak who established Sikhism was its first Guru. After him there were nine more Gurus who were the highest religious authority. The last Guru, Guru Gobind Singh, proclaimed that after him the Guru of the Sikhs would be the holy book of Sikhism, Guru Granth Sahib. Guru Granth Sahib is written in Gurumukhi script. It includes the writings of the Sikh Gurus and the writings of Hindu and Muslims saints. But out of humility Guru Gobind Singh did not include his own writings in the book he had proclaimed as the permanent Guru of the Sikhs. His writings appear in a separate book called Dasam Granth.

Guru Gobind Singh is also the Guru behind the unique appearance of Sikh men. During Guru Gobind's term as the Guru of the Sikhs and also before him, the ruling empire of Punjab region was the Moghul Empire. The Moghuls were Muslims. Some of the Moghul emperors, like Aurangazeb were fanatic Muslims who harassed the non- Muslims, including the Sikhs. Some of the Sikh Gurus were even executed by the Moghul emperors. In order to stop their persecutions, Guru Gobind decided to make his followers, the Sikhs (meaning learners), a community of fighters. He changed his surname to Singh, which means lion.

His followers also changed their surname to Singh. Since then a ceremony of baptizing was established among the Sikhs in which the boys were given the title Singh and the girls were titled Kaur meaning princess. In those days

"Singh" as a surname was very popular among a famous warrior caste of north India, the Rajputs. Some of the first Sikhs were also Rajputs. In order to make it easier for his followers to recognize each other, Gobind Singh, chose five marks, some of which even today symbolize the Sikhs. The five signs were, uncut hair; comb; sword or dagger; bracelet on the right wrist and shorts.

The religious Sikhs dress according to Guru Gobind Singh's order, carrying a sword. Most of the Sikhs even today have uncut hair and gather it in a turban. But some easygoing Sikhs cut their hair or they do not gather their uncut hair in a turban. The emphasis on militant tradition and community service in Sikhism continues even today and many Sikhs serve in the Indian army or police. The Sikhs also have a reputation as experts in steering, from cars to airplanes.They were among the first communities in India who dared to drive vehicles specially Lorries. India being a vast country needed drivers who could also travel at nights. But many Indians believed in superstitions like ghosts and haunted places, while the Sikhs rejected these kinds of beliefs and therefore traveled at nights, since then their reputation as steering masters of India.

10

Christianity in India

Christianity in India is progressively partaking of Indian beliefs and customs, even meditation systems. The doorway of the suburban Mumbai flat, in the southern part of India, is festooned with flowers. Strains of religious songs waft out from within. Some 30 women sit cross-legged on the floor facing a silk sari-clad, flower-covered stone idol. Implements for a traditional Indian puja (prayer ritual), including prasad (food offerings to the deity, in this case plates of fruits) sit on either side. Typically Indian, right? Wrong. For the gathered devotees, this is just another way of celebrating the feast of Mother Mary. Its prime mover Anjali Aranha feels that she is only expressing her conviction that she is a Hindu by culture and a Christian by belief. "I am taking back what is mine. Being Hindu is not opposed to being Christian," says she. A minuscule movement is transforming Indian Christianity.

One that sees Hinduism and Christianity in sync with each other, thereby disentangling the confused strands of identity that make an Indian Christian. "Hinduism helped me become a better Christian," says Eric Pinto, "I found it hard to believe in a vengeful Biblical God who made the universe in six days and rested on the seventh. Learning yoga made me understand that all universal laws operate through God. That made sense." But where does Indianness end and Christianity begin? Are Christians betraying their faith by practicing yoga? What is the exact nature of the sin committed by accepting prasad? The questions compel us to inquire into the nature of faith and nationality.

The Indian Way

For a faith that emphasizes the need for belief, these are radical questions. Yet more Indian Christians are looking to ford the twin halves of their identity. Some institutions, such as the Fr Agnel ashram in Pune, India, will not ordain priests unless they take a Vipassana course. Most Indian seminaries even have courses on Indian philosophy. In many Christian ashrams in India today, you may encounter a vegetarian kitchen, Sanskrit verses, even meditation and yoga. Some ashrams follow Indian architecture. Some present Biblical stories through Indian dance and music. Many Christians adopt Indian names.

The term for this trend is inculturation, and it is primarily happening within the westernized segment of the Catholic Church in India. Inculturation is inspired by the enlightened edict of the Second Vatican Council, 1962-65. In essence, the Vatican recognized the validity of other faiths and directed local churches to align themselves to prevailing cultures. To quote: "All nations form one human family; all of them are guided by the one God, all of them have the same destiny... The church exhorts Christians to preserve and promote the moral and spiritual goods found among the people."

Ironically, inculturation was the basic nature of Indian Christianity long before the West entered. Christianity here is believed to have been introduced in AD 52. This is when Thomas the Apostle came to Malankara, Kerala (a southern Indian State). Thomas converted many caste Hindus and established a church that, in every way save religious, was Indian. Belief in the divinity of Jesus went hand in hand with belief in karma, reincarnation, lighting of lamps and distribution of prasad. Clearly, the early Indian Christians made a distinction between religion and culture. When the Portuguese came to Kerala in the 16th century, they gave Christianity a western orientation. In 1599, they eliminated Indian elements and introduced the Latin rites of Roman Catholicism even though not all Kerala Christians chose to give allegiance to the Pope.

In Goa too the Portuguese influenced the people's cultural moorings. This trend towards fusing religion and culture was reinforced by the British, who brought with them the Anglican Church, to which the Churches of North and South India are aligned. However, there were protests. As far back as in the 19th century, Brahmanbandhab Upadhyay, a passionate Brahmin convert and freedom fighter, wrote that the Christian's faith was "too... mixed up with beef and pork, spoon and fork, too tightly panta-looned and petticoated to manifest its universality".

In many ways, inculturation is a profound pheno-menon. It reflects the willingness within even the highest echelons of church authority to re-examine the truisms of the Christian creed. The clergy, at least, accept that it is old-fashioned to insist that salvation lies only through Christ. Naturally, there is no longer a compulsive need to convert. Says Fr Thomas Malipurathu, director of a Catholic center of mission and missionary work: "Evangelizing has a wider meaning than conversion. It should be a means to translate into reality what Jesus meant by the kingdom of God."

Why this hue and cry over conversions then? The answer lies in the pluralistic nature of Indian Christianity. Even as mainstream Catholic churches are pulling back, Indian Christianity is being influenced by the Pentecostal believers who originated in the USA. Going under names such as Born Again Christians, they practice a form of Christianity that identifies knowledge of God solely within the Biblical context. In contrast, inculturation focuses the discourse within the Christian body, not outside it.

The Way It Works

Fr Hillary Fernandes of the Bombay diocese in Mumbai has done trailblazing work in inculturation. Among his novel reforms was the translation of the worship from Latin to Marathi. He celebrates major Indian festivals with a Mass, of course Indianized. Dressed in Indian clothes, this modest priest says: "Christianity has remained foreign for 2,000 years. But spirituality can never be foreign. Because of the religion's identification with a foreign culture, its spirituality has been rejected." Fr Anthony de Mello, a Jesuit priest, was among the front-runners of inculturation.

Through one of his first published works Sadhana (Contemplation), he helped several Christians realize that Indian forms of contemplation were not only compatible with Christianity, but also complementary. Integration is clearly one of the key benefits of inculturation, for it gives Christians a sanction to discover their Indian roots. Says Fr Michael Rosario, who teaches Indology at St Pius: "As an Indian priest, Indian spirituality is my heritage and culture." Fr Michael Gonsalves goes a step further: "We must substitute the Old Testament of the Bible with Indian history, scriptures and arts. For us, the Holy Land should be India; the sacred river the Ganges; the sacred mountain the Himalayas, the heroes of the past not Moses, or David, but Sri Ram or Krishna."

Crucial to inculturation is the language. Says Fr Fernandes: "You cannot inculturate in English. The language is important to access your culture." In the Vasai diocese in the southern state of Maharashtra, India, weddings are conducted the Indian way. A church proclaims its name in Marathi, the Maharashtrian language. Credit for this peaceful integration goes to Archbishop Roberts of Mumbai, who opened a number of Marathi-medium schools in all the parishes of Vasai 60-70 years ago. The bishop of Vasai, Thomas Dabre, tells me, "There is no alternative to inculturation. Christians must live in accordance with the culture of the local people."

Return to Self

Inculturation strikes a strong chord among its votaries. Many look for ways to relate Christian and Hindu concepts. Fr Lancy Perreira, rector of St Xavier's Institute of Education, has authored a book that traces the spirituality inherent in Christianity, Indian music and science, his three passions. He sees no contradiction between being an Indian and a Christian. "For me," he says, "Christianity is first and foremost a way of life. Through Jesus, I am open to everything that is human." Fr Perreira echoes the thoughts of many others when he says that Christ was a Jew of his time and we are Indians of our time.

Others emphasize Christianity's Asian origin. Says Vandana Mataji, a Parsi-turned-nun who heads Jiva Dhara, an ashram in Rishikesh, at the foothills of the Himalayas in northern India: "Jesus was an Asian. We have no right to live, think and pray like western Christians." Through inculturation, the Indian Christians, so far torn between religion and nationality, are clearly being helped to clarify their identities as Christians and Indians, and to fuse the two without betraying either.

Towards Integration

In looking for integration, many question what it means to be a Christian. Many realize that, essentially, being a Christian has little to do with creed and all to do with remaining faithful to the teachings of Jesus Christ. Fr Saldanha sees this as "loving God and one's neighbor and striving to live in union with Christ". Such a definition eliminates all conflict between nationality and religion. When you love your neighbor in the true Christian sense, you cannot withhold her/his right to live or worship her/his way. Few have carried this examination to as rigorous lengths as Russian writer and mystic Leo Tolstoy. In his *The Kingdom of God and Peace Essays*, he repudiates the entire superstructure of western civilization as being incompatible with the teachings of Christ. Using Christ's injunction to resist not evil, he points out the incongruity of Christian nations with military institutions or law courts.

He says: "Christianity, in its true sense, puts an end to the State." Arguing against the association of Christ with Christianity, he says: "In our time it has reached its logical climax... in a demand for blind belief, not in God or in Christ, or even in the teaching, but in a person (as in Catholicism) or in several persons (as in the Orthodox Greek faith) or in a book (as in Protestantism). So... a man no longer believes in God or in Christ as they have been revealed to him, but in what the Church commands him to believe in." This insistence on belief as opposed to experience is perhaps the greatest limitation of the way Christianity has been interpreted. Christ himself was totally opposed to organized religion. He had thrown the moneychangers out of the temple.

There are other anomalies too—inability to blend with other faiths, exclusivity and sectarianism. Even in India, many find themselves squirming under questions raised by Christianity. Siddhartha, a Buddhist, was born a Syrian Christian. Christened George Kurien, he was uncomfortable with the exclusive aspects of Christianity. Says he: "Christianity is scared of losing itself if it gets into a close dialogue with Hinduism and Buddhism." The externalization of faith makes Christians unable to plumb into the living center of all religions, where alone lies synthesis.

Christ Forever

And yet, almost all the people interviewed for this article remain ardent Christians. What draws them to the faith? Vandana Mataji speaks for many: "I fell in love with Jesus Christ. I became a Christian because I found him fantastic." At the living heart of the faith is the person of Jesus Christ—a towering figure of love, compassion, and wisdom. How does one remain unmoved by his preference for the poor, the prostitute and the publican? How to remain unchanged by his injunction to love the other enough to turn the other cheek?

Writes Tolstoy: "The Christian teaching consists in indicating to man that the essence of his soul is love, that his happiness comes not because he loves this or that man but because he loves the source of all, God, whom he recognizes in himself through love, and so this love will extend to all men and also all things." Those who take the trouble to struggle out of the conventional truisms of Christianity and discover its spiritual core, which Tolstoy calls "progress along the appointed path towards inward perfection by an imitation of Christ, and towards outward perfection by establishment of the kingdom of God" become much more tolerant. Says Fr Fernandes: "There is only one God. Let us have worship where we can all come together."

The Road Ahead

If inculturation reaches its logical conclusion, what kind of Christianity can we expect? Upadhyay had long postulated Christianity, where "Christian truths" are "formulated through Vedantic (ancient Indian scriptures) thought". Adds Raimondu Pannicker, author of *A Dwelling Place for Wisdom*: "If we as Christians... could succeed in undergoing the Advaitic experience... then Christians, at least of Indian origin, would be automatically enabled to live an advaitic-Christian faith, which makes possible both a fully Hindu and a fully Christian life—without the pain of a split personality."

Advaitic Christianity sounds rather good. When Christianity can become one more Indian sect, such as Jainism or Sikhism, seeking union with God through Jesus Christ, yet with an undisturbed fidelity to the cultures and lifestyle of the land, inculturation will have completed its task. But inculturation is still to penetrate the masses. Says Fr Gonsalves: "The European missionaries in the past have instilled an aversion in the minds of the Indian Christian to whatever smacks of Hinduism." Brought up to believe that salvation lies solely within the church and to think otherwise is blasphemy, it is not easy for Christians to shed the conditioning of a lifetime.

Another factor inhibiting this delicate process of expansion is the aggressive anti-Christian stand adopted by fundamental Hindu organizations. Inculturation will integrate Christianity within the Indian ethos, but it must be allowed to happen in its own pace. Changes are occurring—slowly but surely. Much of the West itself has already penetrated the value of Indian spirituality. It won't be long before Indian Christians do likewise and take back their own heritage with pleasure and gratitude.

Christian Ashrams

Nowhere is the impact of inculturation more evident than in India's 50-odd Christian ashrams. A pioneer here is Bede Griffiths, a British Benedictine monk who recognized the profundity of Indian philosophy and pursued its integration with Christianity. Along with another monk, he set up the Kurusumala ashram in Kerala before taking over the Shantivanam ashram in Tamil Nadu. Shantivanam was started by two French priests who adopted Indian names, wore saffron, and lived spartan lives. Under Griffith, the ashram became a melting pot of Hindu and Christian thought with emphasis on contemplation.

A three-headed figure at the entrance represents the trinity of both Hinduism and Christianity. Then comes the cross, enclosed in the wheel of dharma (Buddhist spiritual symbol). At the center of the cross is the sacred Hindu word Om and it rests on a lotus. The liturgy is Indian. Other well-known Christian ashrams in India are the Jiva Dhara at Rishikesh run by Vandana Mataji, the Anjali ashram at Mysore, run by Fr Amolorpavdas, and the 'Christa Prema Seva' started by Jack Winslow, a Protestant, in Pune.

In Jive Dhara, Ashramites wake up at 4 a.m., practice yoga and meditation, and stick to a vegetarian diet. The routine even includes noble silence. On my visit to the Christa Prema ashram, I find it undergoing a change of guard. In the dining room with seats on the floor, a Sanskrit sloka hangs framed on the wall. In one of the two chapels (one set in the garden), straw matting covers the ground. A lamp burns before pictures of Christ. There are flowers by the lamp. Instead of the distant sense of awe that most altars convey, this arrangement makes God seem approachable. I find myself deeply satisfied, for here is a form of worship I can relate to. "It's a deeply human place," says Sr Brigitta, the outgoing head. I couldn't agree more.

Authentic Indian religion or a Western import? Christianity came to India in two main periods: the first century missionary activity of Thomas, the disciple of Jesus, and the Western missionary activity from 1500 to 1975. Today there are about 27 million Christians in India, nearly the total population of Canada. This large community represents less than three percent of the total population of India. Missionaries came to India in response to famine and poverty.

People who came to faith were frequently put out of their own communities with no place to go but to the mission. Many children were orphaned by famine and they also became dependent on the mission. One mission in the 1930s reported that 80 percent of their converts were financially dependent on the mission. These factors removed the converts from their own culture. They became strangers in their own land. These new Christians were perceived as giving allegiance to a foreign land and culture. A pastor related that a tribal person came to him and said, "I have cut my hair and put on long trousers. What else do I have to do to be a Christian?"

Indian Christians in Society

India, which is 83 percent Hindu, is a country of minorities, with 180 million Muslims, 70 million tribal people, 60 million Sikhs and uncounted millions of others. Each of these groups represents a potential voting block in India's democracy. However, Christians are not in significant numbers to be catered to by the national politicians. Christians in India are discriminated against in certain government programs. The government has a program of reservations for jobs and university education. This program gives preference to people of the lower castes and those below caste. To qualify for these benefits, applicants must state their caste origin. Christians, having denounced caste, are unable to do this. Yet many Christians come from the very groups for whom these programs were devised. This represents a major loss to these people struggling for education and jobs.

Government jobs are widely sought and highly valued. The perception of many Christians is that they do not have an equal opportunity for these jobs and subsequent promotions. On the other hand, some Christians benefit by being perceived as more honest, resulting in more rapid promotions. Despite minority status, Christians are seen as leaders in medical care and education. This reflects the emphasis of many foreign missions. There are disproportionately more Christian doctors and nurses compared to the general population. It is estimated that more than 30 percent of the nurses in India are Christian. The quality of medical care and education in Christian institutions is believed to be higher than that available through government institutions.

Indians concede that the conditions for Christians in the south differ from the north. Christians in the north go about their business quietly. The programs of some churches appear to be aimed at survival more than an open involvement in the larger community. One church leader in the south said, "To be Christian in the north means Western clothes, speaking English and eating beef. In the south Christians are part of the fabric of society. We have always been here." Christians in southern India date their origins back to the landing of Thomas on their shores. Thomas established churches throughout southern India. Catholic missionaries came in 1505 with Vasco de Gama and instituted changes including penance, prayers for the dead and the confessional. Two hundred years later church leaders became aware of their history though the help of British missionaries.

Subsequently a reform movement started from within the church. These reforms represent a return to the original tenets of the church prior to 1600. Southern Christians have a strong sense of continuity from the first century to the present. Their liturgy is 2000 years old. Members are happy to be known as part of the church. There is a strong lay movement. Since government workers are required to retire at age 55, an impressive amount of social work is done by lay members of the church. The church in India is a mosaic of places where the church is thriving and places where it is merely suviving. Christians face the future with caution of persecution, and hope in a loving God.

The First Christians in India

The first Christians in India, according to tradition and legend, were converted by Saint Thomas the Apostle, who arrived on the Malabar Coast of India in A.D. 52. After evangelizing and performing miracles in Kerala and Tamil Nadu, he is believed to have been martyred in Madras and buried on the site of San Thom Cathedral. Members of the Syro-Malabar Church, an eastern rite of the Roman Catholic Church, adopted the Syriac liturgy dating from fourth century Antioch. They practiced what is also known as the Malabar rite until the arrival of the Portuguese in the late fifteenth century.

Soon thereafter, the Portuguese attempted to latinize the Malabar rite, an action which, by the mid-sixteenth century, led to charges of heresy against the Syro-Malabar Church and a lengthy round of political machinations. By the middle of the next century, a schism occurred when the adherents of the Malankar rite (or Syro-Malankara Church) broke away from the Syro-Malabar Church.

Fragmentation continued within the Syro-Malabar Church up through the early twentieth century when a large contingent left to join the Nestorian Church, which had had its own roots in India since the sixth or seventh century. By 1887, however, the leaders of the Syro-Malabar Church had reconciled with Rome, which formally recognized the legitimacy of the Malabar rite.

The Syro-Malankara Church was reconciled with Rome in 1930 and, while retaining the Syriac liturgy, adopted the Malayalam language instead of the ancient Syriac language. Throughout this period, foreign missionaries made numerous converts to Christianity. Early Roman Catholic missionaries, particularly the Portuguese, led by the Jesuit Saint Francis Xavier (1506-52), expanded from their bases on the west coast making many converts, especially among lower castes and outcastes. The miraculously undecayed body of Saint Francis Xavier is still on public view in a glass coffin at the Basilica of Bom Jesus in Goa. Beginning in the eighteenth century, Protestant missionaries began to work throughout India, leading to the growth of Christian communities of many varieties.

The total number of Christians in India according to the 1991 census was 19.6 million, or 2.3 percent of the population. About 13.8 million of these Christians were Roman Catholics, including 300,000 members of the Syro-Malankara Church. The remainders of Roman Catholics were under the Catholic Bishops' Conference of India. In January 1993, after centuries of self-government, the 3.5-million-strong Latin-rite Syro-Malabar Church was raised to archepiscopate status as part of the Roman Catholic Church. In total, there were nineteen archbishops, 103 bishops, and about 15,000 priests in India in 1995.

Most Protestant denominations are represented in India, the result of missionary activities throughout the country, starting with the onset of British rule. Most denominations, however, are almost exclusively staffed by Indians, and the role of foreign missionaries is limited. The largest Protestant denomination in the country is the Church of South India, since 1947 a union of Presbyterian, Reformed, Congregational, Methodist, and Anglican congregations with approximately 2.2 million members. A similar Church of North India has 1 million members. There are 473,000 Methodists, 425,000 Baptists, and about 1.3 million Lutherans. Orthodox churches of the Malankara and Malabar rites total 2 million and 700,000 members, respectively.

All Christian churches have found the most fertile ground for expansion among Dalits, Scheduled Castes, and Scheduled Tribe groups. During the twentieth century, the fastest growing Christian communities have been located in the northeast, among the Khasis, Mizos, Nagas, and other hill tribes. Christianity offers a non-Hindu mode of acculturation during a period when the state and modern economy have been radically transforming the life-styles of the hill peoples. Missionaries have led the way in the development of written languages and literature for many tribal groups. Christian churches have provided a focus for unity among different ethnic groups and have brought with them a variety of charitable services.

The exact date of the arrival of Christianity to India is not established. By tradition, Christianity is said to have arrived in South India with the arrival of St. Thomas, one of the apostles of Jesus Christ, at the Malabar Coast in 52 AD. He spent some years in South India and died near Madras. However, others believe that the first missionary to arrive in the country was Saint Bartholomew. Historically, Christian missionary activity started with the advent of St. Francis Xavier in 1544 AD, who was followed by other missionaries from Portugal, Denmark, Holland, Germany and Great Britain. Throughout the 18th and 19th centuries Catholic as well as Protestant missionaries preached Christian doctrines in India and also made important contributions to social improvement and education in India.

The great period of expansion of Christianity in India began in 1858, when the British government took over rule in India from the East India Company. Christians from many countries came as missionaries and in 50 years the faith was rooted in large parts of India. Christians, numbering about 30 million, comprise 2.34% of the Indian population. Most of them are concentrated in the Northeast and in Kerala and other southern states, although they are scattered all across India. Today, there are 23 dioceses in India with 11 of them being located in Kerala.

The Syrian Church

The Christians belonging to the Syrian Church are found in South India and claim an apostolic foundation for their Church. They believe that Christianity was introduced in India by St. Thomas, who arrived in Cranganore at the Malabar Coast in 52 AD. St. Thomas established seven Christian communities or churches in Kerala at Cranganore, Paravur (Kottakavu), Palayoor, Kokkamangalam, Malayattoor, Niranam, Chayal (Nilackal) and Kollam (Quilon). He was followed by a group of Christian immigrants from Persia, led by Thomas Cananaus, who arrived on the Malabar Coast in 345 AD.

The earliest historical evidence regarding the existence of a Church in South India is found in the book *Christian Topography* written by an Alexandrian merchant Cosmas Indicopleustes, which is dated at the second quarter of the 6th Century AD. Persian crosses ("Thomas Crosses") discovered in Madras and Kottayam point towards the existence of a connection of the Malabar Church with the Church in Persia, which eventually came to be known as the *East Syrian or Nestorian Church* and was visited by Marco Polo in 1293 AD.

After briefly paying obedience to the Roman Church, under the influence of Alexio de Menezes, the Archbishop of Goa in 1599 AD, the Malabar Church renounced the authority of the Pope and asserted its independence in 1653 AD. This is known in history as the 'Coonen Cross Declaration'. The Christian communities then split into many groups - East Syrian Catholics, West Syrian Catholics, Syrian Orthodox, Jacobite Syrian Orthodox, Marthoma (those who accepted the Anglican Church but with the Eastern Liturgy), Church of the East (those who accepted the Nestorian Patriarch) and the Latin Church. In 1887 Pope Leo XIII issued the bull of "Quod Jam Pridem", which liberated the Syrian Christians from the jurisdiction of the Latin prelate of Verapoly and placed them under two Eparchies - one in Trichur and the other in Kottayam in Kerala. More recently, on January 23, 1993, a papal declaration again upgraded Ernakulam to major Arch Episcopal Church with the title of *Ernakulam Angamaly*.

The Roman Catholic Church

The arrival of Vasco da Gama in Calicut in 1498 AD is a landmark in the history of Church in India. With the arrival of the Portuguese to India, the visits of Roman Catholic Missions to India became more organised, and were initially concentrated to Goa, Cochin, Tuticorin and other coastal areas. St. Francis Xavier (1506-52 AD) became the first Jesuit missionary to arrive in India. He was followed by Robert de Nobili (1577-1656 AD). Christianity was spread in the sixteenth and the seventeenth centuries under the auspices of the *Society of Jesus*. After the Portuguese retreated from the Indian political scene, many other missionaries like the Franciscans, the Dominicans, the Augustinians and the Carmelites began their visits.

The Franciscans, who were the first to come to India in 1517 AD, chose Dom John de Albuquerque (1537-53 AD) as the first bishop of Goa. In 1557 AD, Pope Paul IV declared Goa an archdiocese with its supremacy extending from the Cape of Good Hope at the southern tip of Africa to China, and all Christians, including the East Syrian Church, brought under its jurisdiction.

The Protestant Missions

The first Protestant missionaries, German Lutherans, came to India in 1706 AD at Tranquebar, near Tiruchinapally, under the protection of the King of Denmark. By the 19th century several other missions were established in different parts of South India.

The North Indian Church

The origin of Christianity in North India is a matter of conjecture. Some consider that St. Thomas had travelled to North India and introduced Christianity. Others consider it to be the influence of merchants from the Persian Gulf and the Arabian Sea. Marco Polo describes the existence of Christian kingdoms in Central India during the end of 13th century. Under the influence of the Portuguese, several missionaries began to visit North India between 16th-18th Centuries. The Jesuit missions were sent regularly to the Mughal Courts from the time of Akbar to that of Aurangzeb, but it became weaker thereafter due to the decline of the Portuguese influence in India.

The arrival of William Carey in 1793 AD changed the entire dimension of missionary work in India. Carey's pioneering work in Bible translation, primary education and journalism had a profound influence in Bengal and other parts of India. Numerous other missionaries began visiting India after the passing of Charter Acts by the British Parliament in 1813 and 1833 AD. These missions set up several colleges and educational institutions in India.

11

Buddhism in Modern India

"Sometime during the sixth century BC a solitary, wandering ascetic sat to meditate beneath a shady tree, resolving not to rise until he had attained the ultimate knowledge of spiritual enlightenment. Thus began Buddhism, one of the world's great religions and pilgrimage traditions." It began with the life of Siddhartha Gautama (ca. 563-483 B.C.), a prince from the small Shakya Kingdom located in the foothills of the Himalayas in Nepal. Brought up in luxury, the prince abandoned his home and wandered forth as a religious beggar, searching for the meaning of existence. The stories of his search presuppose the Jain tradition, as Gautama was for a time a practitioner of intense austerity, at one point almost starving himself to death.

He decided, however, that self-torture weakened his mind while failing to advancc him to enlightenment and therefore turned to a milder style of renunciation and concentrated on advanced meditation techniques. Eventually, under a tree in the forests of Gaya (in modern Bihar), he resolved to stir no farther until he had solved the mystery of existence. Breaking through the final barriers, he achieved the knowledge that he later expressed as the Four Noble Truths: all of life is suffering; the cause of suffering is desire; the end of desire leads to the end of suffering; and the means to end desire is a path of discipline and meditation. Gautama was now the Buddha, or the awakened one, and he spent the remainder of his life traveling about northeast India converting large numbers of disciples.

At the age of eighty, the Buddha achieved his final passing away (parinirvana) and died, leaving a thriving monastic order and a dedicated lay community to continue his work. By the third century B.C., the still-young religion based on the Buddha's teachings was being spread throughout South Asia through the agency of the Mauryan Empire. By the seventh century A.D., having spread throughout East Asia and Southeast Asia, Buddhism probably had the largest religious following in the world. For centuries Indian royalty and merchants patronized Buddhist monasteries and raised beautiful, hemispherical stone structures called stupas over the relics of the Buddha in reverence to his memory. Since the 1840s, archaeology has revealed the huge impact of Buddhist art, iconography, and architecture in India.

The monastery complex at Nalanda in Bihar, in ruins in 1993, was a world center for Buddhist philosophy and religion until the thirteenth century. But by the thirteenth century, when Turkic invaders destroyed the remaining monasteries on the plains, Buddhism as an organized religion had practically disappeared from India. It survived only in Bhutan and Sikkim, both of which were then independent Himalayan kingdoms; among tribal groups in the mountains of northeast India; and in Sri Lanka. The reasons for this disappearance are unclear, and they are many: shifts in royal patronage from Buddhist to Hindu religious institutions; a constant intellectual struggle with dynamic Hindu intellectual schools, which eventually triumphed; and slow adoption of popular religious forms by Buddhists while Hindu monastic communities grew up with the same style of discipline as the Buddhists, leading to the slow but steady amalgamation of ideas and trends in the two religions.

Buddhism began a steady and dramatic comeback in India during the early twentieth century, spurred on originally by a combination of European antiquarian and philosophical interest and the dedicated activities of a few Indian devotees. The foundation of the Mahabodhi Society (Society of Great Enlightenment) in 1891, originally as a force to wrest control of the Buddhist shrine at Gaya from the hands of Hindu managers, gave a large stimulus to the popularization of Buddhist philosophy and the importance of the religion in India's past. A major breakthrough occurred in 1956 after some thirty years of Untouchable, or Dalit, agitation when Bhimrao Ramji (B.R.) Ambedkar, leader of the Untouchable wing within the Congress, announced that he was converting to Buddhism as a way to escape from the impediments of the Hindu caste system.

He brought with him masses of Untouchables—also known as Harijans or Dalits—and members of Scheduled Castes, who mostly came from Maharashtra and border areas of neighboring states and from the Agra area in Uttar Pradesh. By the early 1990s, there were more than 5 million Buddhists in Maharashtra, or 79 percent of the entire Buddhist community in India, almost all recent converts from low castes. When added to longtime Buddhist populations in hill areas of northeast India (West Bengal, Assam, Sikkim, Mizoram, and Tripura) and high Himalayan valleys (Ladakh District in Jammu and Kashmir, Himachal Pradesh, and northern Uttar Pradesh), and to the influx of Tibetan Buddhist refugees who fled from Tibet with the Dalai Lama in 1959 and thereafter, the recent converts raised the number of Buddhists in India to 6.4 million by 1991.

This was a 35.9 percent increase since 1981 and made Buddhism the fifth largest religious group in the country. The forms of Buddhism practiced by Himalayan communities and Tibetan refugees are part of the Vajrayana, or "Way of the Lightning Bolt," that developed after the seventh century A.D. as part of Mahayana (Great Path) Buddhism. Although retaining the fundamental importance of individual spiritual advancement, the Vajrayana stresses the intercession of bodhisattvas, or enlightened beings, who remain in this world to aid others on the path. Until the twentieth century, the Himalayan kingdoms supported a hierarchy in which Buddhist monks, some identified from birth as bodhisattvas, occupied the highest positions in society.

Initial Spread

Initially, Buddhism remained one of the many small sects in India. The main breakthrough came when King Asoka (ca. 270-232 BCE) converted to Buddhism. He did not make it a state religion, but supported all ethical religions. He organised the spreading of Buddhism throughout India, but also beyond; most importantly to Sri Lanka. This occurred after the Third Council.

The Buddhist Councils

The First Council: Three months after the Buddha's Mahaparinirvana (passing away), his immediate disciples convened a council at Rajagaha. Maha Kassapa, the most respected and senior monk, presided at the Council.

Two very important personalities who specialised in the two areas of the teachings:

- *The Dharma*: Ananda, the closest constant companion and disciple of the Buddha for 25 years. Endowed with a remarkable memory, Ananda was able to recite what was spoken by the Buddha.
- *The Vinaya*: Upali remembered all the Vinaya rules.

Only these two sections - the Dharma and the Vinaya - were recited at the First Council (no mention was made of the Abhidharma yet). Though there were no differences of opinion on the Dharma there was some discussion about the Vinaya rules. Before the Buddha's Parinirvanana, he had told Ananda that if the Sangha wished to amend or modify some minor rules, they could do so. But Ananda forgot to ask the Buddha what the minor rules were. As the members of the Council were unable to agree as to what constituted the minor rules, Maha Kassapa finally ruled that no disciplinary rule laid down by the Buddha should be changed, and no new ones should be introduced.

No intrinsic reason was given. Maha Kassapa did say one thing, however: "If we changed the rules, people will say that Ven. Gautama's disciples changed the rules even before his funeral fire has ceased burning." At the Council, the Dharma was divided into various parts and each part was assigned to an Elder and his pupils to commit to memory. The Dharma was then passed on from teacher to pupil orally. The Dharma was recited daily by groups of people who regularly cross-checked with each other to ensure that no omissions or additions were made.

The second Council: According to the Theravadin School (Rahula), about one hundred years after the Buddha's passing away, the Second Council was held to discuss some Vinaya rules, and no controversy about the Dharma was reported. The orthodox monks (Sthavarivada) said that nothing should be changed, while the others insisted on modifying some rules. Finally, a group of monks left the Council and formed the Mahasanghika - the Great Community. (The Mahasanghika should not to be confused with Mahayana.)

According to another version (Skilton), the Second Council may have had two parts: initially in Vaisali, some 60 years after the Buddha, and 40 years after that, a meeting in Pataliputra, where Mahadeva maintained five theses on the Arhat. The actual split may have occurred at Pataliputra, not Vaisali over details of the Vinaya. In the non-Theravadin version of events, the Mahasangha followed the original vinaya and the Sthaviravada (the Elders) wanted changes. What exactly happened is unlikely to be ever revealed, but the first split in the Sangha was a fact.

The Third Council: During the reign of Emperor Asoka in the 3rd Century BCE, the Third Council was held to discuss the differences of opinion among the bhikkhus of different sects. At this Council differences of opinion were not confined to the Vinaya, but also concerned the Dharma. The President of the Council, Moggaliputta Tissa, compiled a book called the Kathavatthu which refuted the heretical, false views and theories held by some sects occurring at the time. The teaching approved and accepted by this Council became known as Sthaviras or Theravada, "Teaching of the Elders". The Abhidhamma Pitaka was included at this Council. After the Third Council, King Asoka sent missionaries to Sri Lanka, Kanara, Karnataka, Kashmir, Himalaya region, Burma, even nowadays Afghanistan. Asoka's son, Ven. Mahinda, brought the Tripitaka to Sri Lanka, along with the commentaries that were recited at the Third Council. These teachings later became known as the "Pali-canon".

The Fourth Council: The Fourth Buddhist Council was held under the auspices of King Kaniska at Jalandhar or in Kashmir around 100 CE, where 499 monks of the Sarvastivadin School compiled a new canon. This council was never recognised by the Theravada school.

The Fifth Council (Burma): The 5th Buddhist Council was held from 1868 to 1871 in Mandalay, Burma where the text of the Pali Canon was revised and inscribed on 729 marble slabs.

Ancient Buddhism in India

Buddhism in India began with the life of Siddhartha Gautama (ca. 563-483 B.C.), a prince from the small Shakya Kingdom located in the foothills of the Himalayas in Nepal. Brought up in luxury, the prince abandoned his home and wandered forth as a religious beggar, searching for the meaning of existence. The stories of his search presuppose the Jain tradition, as Gautama was for a time a practitioner of intense austerity, at one point almost starving himself to death. He decided, however, that self-torture weakened his mind while failing to advance him to enlightenment and therefore turned to a milder style of renunciation and concentrated on advanced meditation techniques.

Eventually, under a tree in the forests of Gaya (in modern Bihar), he resolved to stir no farther until he had solved the mystery of existence. Breaking through the final barriers, he achieved the knowledge that he later expressed as the Four Noble Truths: all of life is suffering; the cause of suffering is desire; the end of desire leads to the end of suffering; and the means to end desire is a path of discipline and meditation. Gautama was now the Buddha, or the awakened one, and he spent the remainder of his life traveling about northeast India converting large numbers of disciples.

At the age of eighty, the Buddha achieved his final passing away (*parinirvana*) and died, leaving a thriving monastic order and a dedicated lay community to continue his work. By the third century B.C., the still-young religion based on the Buddha's teachings was being spread throughout South Asia through the agency of the Mauryan Empire (ca. 326-184 B.C.). By the seventh century A.D., having spread throughout East Asia and Southeast Asia, Buddhism probably had the largest religious following in the world. For centuries Indian royalty and merchants patronized Buddhist monasteries and raised beautiful, hemispherical stone structures called stupas over the relics of the Buddha in reverence to his memory. Since the 1840s, archaeology has revealed the huge impact of Buddhist art, iconography, and architecture in India.

The monastery complex at Nalanda in Bihar, in ruins in 1993, was a world center for Buddhist philosophy and religion until the thirteenth century. But by the thirteenth century, when Turkic invaders destroyed the remaining monasteries on the plains, Buddhism as an organized religion had practically disappeared from India. It survived only in Bhutan and Sikkim, both of which were then independent Himalayan kingdoms; among tribal groups in the mountains of northeast India; and in Sri Lanka. The reasons for this disappearance are unclear, and they are many: shifts in royal patronage from Buddhist to Hindu religious institutions; a constant intellectual struggle with dynamic Hindu intellectual schools, which eventually triumphed; and slow adoption of popular religious forms by Buddhists while Hindu monastic communities grew up with the same style of discipline as the Buddhists, leading to the slow but steady amalgamation of ideas and trends in the two religions.

Buddhism began a steady and dramatic comeback in India during the early twentieth century, spurred on originally by a combination of European antiquarian and philosophical interest and the dedicated activities of a few Indian devotees. The foundation of the Mahabodhi Society (Society of Great Enlightenment) in 1891, originally as a force to wrest control of the Buddhist shrine at Gaya from the hands of Hindu managers, gave a large stimulus to the popularization of Buddhist philosophy and the importance of the religion in India's past. A major breakthrough occurred in 1956 after some thirty years of Untouchable, or Dalit, agitation when Bhimrao Ramji (B.R.) Ambedkar, leader of the Untouchable wing within the Congress, announced that he was converting to Buddhism as a way to escape from the impediments of the Hindu caste system. He brought with him masses of Untouchables—also known as Harijans or Dalits—and members of Scheduled Castes, who mostly came from Maharashtra and border areas of neighboring states and from the Agra area in Uttar Pradesh.

By the early 1990s, there were more than 5 million Buddhists in Maharashtra, or 79 percent of the entire Buddhist community in India, almost all recent converts from low castes. When added to longtime Buddhist populations in hill areas of northeast India (West Bengal, Assam, Sikkim, Mizoram, and Tripura) and high Himalayan valleys (Ladakh District in Jammu and Kashmir,

Himachal Pradesh, and northern Uttar Pradesh), and to the influx of Tibetan Buddhist refugees who fled from Tibet with the Dalai Lama in 1959 and thereafter, the recent converts raised the number of Buddhists in India to 6.4 million by 1991. This was a 35.9 percent increase since 1981 and made Buddhism the fifth largest religious group in the country.

The forms of Buddhism practiced by Himalayan communities and Tibetan refugees are part of the Vajrayana, or "Way of the Lightning Bolt," that developed after the seventh century A.D. as part of Mahayana (Great Path) Buddhism. Although retaining the fundamental importance of individual spiritual advancement, the Vajrayana stresses the intercession of bodhisattvas, or enlightened beings, who remain in this world to aid others on the path. Until the twentieth century, the Himalayan kingdoms supported a hierarchy in which Buddhist monks, some identified from birth as bodhisattvas, occupied the highest positions in society.

Most other Buddhists in India follow Theravada Buddhism, the "Doctrine of the Elders," which traces its origin through Sri Lankan and Burmese traditions to scriptures in the Pali language, a Sanskritic dialect in eastern India. Although replete with miraculous events and legends, these scriptures stress a more human Buddha and a democratic path toward enlightenment for everyone. Ambedkar's plan for the expanding Buddhist congregation in India visualized Buddhist monks and nuns developing themselves through service to others. Convert communities, by embracing Buddhism, have embarked on social transformations, including a decline in alcoholism, a simplification of marriage ceremonies and abolition of ruinous marriage expenses, a greater emphasis on education, and a heightened sense of identity and self-worth.

The Tradition of the Enlightened Master

A number of avowedly Hindu monastic communities have grown up over time and adopted some of the characteristics associated with early Buddhism and Jainism, while remaining dedicated to the Hindu philosophical traditions. One of the oldest and most respected of the Hindu orders traces its origin to the teacher Shankara (788-820), believed by many devotees to have lived hundreds of years earlier. Shankara's philosophy is a primary source of Vedanta, or the "End of the Veda," the final commentary on revealed truth, which is one of the most influential trends in modern Hinduism. His interpretation of the Upanishads portrays *Brahman* as absolutely one and without qualities. The phenomenal world is illusion (*maya*), which the embodied soul must transcend in order to achieve oneness with *Brahman*.

As a wandering monk, Shankara traveled throughout India, combating Buddhist atheism and founding five seats of learning at Badrinath (Uttar Pradesh), Dwaraka (Gujarat), Puri (Orissa), Sringeri (Karnataka), and Kanchipuram (Tamil Nadu). In the 1990s, those seats are still held by successors to Shankara's philosophy (Shankara Acharyas), who head an order of orange-clad monks that is highly respected by the Hindu community throughout India. Activities of the *acharyas*, including their periodic trips away from their home monasteries to visit and preach to devotees, receive exposure in regional and national media. Their conservative viewpoints and pronouncements on a variety of topics, although not binding on most believers, attract considerable public attention.

The initiation of a renunciant usually depends on the judgment of an *acharya* who determines whether a candidate is dedicated and prepared or not; he then gives to the disciple training and instructions including the initiate's own secret formula or mantra. After initiation, the disciple may remain with his teacher or in a monastery for an indefinite period or may wander forth in a variety of careers. The Ramanandi order in North India, for example, includes holy men (sadhus) who practice ascetic disciplines, militant members of fortified temples, and priests in charge of temple administration and ritual. There are other orders of renunciants who lead still more austere existences, including naked ascetics who wander begging for their food and assemble for spectacular parades at major festivals.

A few dedicated seekers still withdraw to the fastness of the Himalayas or other remote spots and work on their meditation and yoga in total obscurity. Others beg in populated areas, sometimes engaging in fierce austerities such as piercing their bodies with pins and knives. They are a reminder to all people that the path of renunciation waits for anyone who has the dedication and the courage to leave the world behind. Another kind of renunciation appears in the cult of Sai Baba, who achieved national and international fame in the twentieth century. The first person known by this name was a holy man—Sai Baba (died 1918)—who appeared in 1872 in Maharashtra and lived a humble life that blended meditation and devotional techniques from a variety of sources. This saint has a small but dedicated following throughout India.

A later incarnation was Satya Sai Baba (*satya* means true), born in 1926 in Andhra Pradesh. At age thirteen, he experienced the first of several seizures that resulted in a changed personality and intense devotional activity, leading to his statement that he is the second incarnation of Sai Baba. By 1950 he had set up a retreat at Puttaparti in what later became Andhra Pradesh and was accepting disciples. His fame spread along with numerous apocryphal stories of his ability to perform miracles, including the manifestation of sacred ash and, according to some accounts, watches or other objects, from thin air or from his own body.

The cult has expanded to include publishing, social service, and education institutions and includes an international association of thousands of believers. Devotion to Satya Sai Baba does not preclude attachment to other religious observances but concentrates instead on worship and veneration of the holy man himself, often in the form of a photograph. Thousands of pilgrims have traveled to his retreat annually to participate in group activities, obtain mementos, and perhaps a view of the teacher himself.

Revival in India in the 20th Century

The disappearance of Buddhism from the land of its birth, a gradual process that extended from the latter part of the 1st millennium AD until about 1200-1300 AD, is a phenomenon that has been commented upon quite often. Another part of this story is surely the revival of Buddhism, a reawakening with which the name of B. R. Ambedkar is indelibly linked. Indeed, the story of modern-day Indian Buddhism generally commences with Ambedkar's conversion to Buddhism in 1956, a mere couple of months before his death. By the early 1990s, there were an estimated 7 - 10 million Buddhists in India, the bulk of them in the western state of Maharashtra.

However, the narrative of Buddhism's revival in India can more accurately be traced back to the 19th century, and a more complex account of it would have to take stock of various Dravidian, anti-Brahminical, and self-respect movements that, in various ways, impinged on the fortunes of Buddhism in India from the late nineteenth century onwards. The names of reformers such as Jotiba Phule (1826-1890) and much later E. V. Ramaswami 'Periyar' (1879-1973) are, of course, well-known, but one can also point to other tendencies.

Mahima Dharma, or the "religion" founded by Mahima Gosain [previously known as Mukunda Das] in Orissa in 1862, stood for the rejection of caste and idol worship, and Gosain embraced such Buddhist practices as begging for cooked food. Gosain's teachings were spread through many followers, none as famous as the blind adivasi poet, Bhima Bhoi, whose bhajans popularized Mahima Gosain's teachings. Ambedkar's closest forerunner may well have been Pandit Iyothee Thaas, a Tamil Siddha physician (1845-1914) who not only urged the Untouchables (as they were then known) to view themselves as non-Hindus, as casteless Dravidians, but also set another example for them by taking *diksha* at the hands of a Buddhist monk in Sri Lanka. Thaas went on to found the Sakya Buddhist Society in Madras.

Various other trajectories fed into Buddhism's revival, among them the arrival in India in 1891 of David Hewavitarne, more well-known as Angarika Dharmapala. The restoration of Bodh Gaya, the site of the Buddha's enlightenment, was undertaken at his behest, and Dharmapala also founded the Maha Bodhi Society. Before Ambedkar's conversion in 1956 and the advent of what we might call Dalit Buddhism, the Maha Bodhi Society, which also wrested control of Bodh Gaya from the hands of its Hindu managers, would become the custodian of Buddhism's fortunes. Dharmapala's visit to India coincided with a spurt of scholarly interest in Buddhism among Indologists, including such famous ones as the Sanskritist R. G. Bhandarkar, and something of what might be called an antiquarian and spiritual interest in Buddhism among intellectuals and truth seekers in the West.

In 1881, the Pali Text Society had been founded, and authoritative versions of Buddhist texts soon came to be published and disseminated under its auspices. One convert to Buddhism in India who was to acquire considerable fame in later years was Dharmanand Kosambi, who was born in Goa in 1876 and was ordained as a Buddhist monk in 1902. Though his fame has been eclipsed by that of his son, D. D. Kosambi, the most eminent Indian Marxist historian of his generation, Dharmanand Kosambi authored one of the most popular biographies of Buddha, *Bhagwan Buddha* (1940, and still in print from Bharatiya Vidya Bhavan).

Ultimately, however, Buddhism's revival owes the most to Ambedkar's alienation from Hinduism and his embrace of Buddhism, which by no means seemed inevitable to him even when he had emphatically denounced Hinduism, in October 1956. That story has been taken up in great detail by Ambedkar's biographers and is now part of Dalit lore; and consequently it will not be rehearsed now at any length. It is worth recalling that as late as 1929, when a group of Dalits threatened to convert to Islam or Christianity, Ambedkar did not really see Buddhism as a viable alternative for low-caste Hindus. As he then wrote, "No particular effect will be felt on the bullying of the so-called upper castes by becoming Buddhist or Arya Samajist, so we see no meaning in following this path.

To successfully confront the domination of Hindus, we should become Christians or Muslims and win the support of a powerful community and with this erase the mark of Untouchability." Ambedkar was fully conversant with the problem that in India the tendency to view Buddhism as an off-shoot of Hinduism meant that converts to Buddhism would be treated with something like indifference, and that they would not be able to escape the liabilities of low-caste Hinduism. Upper-caste Hindus were not likely to perceive conversion to Buddhism as anything of a threat.

By the mid-1930s, however, Ambedkar had certainly come around to the view that he could not remain within the fold of Hinduism. As he was to declare on 13 October 1935, "Unfortunately, I was born a Hindu. It was beyond my power to prevent that, but I solemnly assure you that I will not die a Hindu." He only took the final plunge in October 1956. Perhaps not coincidentally, or not without its own symbolic politics, Ambedkar's conversion, accompanied by the conversion of thousands of his followers, took place at a large field in the city of Nagpur, a place associated with the rise of Hindu nationalist sentiments. The field where Ambedkar converted would be sanctified as "Diksha Bhoomi", the field or earth of vow-taking.

Though Buddhism has gained adherents over the last five decades, Indian Buddhists are still relatively miniscule in numbers. Buddhism's presence in India is, of course, another matter, with the landscape in many parts of the country still dotted with remains of Buddhist monasteries, Buddhist sculptural art, and other reminders of the supreme presence that Buddhism once occupied in Indian life. The hill regions of north-east India, Uttaraanchal, and Himachal Pradesh, as well as Ladakh in Jammu & Kashmir are other areas where sizable Buddhist communities are found.

Japanese tourists arriving in India to take the Buddhist pilgrimage route are writing yet another chapter of the history of Indian Buddhism, as are, in more profound ways, Tibetan Buddhists. There is a sizable population of Tibetan Buddhists, over 150,000 people, in India; and the Dalai Lama heads the Tibetan government in exile at the hill station of Dharmashala. In the 12th and 13th centuries, as Buddhism was pushed further east and north, it eventually made its way to Tibet and found refuge in the mountainous retreats of that country. It is, thus, perfectly apposite that Buddhism should now have come back to India from Tibet to nourish the soil on which it once grew.

12

Reform Movements in Jainism

The diversity of sects and sub-sects in Jainism is a characteristic feature of its long history as well as of its manifestations of religious reform in the contemporary period. As one distinguished western observer of Jainism, Kendall W. Folkert, pointed out that the true nature of this great religion can be understood only if we emphasise not so much the broad divisions into Digambara and Shvetambara sects but direct our probe into the importance and rationale of small sub-divisions. There are two major factors behind the unity of Jainism despite these divisions: one, attempts by all to unravel the original doctrine and practice of the followers of Jina, and, two, the overarching philosophical credo of 'the many- pointed nature of truth' (anekanta and syadavad) in Jainism.

There is scope for a variety of interpretations to be subsumed under the umbrella of a united Jain faith. The emergence of sub-divisions is not an attempt at deviation from the earlier charters, but a constant return to the roots and an effort to build up on those foundations what is conceived as the 'original' or authentic structure by cutting away the accretions of sectarianism and false doctrine. An examination of the nature of reform movements within

Jainism further elucidates as to why the faith of the Jina has coexisted in a symbiotic relationship with Hinduism and how-unlike Buddhism, for example, it has shown remarkable continuity of precept and practice within the geographical confines of India with almost negligible spread beyond Indian borders (except in very recent times). The following diagram represents the 'lineage' of Jain sects.

Religious Divisions and Their Social Impact

A common feature of all religious reform movements in Jainism is the use of the Hindi and Gujarati term "uddhar" which is often seen as the equivalent of English 'reform' but signifies literally 'a raising up' (it can also be used to describe the restoration of a ruined temple). This term is employed by sympathetic Jain writers in the sense both of a retrieval and reactivation of a basic doctrine of non-violence and renunciation taught by Mahavira and a concomitant rejection of what are regarded as the debased practices, which attend this particular period of the world era. Interestingly enough, given the individualistic bias of Jainism (viz., for attaining moksa or salvation) these reform movements are usually spearheaded by known individuals who may or may not start a line of pupillary succession. Thus the three sectarian movements that we shall discuss were led by individuals : Sthanakvasi and Terapanth (anti-image or aniconic sects among the Shvetambaras); Sthanakvasi by Lonka or Lonka Shah as well as a merchant called Lavaji, Terapanth by Acharya Bhikshu and Kanji Swami Panth (originally Shvetambara but subsequently Digambara) by Kanji Swami.

The Sthanakvasi

A somewhat mysterious individual in Jainism, Lonka or Lonka Shah existed in Gujarat during the fifteenth century. Tradition is unanimous that an inspection of the Shvetambara scriptures led him to deny that image-worship could have any place in true Jainism. The Sthanakvasi whose remote founder he is see him as a rich, mighty and learned layman with powerful connections among the Moslem authorities in Ahmedabad, whose skills in calligraphy led to an invitation to copy the scriptures. After serious study of the scriptures he became convinced that the practice of Jainism he saw around him was without any textual basis and totally corrupt. Accepting the authority of only thirty-two of the scriptural texts and rejecting a great deal of ritual of all kinds, he took some sort of ascetic initiation and became a charismatic teacher who weaned away large number of Shvetambaras from their image-related practices.

A balanced picture of Lonka's career is presented recently by Pandit Dalsukh Malvania, a Sthanakvasi layman and one of the most distinguished twentieth century interpreters of the Jain intellectual tradition. The aniconic ideal of Lonka's followers did not long survive the death of its inspiration. The pupillary descent started by him (Lonka gaccha) gradually reverted to image-worship as there is inscriptional evidence to prove the consecration of temples and installation of images by acaryas of that gaccha. However, in 1644 the Mughal emperor issued an edict to exclude the lay members of the Lonka gaccha from communal meals with Shvetambara community in Ahmedabad, which not only seriously impeded their business activity but also suggests that they were not fully assimilated into the image-worshipping community. The Lonka gaccha today has no fully initiated ascetics and exists only at the fringes of Shvetambara society. The Sthanakvasis were formed by the seventeenth century Gujarati merchant called Lavaji who along with another merchant Dharmasimha broke away from the Lonka gaccha.

As with Lonka there is some doubt about whether Lavaji took formal ascetic initiation but there is no doubt that the substance of his criticism of the Lonka gaccha was directed to its general laxity and he consequently expressed a wish to revert to the model of monastic behaviour found in the Dashavaikalika which did not, of course, include image-worship. The three monks who came after him in pupillary succession followed the practice envisaged in the earliest scriptures of lodging in ruined and deserted building as a result of which the ascetics of this nascent sub sect were called Dhumdhiya, 'Searchers' (for suitable lodgings).

The Sthanakvasis, as they are known today, evolved from these monks, the name meaning 'Living in Lodging Houses (Sthanaka), a reference to the fact that the monks of this sect shunned the upashrayas lodgings which the image-worshippers erected in the vicinity of temples. Lavaji was responsible for the introduction of a practice which has continued to distinguish Sthanakvasi and Terapanthi ascetics from those of other Shvetambara sects : the permanent wearing of a strip of cloth across the mouth, tied behind the ears, known as muhpatti, mouth-shield (square in shape for the Sthanakvasis, rather more narrow and elongated for the Terapanthis), which by minimizing the destruction of air-bodies and tiny insects through the outflow or inflow of breath is an outward sign of the ascetic's commitment to non-violence. Shvetambara image-worshipping ascetics today all possess muhpattis and one of their most conventional poses in portraits and photographs is with a book in one hand and a muhpatti in the other, symbolising knowledge and compassion.

These ascetics tie or hold in hand the muhpatti only on special worship or ritual occasions. In fact, with the image-worshipping Shvetambaras even the lay people tie up a handkerchief over their mouth and nostrils while praying close to the image. However, what distinguishes the practice of muhpatti by aniconic Sthanakvasis and Terapanthis is that the muhpatti be worn permanently by ascetics. It is worth-noting that although the ostensible reason for their emergence was a process of ascetic reform initiated by Lavaji and Dharmasimha, it has been suggested with some plausibility that those who became Sthanakvasis were in fact trying to break away from high caste domination and in reality the origins of the sect may well lie in the realm of lay business competition.

As with other Jain sects, the Sthanakvasis split at a fairly early stage into branches, in this case as many as twenty-two based on regional and perceptorial connections. The Sthanakvasis have remained a resilient component of the Jain community whose reputation for adherence to the principles of non-violence and compassion is high. In the past, the Sthanakvasis were located mainly in the north and the west in towns such as Ludhiana in Punjab and Limbdi in Gujarat. Now, however, as a result of increasing internal migration by the Sthanakvasi laity in India, they have become more widespread and Sthanakvasi ascetics can often be found passing caturmas (the four month rainy season retreat) in the south of the subcontinent.

Recently, the Sthanakvasi monk, Sushil Kumar Muni (1926-1994) gained comparative fame in public life for his attempts to intervene positively in the various communal disputes, which plague contemporary Indian society. Having been denied his wish to proselytize Jainism in the West by his religious superiors, in 1974 Sushil Muni split off the aniconic Sthanakvasi Sraman Sangha together with twenty other ascetics and founded his own religious order, the Arhat Sangha. He then headed to New Jersey, where he founded first the International Mahavir Jain Mission and later, in 1983, Siddhacalam, the first asrama for Jain ascetics and laity in the West. Sushil Muni also organized the first World Jain Conference in New York (1981), which was succeeded by meetings in Leicester (1983) and Delhi (1985, 1987), and Asian Jain Conferences in Bangkok (1988) and Singaore (1989).

Acarya Bhikshu and the Terapanth

Acarya Bhikshu, the eighteenth century Shvetambara

reformer and founder of the Terapanth sect, is one of the best-documented figure in the history of Jainism. Bhikshu (often known by the Rajasthani version of his name, Bhikhanji) was born in 1726 in the desert region of Marwar in Rajasthan. It is likely that the vigorous and uncompromising variety of Jainism he preached had something to do with the rugged ecology of his birth and activity. Bhikshu belonged to the fairly numerous Bisa Oswal caste and originally took initiation in 1751 as a Sthanakvasi monk under Acarya Raghunathji. He maintained that the Jain path could involve nothing but total commitment and his experiences as a Sthanakvasi monk revealed to him a host of imperfections in the sect, which led to his breaking away from it in 1759.

Along with thirteen other monks who followed him, Bhikshu formed the Terapanth ('tera' means thirteen in Rajasthani and Hindi). In keeping with its rigorous nature, the monks of Terapanth undertook elaborate and lengthy fasting and observed the strictest non-violence, viz. tying the muhpatti all the time. Bhikshu made a distinction between laukika (worldly) and lokottara (transcendent) religious practices and emphasized the latter urging even the laity to aspire to them. The full community of Terapanthis, including lay supporters, was formed in 1765. When Bhiksu died in 1803, he had initiated fifty-six nuns and forty nine monks which, in the light of what little is known of Shvetambara ascetic demography at the time, probably represents a reasonably substantial number. What was distinctly new in Terapanth was its insistence on the centrality of the acarya, the assumption by him of all monastic offices and the subordination of all Terapanth ascetics to him. The ninth acarya (from 1936 to 1998), Tulsi presided over a recent remarkable expansion of Terapanthi activity and was responsible for the high profile of the sect in post-independence India.

He carried out the largest number of initiations of any Terapanthi acarya and planned for the first Jain University in Ladnun, his birthplace in Rajasthan. In 1949, he founded the Anuvrata movement, dedicated to raising the moral tone of Indian public and commercial life by taking Jainism beyond the Jains, which was to become the best-known Terapanthi enterprise in India and an outward expression of the sect's identity. The movement had some of the trappings of an internationalist western-style peace movement. To quote Tulsi, 'If an atom (anu) has in it the monstrous power to destroy the world, amply demonstrated in the unprecedented holocaust at Hiroshima and Nagasaki, I want to tell the world that we have its counterpart in anuvrata- a small or atomic vow-which alone has the power to ward off and counter the threat of an atom bomb." (Cited in Dundas, 1992). A member of this movement, as conceived by Tulsi, would take both a general, and depending on his or her status and walk of life, a modified version of the anuvratas, the lay lesser vows, which through effecting a moral reformation would "inspire people to cultivate self-restraint irrespective of their caste, colour, creed, country and language, to establish the values of friendship, unity, peace and morality, to create an unfettered society free from exploitation." (Cited in Dundas).

Another Terapanthi innovation, associated with Acarya Tulsi's successor and present head, Yuvacarya Mahaprajna, is the development of a modern form of Jain meditation known as prekshadhyana, 'insight-meditation', which is designed to "engage the mind fully in the perception of subtle, internal and innate phenomena of consciousness" (cited in Dundas). As Dundas has pointed out, "this system, takes its inspiration from scattered scriptural statement about perceiving the self with the self, while also drawing eclectically on a wide range of sources in other traditions, provides a meditative structure...for a religion which seems to have lost contact with its original system of contemplation at least one thousand years ago." (Dundas). Another remarkable feature is the Terapanthi leadership's willingness to break with Jain tradition's longstanding prohibition of ascetics traveling into 'non-Aryan' lands. Here, lower-order male and female ascetics called saman and samani have been trained and granted special dispensation to travel abroad. Although they take the five Great Vows, they are unlike normal ascetics in that to facilitate their activities outside India they are allowed to use mechanical means of transport and to accept food, which has been specially prepared for them.

The Kanji Swami Panth

The most successful twentieth century Jain movement has unquestionably been the Kanji Swami Panth. Kanji Swami was born in 1889 into a Sthanakvasi family in a small village in the Kathiawar region of Gujarat. Orphaned at an early age, he gradually became inclined towards the ascetic life and in 1913 took initiation as a Sthanakvasi monk. Although he soon became a learned and famous monk, carrying the title 'Kohinoor of Kathiawar', Kanji Swami was never able to engage fully with the Shvetambara Scriptures, which he felt lacked a sense of soul. The event, which changed the course of Kanji Swami's life, was his discovery around 1921 of Kundakunda's 'Essence of the Doctrine'. Soon afterwards he studied other Digambara scriptures such as the writings of Todarmal and Shrimad Rajacandra, as a result of which he became convinced that Digambara Jainism was the true path.

However, for some time he led a kind of double life, nominally a Sthanakvasi monk but regarded himself as a Digambara until 1934 when his spiritual crisis came to an end. In that year during the celebration of Mahavir Jayanti in the small town of Songarh he threw away his muhpatti and proclaimed himself to be a Digambara layman. Kanji Swami never became a Digambara monk, however. Initially the Shvetambara Sthanakvasi community of Gujarat was resentful of what it conceived to be an apostasy towards Digambara doctrine in Kanji Swami's teachings as also of the movement's un-Gujarati character. Eventually the local

Sthanakvasis seem to have become reconciled to Kanji Swami and indeed virtually all of the three hundred or so families who today live at Songarh and belong to the Kanji Swami Panth claim to be of Sthanakvasi background. As regards the doctrines of the Panth, there is insistence on the primacy of the higher level of truth (nishcaya naya) over the lower one of ordinary life (vyavahara naya).

For Kanji Swami, the three Jewels of right faith, knowledge and practice could only function properly on the basis of a prior experience of the soul, and the various rituals and merit-making practices of Jainism were regarded as subordinate and essentially irrelevant through their being linked to the passions. According to Kanji, it was only the pure soul, which could bring about spiritual deliverance. The Kanji Swami Panth has always been a lay movement and initiated ascetics are accorded no special status. Nonetheless, Kanji Swami was respectful of monks since he regarded them as personifying the fundamental principles of Jainism. Similarly, though he was critical of elaborate worship and rituals, yet he accepted the worship of images in temples of Digambara Jain tradition some of which he himself consecrated.

He also undertook extensive pilgrimages (by motor vehicle) to Digambara holy places throughout India. Whereas Songarh in Gujarat was the founding place of this Panth, another leading center was established in Jaipur and today a large number of its devotees are found among the born-Digambaras as well as the Digambara-converts all over North India. The Kanji Swami Panth got embroiled in the politics of the Digambara Jains but its adherents continued to increase. Due to its insistence on simplified procedures of ritual and worship, it also became increasingly popular in the diasporic Jain community. Kanji Swami died at Mumbai in 1981. We have so far seen how sects and subsects arose around certain key individuals in the Jain tradition. Among Sthanakvasis and Terapanthis, these leaders gave rise to pupillary succession. Particularly among the

Shvetambara Terapanthis the office of the acarya became the pivot of centralization and unity among both its lay and ascetic followers. The Kanji Swami movement, on the other hand, has remained a lay movement without initiating pupillary succession. Nevertheless, Kanji Swami too started a new sect or Panth. We shall now discuss the career and teachings of Shrimad Rajacandra who was a leader of Jain reform without even founding a sect but whose socio-religious influence radiated far and wide.

Social Reform Movements

Although it is difficult to separate social and religious reform movements in a world-religion like Jainism, yet it may be pointed out that the above-mentioned religious movements have often been either accompanied by social reform or co-existed with it. A sociological analyst of the Jain community, Dr. Vilas Sangave, has given an account of social reform movements in Digambara and Shvetambara sects.

Reform Movements in the Digambara Sect

Leaders of different sects among Jains launched several reform movements pertaining to issues and problems, which they considered imminent, and pressing both from religious and social points of view. In reform movements among the Digambara sect, the 'Das Pujadhikara Andolana' i.e., 'the Dasas' Right to Worship Movement' occupies a prominent position. The 'Dasas' are persons belonging to the 'Dasa' divisions of Jain castes. The use of 'Visa' and 'Dasa' as names of divisions of castes is common among the Jain castes like Agarwala, Osavala, Hummada, and Porvada in northern and western India. The term 'Visa' signifies 'twenty in the score' i.e. pure, and 'Dasa' signifies 'ten in the score', i.e., half-pure. Such Visa and Dasa divisions are treated in a descending order of social respectability and are considered as heterogamous divisions for marital purposes.

As Dasa persons were assigned a lower position in the

caste system, various social restrictions were imposed on their interdining and inter-marriage relations. Along with these social restrictions, certain religious disabilities were also forced on them. The Dasa persons were not allowed to perform puja or worship in the temples. This form of religious discrimination and social injustice was not liked by the leading intellectuals and was strongly opposed by the Dasa persons among the Digambara Jains. Pandit Gopaladasaji Baraiyya of Banaras spearheaded the movement and declared in unambiguous terms that 'in accordance with the liberal principles of Jainism the Dasas have the equal right to worship like the non-Dasa persons'. This stand taken by the pandits and the intellectuals was opposed by rich persons and after a protracted controversy, the matter was referred to a court of law where the judge gave the decision that the Dasas have no right to worship as there is no custom or practice in prevalence to that effect.

The court decision gave rise to widespread disquiet between the Visa and Dasa sections for a long time and considering the stiff and adamant attitude of the Visa sections, many Dasa persons left the Digambara sect and joined the Shvetambara sect. Later, the All India Digambara Jain Parishad, Delhi, the national representative organisation of the Digamabara Jains, revived the movement and, due to its strenuous efforts, conditions changed and the Dasa persons in practice began to enjoy in full measure their right to worship in Jain temples and even built temples from their own funds for common use.

The second important movement of a socio-religious nature with far-reaching effects was launched by the Digamabara Jains at the beginning of the twentieth century. The movement was known as 'shastra-mudrana Virodhi Andolana' i.e. the Anti-Scripture Printing Movement and it aimed at preventing the Shastras, the sacred literature preserved in manuscript form, from being printed and published in book form. Several intellectual and social leaders from north India like Babu Suraja-bhanaji, Babu

Jyotiprasadaji Jain and Pandit Chandrasen Vaidya strongly pleaded for the printing and publication of ancient scriptures on all subjects in book form so that they could be easily accessible to the general public and be useful in guiding their social and religious practices. This was opposed by the orthodox sections because they believed that printing the scriptures in book form was an anti-religious act.

They considered that it was sin to touch a printed religious book and hence they not only prohibited keeping the printed religious books in temples but also imposed a social and religious boycott on the publishers of such books. This opposition could not stand for a long time in the changed conditions of life when leaders of all other religions had started to make use of the printing machine. Slowly the opposition fizzled out, the printing of ritualistic literature and sacred books was started, separate Jain scripture publishing concerns were established and publication of many books under the 'Jain Sacred Literature Series' was undertaken. The commencement of this publication activity on a large scale greatly helped in ushering social reform among Jains in different parts of India.

Reform Movements in the Shvetambara Sect

In the Shvetambara sect also, some important movements of a socio-religious nature took place in the early decades of the twentieth century. Among the Murti-pujaka Shvetambara Jains, the 'Bala-diksha Pratibandha Andolana' i.e. the 'Prevention of Initiation of Children Movement' was started by prominent intellectuals and social workers. It was directed against the prevailing largescale practice of initiating adolescents and young children (sometimes children of below 10 years) to the ascetic order of the sect because it was felt that small children are not at all in a position to take an independent decision regarding the adoption of the ascetic career as a goal in their life. The movement dragged on for a long time and, due to protracted controversies, the general public opinion moved in favour of putting a virtual ban on such initiation of children and in favour of prescribing an age limit for entry into the ascetic order.

In spite of forceful propaganda and general awakening, the movement could not succeed in completely stopping the practice, but the actual frequency of such initiations became much less. The youth among the Shvetambara Jains took a lead in this movement and established a new organization known as Jain Yuvak Sangh for carrying out this and other social reforms among Jains. As a result of this agitation the old princely State of Baroda passed legislation prohibiting initiation of children in the state. Among the Sthanakvasi Shvetambara Jains, the 'Ek Acharya Andolan', i.e. the 'One Religious Head Movement, was started by intellectuals and social workers with a view to establishing the authority of one acharya (pontiff) on the entire ascetic order of the Sthanakvasi sect.

As we have seen, the movement succeeded and the system of supremacy of one acharya was recognised and accepted by the Sthanakvasi Jains. Accordingly, ascetics of the Sthanakvasi section from all over India were brought under the direct control of one acharya. This resulted in bringing essential unity among the laity of the Sthanakvasi section also, as the lay members were dependent on the ascetics for the performance of religious rites and ceremonies on account of the total absence of idol worship. Thus, unity among the ascetics and lay members of the Sthanakvasi sect under the authority of one acharya was forged and continued. This kind of unity is not found among the Digambara Jains and the Murtipujaka Shvetambara Jains.

In addition to movements of a socio-religious nature mentioned above, from the early years of the twentieth century purely social reform movements were also launched by intellectuals and social workers among Jains in different parts of India. These movements were mainly directed towards brining about essential reforms in the fields of marriage, education, and social customs and tradition. The chief concern of the social reform movement among Jains was to introduce radical changes in several practices connected with different aspects of marriage, like age of marriage, preliminaries to marriage, selection of marriage partners, celebration of marriage ceremony, and widow remarriage. In the field of education also, several efforts were made by Jains from the beginning of the twentieth century, so that they did not lag behind other communities in the race for advancement started under the impact of western culture.

In the early stages, a protracted controversy raged as to whether to continue the orthodox system of religious education through 'Pathsalas' (i.e. indigenous schools) or to adopt the new system of secular education imparted through schools and colleges especially started for the purpose by the government or by the other public bodies. The leaders of the community ultimately decided to popularize and spread secular education but, at the same time, to continue to keep the base of religious education to the maximum extent possible. As a result, along with religious education, secular education was also brought within the reach of all members of the Jain community. Residential schools and colleges known as Gurukulas were started where students are prepared for various university courses but, at the same time, care is taken that they lead a strictly religious life. This Gurukula system of education is becoming popular because the students trained by these institutions remain religiousminded throughout their life and are also in a position to maintain themselves.

The Mahavira Brahmacharyashrama, the Gurukula at Karanja in Maharashtra, and the Yashovijayaji Jain Gurukul at Palitana in Gujarat are notable institutions of this kind. The number of such Gurukulas is small because of the heavy expenditure required. Where Gurukulas could not be established, boarding houses or hostels have been started at practically all big places and centres of education throughout India. Here, residential accommodation is given to Jain students free of rent or on nominal rates. Students residing in such hostels are free to join any institution for their education, but they are required to take elementary religious education for which provision is made by the authorities, and to lead a religious life (that is, to visit the temple daily, to refrain from eating at night or eating prohibited things, etc.). Poor and deserving hostel students are given financial help in one form or another. With a view to accelerating the spread of education, special funds are constituted to give scholarships or loans to deserving Jain students wherever they may be.

Generally, the scholarship amount is given on the condition that the receiver has to refund it by instalments when he completes his education and is settled in life. In awarding the scholarships, preference is shown to those who wish to pursue higher studies in Jainology or desire to take specialized courses. The spread of higher education among Jains at present is mainly due to the help rendered to them through various means provided by the Jain community. Adequate attention was also paid by Jains towards the spread of female education. Like boarding houses or students' hostels for boys, Shravikashrams (women's homes) were started by Jains at important places. The Shravikashrams were specially designed and organized to impart religious and secular education to female students, to provide accommodation for working women, to give residential facilities to female students enrolled in other institutions, to provide shelter to orphans, widows and deserted women and, in recent times, to arrange vocational training and run small scale industries for the benefit of women.

In some places special scholarship funds have been created with a view to rendering help to poor and deserving women students and to encourage talented girls to take specialized training courses required for different vocations and professions. In the field of social customs and traditions, it can be stated that many undesirable and anti-social practices, which were prevalent in other societies, were not found among the Jains. For example, in ancient times, in almost all patriarchal societies, the birth of a girl was not a welcome event and this gave rise to practices like female infanticide and neglect of female children. This custom of infanticide of girls crept into some sections of Hindu society during the medieval period and was in vogue till it was prohibited by the early British rulers.

Since Jain philosophy is based on the main principle of Ahimsa or non-injury to living beings, female infanticide was not even thought of in the Jain community at any time. For the same reason, female children were not purposefully neglected even though sometimes they might have been regarded as a burden on the family. Similarly, the practice of 'sati' (self-immolation by widows), which was common among the Hindus, was conspicuous by its absence among the Jains. Further, the custom of tonsure was practiced by Hindu widows from about 1200 A.D. and was in vogue in many quarters till recent times. But the Jain widows never followed this custom. Among the Jain women only the Sadhvis (nuns) used to be shaved in accordance with the rules of asceticism prescribed for them.

In respect of observance of social customs and traditions, it may be said that several Jain associations and Jain journals and newspapers started during the British period at the national, regional and social levels tried by all means of propaganda and education to eradicate bad and irreligious practices which had crept into the Jain community from medieval times due to lack of knowledge of Jain philosophy and scriptures and the impact of followers of other religions and customs on Jains. Mainly due to their efforts, the worship of Hindu gods has declined, the observance of Hindu festivals like Holi and Shitalasaptami has been discontinued, the performance of Shraddha ceremony for religious reasons is declining and undesirable social practices like bride-price, child marriage, extra expenditure on ceremonies connected with pregnancy and death, beating breasts while sorrowing over the death of a person, etc. are becoming infrequent. Further, interest has been generated in Jain religion, history, literature, and culture. But the efforts made have not yet succeeded in bringing about a sense of oneness among all Jains, irrespective of differences of sect, caste, religion, language or occupation.

Jainism Enters the Modern Age

As has been mentioned, Jains declined in numbers after the medieval period. In some ways this strengthened Jainism for it produced tight-knit communities of Jains with common interests and a devotion to the faith reinforced by their closeness within the group. In the early nineteenth century we must speak of communities, rather than of a single Jain community, for within the wider structure of the Jain religion Jainism provided, and indeed still provides, for a number of sometimes overlapping allegiances. Besides the broad division between the Svetambara, strongest in western India, and the Digambara, mainly in the south, there is the Sthanakvasi sect (within the Svetambara division) which rejects the worship of images. The Terapanthi, an offshoot of the Sthanakvasi, dates from 1760 and has become a well- organized and active movement. The Svetambara, more than the Digambara, have always shown a tendency to form groupings around particular teachers and their successors.

Allegiance to a particular temple often can run parallel to family or caste allegiance. We must be honest about the fact that, as in any live and active organization, religious or secular, differences of opinion can arise within the broad unity of the Jain faith. In the nineteenth and twentieth centuries we can pick out certain mainstreams of development. With the growth of modern communications there has been a notable development of all- India federations of various sorts. Secondly, Jain scholarship, education and writing have broadened out at all levels, whether simple aids for children or learned editions of the sacred texts and university theses on Jain topics. Thirdly, Jains have become much more conscious of the wider public: without seeking to count heads of converts like many religions, Jains have become concerned to spread knowledge of the Jain religion and to encourage adherence to its principles.

Parallel to this there has been a growing (though still small) interest by scholars and others in the West and by non-Jains in India. Lastly, for the first time in Jain history, Jainism has been carried to Africa, Europe and North America, where Jain communities have settled and flourished. Jains have a long association with finance and commerce and many were well placed to play a leading role in the economic development of modern India. There was an influx to the big commercial and manufacturing centers of Bombay and Calcutta in the nineteenth century. Development was not without its traumas: when Jain businessmen first became involved in the cotton industry in Ahmedabad they were criticized by co-religionists fearful of the harm to tiny living beings implicit in the operation of the great new machines.

The reputation of Jain businessmen for honesty and fair dealing, together with a simple way of life, stood them in good stead and many prospered exceedingly. Prosperity reinforced the traditional Jain devotion to charitable causes. The building of temples, some of great beauty and richness like the great white marble edifice to the fifteenth Tirthankara erected in Ahmedabad in 1848 by a prominent businessman, went ahead in the nineteenth and twentieth centuries. Educational institutions have been endowed and publishing of religious works supported. Peculiarly Jain institutions, the refuges for sick animals are maintained. Generosity to Jain causes, by people of all income groups, is a major Jain characteristic, but generosity is not confined to Jain causes alone. Let us now pick up a few, only a few, examples of the prominent people who have been particularly concerned with the promotion of Jain faith and principles over the past century. In 1893, a 'World Parliament of Religions' was held in the United States and the organizer sought a Jain representative.

The invitation went to Acharya Atmaramji but as a monk it was not possible for him to travel so the task of being the Acharya's representative and the first Jain to explain his religion to a major overseas gathering fell to Sri Virchand Gandhi, Honorary Secretary of the Jain Association of India. His lectures in the U.S.A. earned him a silver medal from the Parliament of Religions for his scholarly oratory. He received other honors and a philosophical society named after him was established. Going on to England he continued his lecturing (he gave 535 lectures in all). One of his students was Herbert Warren who became secretary of the Jain Literature Society founded with Virchand Gandhi's help. Herbert Warren wrote two successful books on Jainism explaining the subject in a straightforward up-to-date way. Virchand Gandhi died at the very early age of thirty-seven. Another learned layman was Champat Ray Jain, a barrister by profession. Fluent in Hindi, Urdu and English, he studied the Christian and Muslim religions and claimed that their message was essentially the same as that of Jainism.

He published a dozen books in the 1920s and '30s, including The Key of Knowledge, Jain Law, and what is Jainism? In his writings and lectures he explained religion in twentieth century terms, using the concepts of modern psychology and science. Srimad Rajchandra is especially remembered as the spiritual mentor of Mahatma Gandhi. The Mahatma, though not he a Jain, was deeply influenced by Jain doctrines, particularly non-violence. Rajchandra wrote many books, with emphasis on the soul and its purification. He died young but his work survives in a number of religious centers or foundations established by his followers. The monastic order has known many who have made significant contributions to Jain learning and Jain religion in the past century. Acharya Vallbhvijay Suri was born in 1870 and lived to be 84. The shock of losing both his parents as a child turned him to spiritual quests and at the age of seventeen he became a monk as a disciple of the famous Atmaramji.

It was the dying wish of his teacher that Vallabhvijay should devote himself to the establishment of educational institutions. It is for this work that he is especially remembered. In his long life he established schools and colleges. Mahavir Jain Vidhyalaya, founded under his guidance to provide university hostels and religious education, and help with higher education for poorer students, now has seven branches and has produced very many graduates. Acharya Vallabhvijay was a simple and effective preacher, free from sectarian bias, with a love for people of all faiths and a devotion to his native land and the cause of its independence. The Terapanthi sect, which, like the Sthanakvasi from which it separated in the eighteenth century, does not worship images, has a single spiritual leader or Acharya. In 1936 his position passed to twenty-one year old Acharya Tulsi. It was an inspired choice, for this young man was to transform the Terapanthi. He has traveled to almost every part of India.

He has shown particular concern for education and preaching, putting emphasis on study, research and writing by Terapanthi monks, and by nuns as well. The Jain Vishva Bharati which emerged from his work is an institution for higher education in the Jain field. The Anuvrata Movement which he initiated in 1949 works for moral uplift, honesty and a non-violent, non-exploitive society: some of its members are non-Jains. In 1980, he introduced another innovation with the initiation of the first of a new order of 'lay nuns' and 'lay monks', shramani and shramana. Whilst dedicated to the life of nuns and monks, they are dispensed from the prohibitions on traveling in vehicles and on eating with lay people (and cooking for, themselves if essential) as well as from certain toilet rules incumbent on the full-fledged mendicant. Kanji Swami was originally a Sthanakvasi but after much searching found that the Digambara sect best answered his spiritual needs.

He is known for his work on Kunda-Kunda, a great south Indian Jain writer probably of the third or the fourth century A.D. A movement which he started in 1934, which stresses inward thought rather than external ritual, attracted followers who hold him in great reverence. Another distinguished scholar was Vijay Dharma Suri (1868- 1922) who wrote many books on Jain philosophy and ethics in Sanskrit, Gujarati and Hindi, edited texts and inscriptions, started an important series of published texts, the Yashovijaya Jaina Granthamala (named after the seventeenth- century scholar Yashovijaya), established schools and corresponded with many Indian and European scholars. The list could go on for pages! Let us end by mentioning Ratnachandraji Maharaj who completed in 1932 the publication of a four-volume dictionary of Ardhamagadhi, the language of the ancient Jain scriptures, with explanations in Sanskrit, Gujarati, Hindi and English.

One important development in recent decades has been the publication of good modern editions, often with translations into modern languages, of the sacred books of Jainism, thus making the scriptures, formerly restricted to monks, available to a wider public. Ray Dhanpati Simha Bahadur initiated the printing of Jain Agama texts in the 1880s. The Sacred Books of the Jains series, started by Kumar Devendra Prasad Jain, published from 1917 various Digambara texts with English translations and commentary.

Baharatiya Jnanpith, of Varanasi, engages in research and publication, and a steady stream of publications comes from the L.D. Institute of Indology in Ahmedabad. The L.D. Institute is building up an important Jain manuscript collection in original and microfilm. There is, in fact, a great deal of publishing in India in the Jain field, ranging from children's books to university theses on specialized topics, from commercial publishers as well as from Jain institutions.

The quality is very varied: magnificent (and often expensive) books on Jain art or works of serious advanced scholarship can be seen alongside amateurish (but certainly sincere) little pamphlets. Periodicals of one sort and another have proliferated since 1857: over 120 titles can be counted, including in English the Jain Journal (Calcutta) and The Jain, trilingual in English, Gujarati and Hindi (published by Jain Samaj Europe). Five universities in India have professors of Jain studies and a new institution in Delhi may well become the major center in this field. The challenge from both Muslim and Christian missionary effort towards the end of the nineteenth century was one factor behind the establishment of a number of nationwide Jain institutions, but they also enable Jains to face the challenges of the modern world in a united way. The All- India Digambara Jain Conference first met in 1893.

A similar Svetambara organization dates from 1903 and a united meeting of 700 Svetambara monks was held in 1934 to reaffirm the traditional rules. The Sthanakvasi held their first national conference in 1906 and took an important step in 1952 when they recognized Atmaranji Sadadi as the single chief Acharya (religious leader) of the sect: his present successor is Acharya Anandarushi. A wider dimension was given to Jain unity with the formation in 1899 of the Jain Young Men's Association which became in 1910 the All-India Jain Association. In 1973 the 2500th anniversary of Mahavira's moksa was the occasion for widespread celebrations and marked the new resurgent spirit of Jainism. Emigration from India has led to Jain communities emerging in East Africa, Europe and North America. Jain temples have been set up in Mombassa and Nairobi, and the first in Europe will be in Leicester.

In North America various Jain associations have come together in a single federation. Western interest in Jainism is growing, though slowly. Much work has been done by Western scholars since Major Colin Mackenzie published his 'Account of the Jains' in the journal of the Asiatic Society of Bengal in 1807. The Germans were to become the most active in the field of Jain research. A landmark was the publication in 1884 of the first two volumes of Jain Sutras, translated into English by Hermann Jacobi. It would not be appropriate here to give a long catalogue of names, but it would include English, German, French, Italian and even Japanese scholars. Although good general accounts of the Jain religion have long been available in French and German, no such work by an English writer has been published except Mrs. Sinclair Stevenson's The Heart of Jainism (1915), a sympathetic book but colored by a strong Christian missionary outlook. At a more popular level, knowledge of Jainism and the Jains is filtering only very slowly into Western consciousness.

Within the Jain community there is a desire to make the principles of Jainism known to a wider world and this cannot do anything but good. There is no doubt that now, in the late twentieth century, Jainism is in a healthy state. The great pilgrimage centers are popular, religious practices and ceremonies attract large numbers, charity towards Jain cause is generous. Jainism has spread beyond the bounds of India and the ambitious Jain Center in Leicester is an example to all.

13

The Baha'i Faith in India

Of the approximately 5 million members claimed world-wide by the Baha'i authorities, nearly 2 million Baha'is are said to reside within the Republic of India. This means that close to 40% of the international Baha'i community is to be found within the borders of this South Asian nation, a statistic that not only reflects the important position India currently holds within the world-wide Baha'i community, but also suggests that this country may have an important impact on the future direction the religion might take. The study of the history and sociology of the movement in the subcontinent is therefore an increasingly vital component of Baha'i studies as an academic field.

I discern five distinct stages of development during the nearly 150 years of Baha'i history in India:

1. The Babi, or pre-Baha'i period;
2. The initial stage of Baha'i community development (1872 -1910);
3. The first steps toward national unity (1910-1921);
4. The period of the Guardianship and the evolution of the community as part of an international administrative order (1921-1957); and
5. The era of mass teaching (1957 to the present).

Beyond containing their own unique personalities and

events, these periods also display distinct patterns of community organization and missionary endeavor. I will here be interested in justifying this periodization of the history of the community, as well as in asking what dynamics (both internal and external) led to the changes that moved the community from one stage to the next. The Baha'i Faith is a contemporary religious movement active nowadays in over three hundred countries and dependencies throughout the world. Evolving from the Babi movement, which spread throughout Iran and Iraq in the mid-nineteenth century, the Baha'i Faith has slowly moved beyond the pale of Shi'ite Islam and thereby established itself as an independent religion.

The movement's founder, Mirza Husayn 'Ali of Nur, Baha'u'llah (1817-1892), is considered by adherents to be a messenger of God equal in station to, among others, Moses, Jesus, Muhammad, Buddha and the Hindu avatars. Banished from Iran in 1853 by the order of Nasiru'd-Din Shah, he lived in exile, being sent to Baghdad, Istanbul (Constantinople), Edirne (Adrianople), and, finally, the prison city of Acre (Akka or now Akko) located in the bay near Haifa in what was then Ottoman Syria and is now Israel. After Baha'u'llah's death the leadership of the community passed to his eldest son, Abbas Effendi, Abdu'l-Baha (1844-1921), who following his release from captivity in 1908 visited both Europe and North America.

In 1921 Abdu'l-Baha's grandson, Shoghi Effendi, succeeded to the head of the Faith, having been named Guardian of the movement in Abdu'l-Baha's will. During the Guardianship (1921-1957) the Baha'i Faith increased both in size and administrative capabilities by establishing communities in over 130 countries and developing local, national and international administrative institutions. From 1957 to 1963 the Baha'I Faith was guided by The Hands of the Cause, a group of initially 27 individuals (22 men and 5 women) who had been personally appointed by Shoghi

Effendi to help him oversee the international activities of the movement. Since 1963 the affairs of the Faith have been directed by the Universal House of Justice, a body of nine men (women are currently prohibited from serving on this body) elected every five years by national representatives, whose headquarters is located in Haifa.

The Babi Period

The Babi movement, the predecessor to the Baha'i faith, had some connections with India. Two of the most important Babi histories make mention of several prominent Indian believers. The major Baha'i historian for this period, Muhammad-i Zarandi, Nabil-i Azam, informs us that one of the Bab's original disciples (Letters of the Living) was an Indian known as Shaykh Sa'id-i-Hindi. Following instructions he took the Bab's claims throughout several provinces of Iran and into his own homeland. The fruits of this latter venture, however, were far from productive, as his only success was the conversion of a certain Sayyid in the town of Multan. After this the Shaykh's activities are not recorded.

Another Indian who was ordered by the Bab to journey to India was a dervish referred to in Mirza Husayn of Hamadan's history *Tarikh-i-Jadid* as "the Indian believer." He came to the prison of Chihriq where the Bab was being held and managed to meet him, receiving from him the title "Qahru'llah." After several encounters with local religious authorities, including a brief arrest in the city of Khuy, he set out for India on foot. Whether or not he completed his journey is unknown.

A third significant convert during this time was a blind Sayyid, Jinab-i-Basir. Nabil states that he was the above mentioned Sayyid converted by Shaykh Sa'id-i Hindi. In contrast the *Tarikh-i-Jadid* claims that Jinab-i-Basir heard of the Bab's appearance in Bombay from where he traveled to Mecca and met him in person.After the Bab's death Jinab-i-Basir, along with several other Babis, made extravagant claims, but he was eventually "faced-down" by Baha'u'llah who made his own claim to divinity. Jinab-i-Basir was later executed for his beliefs in Luristan.

That there were other Indian believers is made evident by Mahjur's monograph on the Babi insurrection in Mazandaran. He lists four Indians as being among the 318 Babis who fought at Fort Shaykh Tabarsi. Moreover, in the 1850s the Afnan clan, relatives of the Bab, established a trading center in Bombay. Although some knowledge of the Bab's claims had thus penetrated into South Asia and fired certain local millenialist expectations, there was lacking the needed doctrinal and ritual coherence that is required of community. Both the physical distance from the sources of inspiration, as well as the disruption and turmoil evident amongst the Babi communites in Iran, especially following the Bab's execution, made community virtually impossible. Thus it would not be until the movement came under the influence of Baha'u'llah and, later, of Abdu'l-Baha, that a true community would begin to develop.

The Indian Baha'i Community (1872-1910)

Two members of the Afnan clan who were resident in Bombay, Haji Sayyid Mirza and Sayyid Muhammad, became Baha'is in the 1860s, and they wrote to Baha'u'llah requesting that a Baha'i teacher be sent to India. Baha'u'llah asked Sulayman Khan Tunukabani (known as Jamal Effendi), who was both a Sufi and a learned scholar of Arabic and Persian, if he would take on the task, and his arrival in Bombay in 1872 can be rightly said to signal the beginning of organized missionary activity in the subcontinent.

After a short stay in Bombay Jamal Effendi began a teaching tour that took him across the entire country and was highlighted by his attending the ceremony in Delhi at which Queen Victoria was proclaimed *The Empress of India*. The proselytizing style he employed can be gleaned from an account penned by one of his Indian converts, Sayyid Mustafa Rumi of Madras:

It was his custom to notify his arrival to the Governor or highest official of the place in British India and the ruling prince in an Indian state. He would then pay a visit to them and deliver the message. His list of those to whom he delivered the Message contains names of almost all the high officials and princes of the land.

Thus Jamal Effendi established an *elitist* approach to teaching the Baha'i Faith in India, and it was this style of teaching that would dominate Baha'i missionary activity in India for decades. It seems that for the most part Jamal Effendi's efforts were met with courteous interest if not overt enthusiasm. The progressive character of many of the Baha'i principles spoke well to reformers, and the universality inherent in many of the religion's teachings was welcomed by those who feared communalism. There were, however, exceptions. Both in Bombay and Calcutta Jamal Effendi raised the ire of conservative religious leaders. What the liberal wing of Indian intellectual leadership saw as forward looking, traditionalists viewed as dangerous. These conservative Muslim and Hindu anti-Baha'i polemics were muted by the relatively small number of converts Jamal Effendi was able to attract by the time of his departure in 1878.

Jamal Effendi left behind him three prominent converts (Rafi u'd-Din Khan of Hasanpur, Haji Ramadan of Rampur and Sayyid Mustafa Rumi), who would begin the slow process of building the Indian community. During this time the Afnan's printing press in Bombay produced the first ever Baha'i books to be printed. The *Book of Certitude* and the *Secret of Divine Civilization* were both published in1882. In order to further the publishing work, prominent Baha'i calligraphers such as Mishkin-Qalam and Mirza Muhammad Ali came to Bombay.

After the death of Baha'u'llah and the inauguration of the ministry of Abdu'l-Baha, the Baha'i community in Bombay was split as a consequence of the activities of the followers of Mirza Muhammad Ali who had challenged his half-brother's right to legitimate leadership. As a result, Abdu'l-Baha directed a number of prominent emissaries to India, both Persian and Western, to guide the community and encourage teaching. Among these were Mirza Mahmud Zarqani, Aqa Mirza Mahram, Mirza Hasan Adib, Ibin-i-Asdaq, Lua Getsinger, Mrs. H. Stanndard, Sidney Sprague, Hooper Harris and Harlan Ober. By 1908 the work of these individuals along with a small group of local converts had produced functioning communities in Bombay, Calcutta, Aligarh and Lahore. Of these, the Bombay community took the forefront in both teaching and translation work. Its advancements in the area of translation marked the first time any of Baha'u'llah's writings had been translated into one of the native languages of India. Bombay also managed to acquire the first Baha'i cemetery in India, and Abdu'l-Baha designed the layout of the sight.

The activities of the Bombay community were commented upon by Sydney Sprague who in 1908 reported: "There are three meetings a week held in Bombay and there are as rule eighty to a hundred men present." He also noted that it was not easy to become a Baha'i: "It often means a great sacrifice on the part of a believer, a loss of friends, money and position." During this period, a number of Indian Zoroastrians ("Parsis") were converted to the Baha'i Faith, thereby forming a nucleus of future Baha'i leadership in India. The conversions came about as a result of the work of agents who had originally been sent abroad by the Indian Zoroastrian community to help their coreligionists in Iran. There they came into contact with the Baha'i Faith and supported its activities. Later, several Iranian Zoroastrian converts to the Faith traveled to Bombay (notably Mulla Bahram Akhtar-Khavari) and actively promulgated their new religion among local Zoroastrians. Although they were met with opposition by some of the conservative dasturs, these missionary converts were quite successful in opening the Zoroastrian community to Baha'I concepts and teachings.

This second stage of development, which manifested the first true signs of Baha'i community in India, was characterized by two main features. The first was the previously noted elitist approach to teaching the Faith. Following the lead of Jamal Effendi, the nascent Baha'i communities focused their efforts on local leaders and members of the intelligentsia. Association with reform movements such as the Theosophical Society and the Brahmo-Samaj proved popular, as did lectures and pamphleteering. The fact that Islamic reform movements of the period were often characterized by strong strains of revivalism and separatism did not make them as fertile grounds for Baha'i interaction, although there is evidence that Baha'is did make an attempt to raise their claims with the leader of the Ahmaddiya movement, Mirza Ghulam Ahmad of Qadiyan.

The main assumption underlying the focus on literate members of the middle and upper classes was that legitimate conversion to the Baha'i Faith required fairly extensive knowledge on the part of a new believer of the religion's doctrines and principles, which in turn required a fairly high level of education. In following this tack the Baha'is were in many ways mirroring the attitudes of the reform movements with which they came into contact. Reform was primarily the prerogative of the upper classes who often looked to English liberal ideas and institutions for inspiration. There was little thought of speaking to the masses.

Even in the secular Indian political arena it was English educated Indians in the professions who came to form, in effect, a new class, which prior to the arrival of Gandhi on the national scene was virtually cut off from the mass of the population. Moreover, the fact that for the most part the Baha'i message was presented in Persian, Arabic, Urdu, or English added to the sense of exclusivity, as these languages were generally associated with cultural elites. The second feature concerned the nature of Baha'i community organization which was almost exclusively local in orientation. Throughout the country various Baha'i communities acted virtually independent of one another. Although they had as their sources of spiritual unity the figures of Baha'u'llah and Abdu'l-Baha, when it came to organizing teaching plans and developing community administration there was little sense of national unity.

In looking at the factors that helped move the Indian Baha'I community into this stage of development, the ability to make contact with the established sources of authority through personally sent emissaries stands out as vital. Up until the time of Jamal Effendi's arrival in Bombay those Babis and then Baha'is who traveled to, or resided in, the subcontinent remained effectively isolated and without central leadership. The use of traveling teachers, especially by Abdu'l-Baha, helped bridge this gap of isolation, and although the individual communities remained relatively autonomous, the symbolic sense of leadership that was now available provided a much needed sphere of spiritual orientation.

Also of considerable importance was the establishment of the Afnan's printing press in Bombay which not only resulted in greater contact with other Baha'i communities in the Middle East but also gave to that city a unique Baha'i cultural identity. Extensive telegraph, rail and steamship networks, initially established by European entrepreneurs and colonial governments for their own purposes, now linked the Middle East and British India and were key technological prerequisites for this greater integration of the community, as well.

The First Steps towards National Unity (1910-1921)

With the advent of a national teaching plan in 1910 a new phase of Baha'i history in India began. In January of that year a convention comprised of members of India's various religious communities was held in Allahabad. The Baha'is were invited to the convention, and Sayyid Mustafa

Rumi presented a talk which was enthusiastically received by the delegates. As a result of this interest it was decided that "teaching" (proselytization) activities in the subcontinent should be accelerated, and before the year had ended a national teaching campaign was launched. The program called for the election of a nineteen member teaching council which would coordinate propagation activities across the entire country. The council officially came into existence in August, 1911.

Although not winning many converts, the teaching campaign of 1911 was of marked importance to the Indian Baha'i community, since it signified the first real attempt systematically to proselytize for the faith on a national basis. The next major step in this direction took place approximately ten years later. In December, 1920, the First All-India Baha'i Convention was held in the city of Bombay. Representatives from India's major religious communities were present as well as Baha'i delegates from throughout the country. For three days the delegates heard speeches, consulted with one another and drafted resolutions that would become the focal point of the community's goals for the next decade. The resolutions included the collection of funds to build a Baha'i temple, the estab-lishment of a Baha'i school and the expansion of teaching and translation work.

While the pattern of missionary elitism continued during this phase of development, the shift toward organi-zational centrism is new and demands explanation. To some degree this movement was a natural consequence of expanded teaching plans that required greater logistical coordination. Thus the resolutions of the 1920 Convention were logically tied to the experiences of the 1910 teaching plan. But why the emphasis in 1910 on the national approach to teaching? I would suggest that one significant factor in this regard was the growing sense of Indian nationalism that was found among Indian intellectuals and reformers of the period.

Indeed the landmark Government of India Act of 1909, although communal in structure, initiated a new kind of association of Indians with Britishers in fashioning legislation for all of British India and has been called by one modern historian the first tentative path toward responsible parliamentary government for India.Thus the political milieu in which the then Baha'i community found itself operating was one that focused its thinking in national terms, and such an attitude may well have influenced the community's view of itself. Here it is important to remember that the Teaching Plan of 1910 was initiated as a result of Baha'i participation in a non-Baha'i, national event - The All-India Allahabad Religious Convention.

The Period of the Guardianship (1921-1957)

In April, 1923, Shoghi Effendi created the National Spiritual Assembly of the Baha'is of India and Burma and thereby formalized the idea of an Indian national community. The role he bequeathed to this body is made evident in the following message sent in November, 1925:

I pray that your newly constituted National Assembly may grow from strength to strength, may coordinate and consolidate the ever expanding activities of the friends of India and Burma and inaugurate a fresh campaign of Teaching that will redound to the glory and power of the Most Great Name.

Under the guidance of the National Spiritual Assembly and the supervision of Shoghi Effendi in Haifa, the Indian Baha'i community slowly began to feel the effects of the emerging worldwide Baha'I administrative system. Increasingly during the period of the Guardianship Indian teaching plans were timed and coordinated with those of other countries. In addition to welcoming "travel teachers" (itinerant missionaries) from different parts of the world, Indian Baha'is gradually began to generate regular teaching campaigns modeled on the lines of those initiated by Shoghi

Effendi in the United States. Thus when in 1937 the American community introduced the Seven Year Plan, the Indian NSA decided they should organize a similar project, and accordingly a Six Year Plan was drawn up and scheduled to commence in 1938.

Although for monetary reasons the start of the plan was delayed until 1940, the first Baha'i summer school was able to be held in Simla in 1938, and when the plan did get underway it produced immediate results. By 1941 three new local communities with functioning assemblies had been established: Hyderabad, Kota and Bangalore. The next year saw three more local spiritual assemblies established, and several Baha'I groups (communities with less than nine members) were also formed. The rigorous teaching efforts continued during the final years of the plan, and by its completion date in 1944 the Indian community was comprised of twenty-nine local spiritual assemblies.

The achievements of the Six Year Plan encouraged the Indian Baha'I community to launch another teaching campaign in April, 1946. Although disrupted by the turmoil accompanying the 1947 Partition of the subcontinent into India and Pakistan, the Four Year Plan met with much the same results as its predecessor. By April, 1947, an additional eight local spiritual assemblies had been created and the same number of groups established. Due to these figures the NSA received nearly 600 pounds sterling from Baha'i communities throughout the world to finance yet another teaching project, and consequently in 1951 the Indian Baha'i community embarked on its third successive teaching campaign. This effort resulted in the formation of eight more local spiritual assemblies and the translation of books and pamphlets into as many as fifteen different languages.

An indication of the new status the Indian Baha'i community (which now numbered approximately seven hundred) had achieved in the worldwide Baha'i community, is that New Delhi was chosen as one of four sites for international teaching conferences in 1953, each held on a different continent. The Delhi convention of October, 1953, helped mark both the completion of India's third major teaching project in the preceding fifteen years and the inauguration of Shoghi Effendi's world-wide Ten Year Crusade. The 450 Baha'is who attended the conference (from such varied countries as the United States, Canada, Iran, Iraq, Australia and New Zealand) outlined strategies for the upcoming Crusade and engaged in an active program of public relations which included a reception in one of New Delhi's large hotels. The event was attended by over a thousand persons.

In addition a delegation was able to meet with the Prime Minister of India, Jawaharlal Nehru. When the conference was concluded on October 15, 1953, Indian Baha'is once again found themselves embarking on a teaching project, a plan which by the time of its completion in 1963 would not only find the Baha'i international community under new leadership, but would also have revolutionized the composition of the Indian Baha'I community. While the period of the Guardianship witnessed important structural and administrative changes in India, the style of teaching remained fundamentally the same as in earlier periods. It was still to the urban, educated members of Indian society that Baha'i teachers primarily directed their message.

The base was broadened to some degree by the fact that literacy rates in India rose during this period, especially in urban areas. Moreover, the translation of Baha'i literature into a number of different Indian languages meant that Baha'i written publications could receive a wider audience, but in terms of logistics the large metropolitan centers such as Bombay, Calcutta and New Delhi remained focal points of activity. Even though as early as 1933 (when referring to translation work) Shoghi Effendi had written: "I would urge you to concentrate your energy on this important and essential preliminary to an intensive campaign of teaching among the masses in India", his suggestion was not followed. Lecture tours and university visits were incapable of reaching the masses, yet these activities remained by and large the order of the day.

There were, however, two important exceptions to this trend. The first originated during the Six Year Plan and proved to be a real stimulus to community growth. This was a decision by a number of Indian Baha'is to leave the large urban centers and establish residences in smaller towns and cities. Significantly these moves added several new local spiritual assemblies to the community's total, and consequently pioneering became a primary goal of all future plans. The second event took place in the central Indian city of Ujjain in 1944 when the newly formed assembly was asked to participate in an Arya Samaj sponsored meeting.

Mr. Mahfuz'l-Haq Ilmi, a well-known Baha'i travel teacher, addressed the group on the subject of Baha'i social principles. His speech attracted the attention of one Kishan Lal Malviya, a scheduled caste leader from Shajapur (a district northeast of Ujjain). Following the conference Kishan Lal came into contact with the Ujjain Baha'i community and eventually declared him a Baha'i. At about the same time another scheduled caste leader, Dayaram Malviya, also converted. Thus in 1944 the first villagers in central India entered the Baha'i Faith, and while their conversions were not immediately capitalized upon by local Baha'is, both men were destined to play prominent roles in the new course the Baha'I teaching mission would take in the 1960s.

There can be little doubt that the impetus which brought the Indian Baha'i community into this stage of its development and allowed it to show the first real indication of being more than just a few loosely connected groups of metropolitan believers was the personage of Shoghi Effendi and his vision of the Baha'i World Order. While it is true that during the first two decades of the twentieth century signs of movement in the direction of a more unified and cohesive community were present in India, it took the power and prestige that an institution like the Guardianship could command, as well as the organizational skills and energy that Shoghi Effendi brought to the position, to help actualize earlier trends. Symbolic of this new identity was the NSA which he created and helped guide. But even with such dynamic leadership and a new sense of being an active part of an expanding international organization, at the time of Shoghi Effendi's death in November, 1957, there were still less than a thousand Baha'is in the entire country.

The Mass Teaching Era - (1961 to present)

Just prior to Shoghi Effendi's death small-scale mass conversion to the Baha'i faith had begun in East Africa. As part of the Ten Year Crusade a new attitude toward missionary work had begun to develop among a certain segment of Baha'i leadership. Whereas the traditional approach to conversion had been based on the assumption that new believers should be well-informed as regards the details of Baha'i theology, history and administration, there were those who believed that if the Baha'i Faith was going to experience significant growth such stringent requirements would have to be removed. Moreover, the traditional approach virtually excluded the illiterate segments of the world's population. In one of his last letters Shoghi Effendi himself had endorsed this perspective.

He wrote to the NSA of South and West Africa that: "The essential thing is that the candidate for enrollment should believe in his heart the truth of Baha'u'llah. Whether he is illiterate, informed of all the teachings or not, is beside the point entirely." The first organized move in the direction of taking the Baha'I message outside of the towns and cities of India took place in 1959. A teaching conference was held in village Rampur (not far from Varanasi/Benares), and although it did not result in mass conversions, it did provide the first close contact between urban Baha'is and large numbers of Indian villagers.

The conference also produced several recommendations that had significant implications for future Baha'i missionary work throughout India. These included the mass prdoduction of simple leaflets for distribution in nearby villages, the establishment of study classes in Rampur and the regular participation of urban Baha'is in Rampur's religious festivals. One of the individuals who were convinced of the benefits of the new teaching approach was Hand of the Cause, Dr. Rahmatullah Muhajir. In early 1960 following the Rampur conference he met with the Indian NSA and advised them to focus their teaching activities on the rural areas. Moreover he suggested that they take the lead in this direction by personally going to villages to proclaim the message.

Shortly thereafter Mrs. Shirin Boman Meherabani traveled to the city of Indore in the state of Madhya Pradesh where she took council with her brother. He informed her of a nearby Bhilala tribal village where some Baha'i contact had been made. The village was named Kweitiopani and was located approximately fifty miles from Indore in the Dewas district. During the next few weeks Mrs. Meherabani made several excursions to Kweitiopani and then invited those who believed in Baha'u'llah to declare themselves as Baha'is. As a result nearly 75% of the village's largely illiterate population of two-hundred put their thumb prints on enrollment cards. Kweitiopani became the first rural community in India to experience mass conversion.

Following the Kweitiopani conversions Dr. Muhajir returned to India and requested that a village teaching conference similar to the Rampur conference be planned for central India. After consultation it was decided that village Sangimanda in Shajapur District of Madhya Pradesh (the region has traditionally been referred to as Malwa) would be a suitable cite. The decision was based on the fact that it was the home village of Kishan Lal Malviya, the scheduled caste leader who had declared back in 1944. With his help arrangements for the conference were made and in late January, 1961, Dr. Muhajir arrived in Ujjain and proceeded by jeep to the village. An open-air meeting was held at which more than 300 people listened to Baha'I speakers. At the conclusion of the conference over two hundred villagers declared.

The Kweitiopani and Sangimanda declarations set in motion a tide of mass conversions in central India. Leaders in the new crusade included Mrs. Meherabani and her son-in-law, Mr. K.H. Vajdi who traveled extensively by jeep in the rural areas of Malwa. Over the next two year period more than 85,000 declarations were received. The majority of these came from the scheduled castes in Malwa and the rural regions surrounding the city of Gwalior.

The impact the conversions had on the Baha'i international community was reflected in a message sent by the Hands of the Cause (who until the election of the Universal House of Justice in 1963 were directing Baha'i international affairs) to the national conventions around the world:

India, one of the first countries in the world to receive the light of a newly-born Revelation has, during the past year, witnessed a tide of mass conversion not only wholly unprecedented in that country but without parallel anywhere in the entire world during the last one hundred years of Baha'i history.

Following the lead of Baha'i teachers in Malwa and Gwalior, Baha'is in other parts of the country began to initiate rural mass teaching campaigns. Successes similar to those in Madhya Pradesh were experienced in areas of Uttar Pradesh, Andrah Pradesh and Gujarat. In response to the continued expansion, in 1964 Shoghi Effendi's widow and Hand of the Cause, Ruhiyyih Khanum, made an extended trip to India where she toured the mass teaching areas and encouraged village teachers to maintain the momentum. The results of the mass teaching campaign in India during its first decade of implementation can be seen in the enormous increase of both numbers of declared believers and local spiritual assemblies.

Whereas in 1961 there were a total of 78 local spiritual assemblies and less than 1,000 believers, by 1970 these figures had risen to 3,350 assemblies and 312,602 believers. There was a slight lull in growth during the mid-1970s, though significant conversions took place following 1977, and there was a steady increase in reported declarations until the late 1980s, after which growth appears to have reached a plateau. In the late 1990s the Indian Baha'i comm-unity claims a membership of over two million persons, though the reliability of this claim is complicated by ques-tions over the meaning of signing a "declaration card" in India's syncretistic religious atmosphere. Special regional teaching projects such as the South Indian Teaching Project (1977 -1980) and the East India Teaching Project (1978-1980) were, and have been, the focal point of missionary activity since that time.

This has been the result of an administrative policy for India adopted by the Universal House of Justice which in the 1980s divided the country into twenty-two state teaching committees that have been delegated the authority and power to manage the administrative and proselytizing work in their respective states. Indeed, these state bodies (now called "state Baha'i councils") are currently in charge of all aspects of administration within their states (except the deprivation of voting rights) that were earlier handled by the NSA. The events of the mass teaching period raise several important questions, and despite the fact that complete answers lie beyond the scope this paper, they should at least be mentioned and commented upon.

The more significant questions would include:

1. What factors caused the shift in Baha'i missionary activity from a more conservative and elitist approach bound to the metropolitan centers to a policy focused upon reaching the rural masses?
2. How can we account for the positive response to the Baha'I message by so many Indian villagers?

3. In light of the new teaching approach, what did/do the declarations *mean* both religiously and sociologically? And
4. What impact has the mass teaching period had on the administrative structure of the Indian Baha'i community?

As mentioned earlier, there are references in the late writings of Shoghi Efendi that demonstrate his support for bringing uneducated believers into the Baha'i Faith, so in openly incorporating this policy into their teaching mission the Indian community was not, theoretically at least, departing on a radical course. The question remains, however, as to why this policy was not established until the early 1960s. Looking at dynamics from within the Faith itself, three answers come to mind, one fairly apparent and the other two more speculative. One significant factor was the personage of Hand of the Cause, Dr. Muhajir. Although he realized that the mass teaching approach would bring with it certain organizational problems, and that there would be individuals opposed to its results on the grounds of "loss of control," it was his constant support and encouragement that led to the initial village teaching sojourns.

As Mrs. Shirin Boman Meherabani indicated in a personal interview in 1973, without his vision and guidance it is questionable as to whether the Indian NSA would have moved in this direction. A second factor which may well have come into play (and was expressed to me by several prominent Indian Baha'is) was the growing awareness among Indian Baha'is that past policies, if not having failed, were at least wanting in terms of building a strong and dynamic community. After close to a century of missionary work there were still less than a thousand believers in the subcontinent. A new strategy was obviously needed. And then there was the fact of Shoghi Effendi's death, which may have created greater space for individual initiative on the one hand, and on the other may also have led those mourning his loss to redouble their efforts to fulfill his stated wishes for mass proselytizing.

There are also external factors to consider. Of primary importance in this regard was the fact that by the early 1960s India had experienced over a decade of democratic government, and although Indian society still remained highly hierarchical in structure, the influences of the democratic spirit, as expressed in both the public education system and the work of leading intellectuals, combined with the Gandhian ideal of social service, had helped chip away at certain elitist attiudes, especially among the young. The more psychologically democratic social milieu likely made mass teaching to low caste and illiterate villagers seem more natural, in a movement which claimed as one of its leading social principles the "Oneness of Mankind," than it may have been in prior decades.

Finally there is the reality of the initial successes experienced by the village teachers. Had the teaching in Kweitiopani and Sangimanda not produced the desired declarations, or had the flood of new converts that followed in surrounding villages and regions failed to materialize, the plan may have been discarded. In other words, one of the causes of the success of the mass teaching policy was success itself! For a movement that within less than two years had increased its enrollment numbers from less than one thousand to over eighty-nine thousand there was cause enough to continue on the new path.

This leads us naturally into our second question. Why did the Baha'i teachers experience such success? Why did large numbers of villagers sign declaration cards? Based on my field research in Malwa in 1973-74 I have come to two basic conclusions. The first has to do with the caste backgrounds of many of those who declared, while the second is related to the teaching approach adopted by Baha'i missionaries. It should be noted, however, that since this research was limited in both time and space these conclusions must remain essentially speculative. Hopefully future researchwill either confirm or amend them. Kweitiopani was a tribal village (Bhilala), and Sangimanda contained large numbers of scheduled caste Hindu inhabitants (Chamar andBalai). It was in these two villages that mass conversions first tookplace, and the pattern set there was largely followed throughout the various regions of Malwa during the initial years of the mass teaching campaign.

This should not be surprising, as it fits a fairly well established pattern of religious conversion in India whereby non-caste tribal groups and lower castes seek to improve their social standing through conversion to a new religion. Here the Baha'i principle of the oneness of mankind, which directly confronts the accepted human inequalities of the traditional caste system, was probably significant. Villagers from these social strata were no doubt open to the egalitarian teachings of urbanized outsiders and may well have thought that by joining such a movement their own social standing might improve. While I do not have specific figures related to other regions and later decades, it is my understanding that Baha'i declarations have continued to be significantly aligned with the lower segments of various regional social hierarchies.

But the teachings of social equality cannot alone account for the declarations. In the first place, there were, and have been, other than scheduled caste converts, and secondly there were, and are, other egalitarian religious movements in the field that could draw lower caste Hindus away from their religion if this were the only issue. Moreover, a one-dimensional secular explanation may not do justice to what many Baha'is might see as the spiritual force and attraction of their message. While not being able to evaluate the belief component of this latter position, I do feel that the manner in which the message was delivered is significant and goes some way to answering our question. Here I am alluding to 1) the conscious effort made by Baha'i village teachers to present their message in Hinduized symbols and concepts and 2) the policy of not requiring new converts to completely reject (either symbolically or behaviorally) their own religious traditions.

Although in theory the Baha'i Faith had long advocated the oneness of the world's great religious traditions, the reality of having to present the message to largely illiterate or semiliterate Hindu villagers resulted in a more systematic attempt to identify with the Hindu tradition. In this vein, Baha'i teachers began to emphasize what might be called a culturally adaptive proselytizing technique whereby indigenous concepts and symbols were used as channels of communi-cation. This can best be seen in the presentation of Baha'u'llah as an avatar. More specifically, he was often associated with the kalkin avatar who according to the *Vishnupurana* will appear at the end of the kali yuga for the purpose of reesta-blishing an era of righteousness.

Other examples of this approach included emphasizing the figures of Buddha and Krishna as past Manifestations of God (avatars), references to Hindu scriptures such as the *Bhagavad Gita*,the substitution of Sanskrit-based terminology for Arabic and Persian where possible (i.e., Bhagavan Baha for Baha'u'llah), and the incorporation in both song and literature of Hindu holy spots, hero-figures and poetic images.In this vein it should also be noted that there appears to have been a fairly deliberate attempt made by Baha'i teachers to distance the movement from its Islamic identification. A good example of this can be seen in the Hindi translations of Baha'i scriptures and prayers that appeared during this period which are so heavily Sanskritized as to make it difficult to recognize their non-Hindu antecedents.

Associated with this more sympathetic approach to Hinduism was the policy of gradualism regarding the introduction of Baha'i institutions and mores into village life. Baha'i administrators and teachers certainly desired eventual structural and behavioral change, yet they did not force new declarants to immediately cast off traditional ways. For example, although Baha'i social teachings are anti-caste in outlook, outside of Baha'i meetings there was no militant attempt to purge new believers of conventional caste behavior. Similarly, while participation in new Baha'i rituals was encouraged, it was not made a requisite for membership. Only declared belief that Baha'u'llah was the avatar for this age was deemed necessary.

In making use of these tactics the Baha'i teachers did not demand that new contacts completely reject their own heritage either in word or deed. Rather they allowed them to maintain both psychological and behavioral links with the past while at the same time opening up new arenas of belief and action. This compartmentalization fit in well with established mechanisms for change within the traditional village social structure and was perhaps the most significant reason for the large numbers of village conversions that took place during this stage of communitydevelopment. The above analysis raises the question of the meaning of these declarations of faith. Were they true conversions, or were they something else? In attempting to answer this question it might be helpful to compare the Baha'i experience with another contemporary conversion movement in India, the Neo-Buddhist movement.

In 1956 close to a half million members of the scheduled Mahar caste converted to Buddhism. In so doing they took part in a conversion ceremony at Nagpur where they were asked to repeat, among other things, twenty-two oaths, eight of which were specifically anti-Hindu. These eight included denunciations of Hindu deities (among which were Rama and Krishna) and prohibitions against taking part in certain Hindu rituals. The oath concluded with the following statement: "I embrace today the Buddha Dharma, discarding the Hindu religion, which is detrimental to the emancipation of human beings other than the Brahmins as low born."

To some degree Baha'i missionary activity shared certain commonalities with the Buddhist movement.

Although unlike the Buddhists, Baha'is made a specific effort to remain free of the political arena, both groups spoke to scheduled caste discontent and both presented the negative elements of the larger tradition as fundamentally alien to the true core of that heritage. The Neo-Buddhist movement did so by presenting Buddhism as the essence of Indian spirituality while Baha'i teachers spoke of regeneration of true Indian spirituality through the teachings of the new avatar, Baha'u'llah. Where the Baha'i Faith departed fundamentally from the approach of the Neo-Buddhists, and where the question of the meaning of Baha'i conversion becomes highlighted, is that the Baha'is saw no need to make their declarants ritually renounce the Hindu tradition.

Moreover, as shown above, they did not require a dramatic behavioral departure from either Hindu ritual or traditional village patterns of social interaction. Now if a symbolic rejection of one's previous religious affiliation is a requirement for conversion, then I think it could be argued within this comparative context that the Baha'i declarants were not converts while the Mahars were. On the other hand, if a more liberal definition of conversion is allowed for, one which does not demand such official rejection, and provides for a compartmentalized approach to change that gradually introduces new theological and behavioral norms over an extended period of time (perhaps generations) then both groups were converts. In this regard it is interesting to note that despite the official rejection of Hindu beliefs and practices, Eleanor Zelliot reported that "Some Buddhists and some observers find no change at all in the lifestyle of Buddhists."

My own analysis would see many of the Baha'i declarations as fitting into a category that shares something in common with conversion yet is somewhat differentiated from the more commonly accepted understanding of this term. Here I make reference to that category of religious movement that has traditionally been called *bhakti*. Bhakti sects have flourished in India for centuries, and many of them have had as part of their internal dynamic anti-caste attitudes. They have differed from conversion movements in that they have come from within the Hindu tradition and have generally been more narrowly religious in orientation. Their primary concern has not been social change but devotion to a specific avatar.

While they have been aware of the conditions of the depressed, they tended to represent "a new symbolic language for the aspirations of the depressed rather than any fulfillment of these aspirations." The Baha'i Faith fits into this category in three ways: its respect for elements in the Hindu tradition; its presentation of Baha'u'llah as avatar; and, at least during the period of time under discussion here, its preference for symbolic and utopian expressions of change rather than direct social action. If this assumption is correct, the Baha'i Faith may have been seen by many mass teaching converts as a half-way house: one which allowed them to express certain deviant ideas without having to reject in word or deed the larger cultural heritage of which they were a part.

Regardless of how many actual converts came into the Faith during the mass teaching period, the impact of the new numbers was definitely felt in terms of structural and organizational changes that subsequently occurred within the Indian Baha'i community. As early as 1962 the process of decentralization was begun with the creation of special area teaching committees, and, as noted above, by the late 1970s state teaching committees had assumed most of the powers of the former NSA. Thus the process of centralization that began as early as 1910 was significantly reversed during this stage of development.

One of the foremost challenges created by the mass teaching campaigns was the need to establish networks of communication linking the villages and the greater administrative system. As one of the main goals of the

Baha'i Faith is to create a world-wide community of believers who are knowledgeable in the teachings of the movement and active in community affairs, it was soon apparent that a follow-up system of "deepening" (education in the tenets and practices of the Baha'i faith) was required. In response to this need, in the early and mid-1960s several Baha'i teaching institutes were founded in the mass teaching areas. During visits to the new village communities Baha'i teachers would encourage certain believers to attend week-end or week-long educational sessions at the institutes. These participants would then return to the rural areas where they would act as instructors in individual villages.

In addition to these institutes, later decades saw the creation of numerous regional and village schools which not only acted as centers for both Baha'i and primary (secular) education but in some instances also became focal points for regional economic and social development projects. Another major structural shift that has occurred during the mass teaching stage of development pertains to the relative number of rural versus urban Baha'is involved in the management of teaching and deepening efforts. Before this time nearly all such activities were in the hands of a small urbanized elite. Since the successes of mass teaching, however, ever-growing numbers of specially trained teachers from the villages have slowly taken on an increasing responsibility in this regard.

Organized along state and regional lines, these corps of indigenous rural believers make periodic village tours during which time they act not only as missionaries and educators (giving deepening classes) but also as vital links of inter-community communication. In this latter role they carry specific information to the village assemblies from the various teaching committees and in return see to it that the greater Baha'i administrative institutions are kept apprised of individual community conditions and needs. Thus, as the Universal House of Justice emphasized in 1966, the village teachers "must increasingly bear the brunt of responsibility for thepropagation of the Faith in their homelands."In so doing they have taken much of the weight of community development from the shoulders of the urban intelligentsia.

In looking back at the various stages of development outlined above, it becomes evident that over time there has been a general shift in the nature of the dynamics that have helped shape both the content and structure of the Indian Baha'i community. The transition from Babism to Baha'i was external to India, having to do essentially with developments in Iran. Likewise the initial stage of community development was primarily influenced by external elements, most notably in the form of traveling teachers and Iranian expatriates. However, by the early years of the twentieth century, when the Indian community began to take its first steps in the direction of national unity, a number of internal factors specific to the Indian context came to the fore.

These factors were largely associated with cultural and nationalist developments among the bourgeoisie and intelligensia (the two groups from which Baha'i converts were mainly drawn) as well as with the technological and commercial means then being used to unite the subcontinent. Although there was an administrative shift during the period of the Guardianship that often focused the community's vision outward to the larger Baha'i international scene, the internal dynamics of the previous period, which were accelerated by the movement toward independence and culmnated in Independence and Partition, continued to have a significant impact on the Indian Baha'i community. And when we come to the mass teaching era, internal factors have become predominant.

Despite the initial influences of the messges of Shoghi Effendi and the administrative proddings of Dr. Muhajir, once the rural campaigns were underway they essentially came to express the yearnings of the scheduled tribes and castes for a new identity in independent, socialist India. Moreover, the policy of not demanding that new declarants completely separate themselves from their former religious affiliation can be seen as an essentially *Indian* approach to conversion which in some ways was actually at odds with the demands that Shoghi Effendi had made on those who had come into the Faith during the period of the Guardianship.

To some extent this may have been due to the "vacuum of power" which the Baha'i Faith experienced between 1957 and 1963. In the absence of a Guardian, Baha'i travel teachers and scheduled caste leaders were able to bring fellow villagers into the community by making use of this compartmentalized approach to proselytization. Thus by the time the first Universal House of Justice was elected such a method had become firmly established in the subcontinent, and the fruits of that approach in the form of a more decentralized administrative system manned by a large number of indigenous believers will likely help maintain,if not increase, the significance of internal forces in the future.

Bibliography

A.H. Armstrong, ed., Classical Mediterranean Spirituality, World Spirituality 15, New York: Crossroad, 1989.

Anderson, H. and E. Foley, Mighty Stories, Dangerous Rituals, San Francisco, CA: Jossey-Bass, 1997.

Angelika Malinar, The Bhagavadgita: Doctrines and Contexts, Cambridge: Cambridge University Press, 2008

Annemarie Schimmel, Mystical Dimensions of Islam, Chapel Hill: University of North Carolina Press, 1975.

Armstrong, Karen. Buddha. New York: Viking Penguin, 2001.

Babin, P., The New Era in Religious Communication, Minneapolis, MN: Fortress Press, 1991.

Barnstone, Willis (Ed.), The Other Bible, HarperSan Francisco, 1984.

Barrett, David V., The New Believers: Sects, Cults and Alternative Religions, Cassell & Co: London, 2001.

Bowker, John (ed.), The Oxford Dictionary of World Religions, Oxford University Press: Oxford, 1997.

Bavinck, J. H., The Church between Temple and Mosque, Grand Rapids: Eerdmans, 1966.

Bruce, S., Religion in the Modern World: from Cathedrals to Cults, Oxford: Oxford University Press, 1996.

Burnett, David, World of the Spirits: A Christian Perspective on traditional and Folk Religions, London: Monarch, 2000.

Chan, Wing-Tsit, trans. and ed. A Source Book in Chinese Philosophy. Princeton: Princeton University Press, 1963.

Chandra, Lokesh, Iconography of the Thousand Buddhas, International Academy of Indian Culture: New Delhi, 1996.

Conze, Edward (translator), Buddhist Scriptures, Penguin Books:New York, 1959 (1981).

Creel, H.G., Chinese Thought: from Confucius to Mao Tse-tung, University of Chicago Press, 1953.

Dawood, N.J., (translated with revisions) The Koran, Penguin Books: NY, 1997.

De Bary, Wm. Theodore (ed.), Sources of Indian Tradition, Columbia University Press: NY, 1958.

Dominic Goodall, ed. Hindu Scriptures with New Translations, Berkeley: University of California Press, 1996

Donald S. Lopez, Jr., ed., Religions of China in Practice, Princeton Readings in Religion, Princeton: Princeton University Press, 1996.

Donald S. Lopez, Jr., ed., Religions of India in Practice, Princeton Readings in Religion, Princeton: Princeton University Press, 1995.

Eichhoefer, Gerald W. Enduring Issues in Philosophy. San Diego: Greenhaven Press, Inc., 1995.

Gitlin, T., The Whole World is Watching, Berkeley, CA: University of California Press, 1980.

Hiebert, R. E., D. F. Ungurait and T. W. Bohn, Mass Media IV: An Introduction to Modern Communication, New York and London: Longman, 1985.

Holm, Jean and John Bowker, eds., Human Nature and Destiny, London: Printer Publishing, 1994.

Jacob Neusner, Judaism as Philosophy: The Method and Message of the Mishnah, Baltimore: Johns Hopkins, 1999.

John Renard, Seven Doors to Islam: Spirituality and the Religious Life of Muslims, Berkeley: University of California Press, 1996.

Johnston, R., Reel Spirituality: Theology and Film in Dialogue, Grand Rapids, MI: Baker Academic, 2000.

Joseph Dan, Jewish Mysticism, 4 vol., Northvale, NJ: Jason Aronson, 1998.

Krishna Sivaraman, ed., Hindu Spirituality I: Vedas through Vedanta, World Spirituality Series 6, New York: Crossroad, 1989.

Kurtz, Lester R., Gods in the Global Village, Thousand Oaks, CA: Sage, 2007.

Lyden, John. Enduring Issues in Religion. San Diego: Greenhaven Press, Inc., 1995.

Malise Ruthven, Islam: A Very Short Introduction, New York: Oxford University Press, 2000.

Melton, J. Gordon, Martin Baumann, eds. Religions of the World: A Comprehensive Encyclopedia of Beliefs and Practices. Vols. 1-4. Santa Barbara: ABC-Clio, 2002.

Mircea Eliade, ed., The Encyclopedia of Religion, 16 vol., New York: Macmillan, 1987.

Ninian Smart, Dimensions of the Sacred : An Anatomy of the World's Beliefs, Berkeley: University of California Press, 1996.

Nouwen, Henri J.M. The Road to Daybreak: A Spiritual Journey. New York: Doubleday, 1988.

O'Flaherty, Wendy Doniger (ed. and trans.), The Rig Veda: An Anthology. Penguin Books, NY, 1981.

Paul Williams, Mahayana Buddhism: The Doctrinal Foundations, New York: Routledge, 2008.

Peter H. Van Ness, ed., Spirituality and the Secular Quest, World Spirituality 22, New York: Crossroad, 1996.

Peter Harvey, An Introduction to Buddhism, New York: Cambridge University Press, 1990.

Renou, Louis, ed. Hinduism. New York: George Braziller, 1961.

Rinpoche, Sogyal. The Tibetan Book of Living and Dying. New York: Harper Collins, 1993.

Shakir, M. H., (trans.) The Holy Qur'an, Tahrike Tarsile Qur'an, Inc: NY, 1997.

Stephen J. Laumakis, An Introduction to Buddhist Philosophy, Cambridge: Cambridge University Press, 2008

Steven Heine and Charles S. Prebish, eds., Buddhism in the Modern World: Adaptations of an Ancient Tradition, New York: Oxford University Press, 2003.

Sushil Mittal & Gene Thursby, eds., The Hindu World, New York: Routledge, 2004.

Tu Weiming & Mary Evelyn Tucker, eds., Confucian Spirituality, World Spirituality 11, New York: Herder & Herder, 2002.

Warms, Richard, James Garber and Jon McGee, eds., Sacred Realms: Essays in Religion, Belief & Society, New York: Oxford University Press, 2004.

William A. Graham, David Burrell & R.J. McCarthy, eds., Al-Ghazali's Path to Sufism: His Deliverance from Error (al-Munqidh min al-Dalal) and Five Key Texts, Louisville: Fons Vitae, 2000.

William C. Chittick, Ibn Arabi, Makers of the Muslim World, Oxford: Oneworld, 2005.

William C. Chittick, Sufism: A Short Introduction, Oxford: One World, 2000.

Xinzhong Yao, An Introduction to Confucianism, Cambridge: Cambridge University Press, 2000.

Zaehner, R.C. (translation), Hindu Scriptures, J.M. Dent & Sons: London, 1966.

Index